SAKHALIN

A History

SAKHALIN

A History

BY

JOHN J. STEPHAN

CLARENDON PRESS · OXFORD

1971

Oxford University Press, Ely House, London W. I

GLASGOW NEW YORK TORONTO MELBOURNE WELLINGTON
CAPE TOWN SALISBURY IBADAN NAIROBI DAR ES SALAAM LUSAKA ADDIS ABABA
BOMBAY CALCUTTA MADRAS KARACHI LAHORE DACCA
KUALA LUMPUR SINGAPORE HONG KONG TOKYO

PRINTED IN GREAT BRITAIN
BY W & J MACKAY & CO LTD, CHATHAM

PREFACE

JUST a few miles off the northeastern coast of the Eurasian continent, there stretches a long, slender island. This island lies across the mouth of the Amur River whose upper reaches form part of the border between China and the Soviet Union. It separates the Sea of Japan from the Sea of Okhotsk except for two narrow straits, and forms a bridge between the northernmost Japanese island of Hokkaido and the Asiatic continent. Cold winds, impenetrable fogs, treacherous tides, earthquakes, and rugged coastal cliffs combine to produce a natural environment inhospitable to man. Moreover, the island acquired a sinister reputation as the most notorious Tsarist penal colony in Siberia. Today, it is no longer a remote, barren monument to human misery. With the dynamic development programmes implemented by the Soviet government, with the emergence of neighbouring Japan as the world's third-ranking economic power, and with growing tension along the Sino-Soviet frontier, it has become an economically and strategically vital part of the Soviet Far East. It is called Sakhalin.

Despite its colourful history and modern importance, there are virtually no modern studies of Sakhalin outside of those published in the Soviet Union. The paucity of works on Sakhalin derives to some extent from the fact that reliable information is difficult to obtain. The island is closed to foreign visitors. With few exceptions, the available written sources are in the Russian or Japanese languages. But even for those who can read Russian or Japanese, there is still another obstacle—the hitherto unbridgeable gap between the Russian and Japanese historiography of Sakhalin.

The fragmented character of Sakhalin's historiography is the product of the island's confused, divided, and occasionally turbulent past. Sakhalin was once under the suzerainty of China. After the eighteenth century, the island became a contested frontier between Russia and Japan. Both countries have at one time ruled all or part of Sakhalin during 150 years of rivalry punctuated by wars, occupations, and treaties. Today, Sakhalin's status is still an unresolved issue between the two countries.

These historical forces have led to the formation of two insular bodies of literature exhibiting widely divergent viewpoints. Political and linguistic barriers have prevented any significant intellectual interchange by Soviet and Japanese historians of Sakhalin. For example, the prewar Japanese accounts of the island generally treated only the southern half (Karafuto) without reference to Russian written sources or to the northern part of the island. There is still no Japanese study of Soviet Sakhalin since 1945, although the island is a mere twenty-five miles away from Hokkaido. Conversely, Soviet historians have ignored the Japanese role in Sakhalin's history (except as 'aggressors' or 'plunderers') and have studiously avoided referring to Japanese sources. As a result, there is no truly comprehensive history of Sakhalin, in *any* language.

This is the first modern history of Sakhalin that incorporates both the Russian and the Japanese accounts of the island. In addition, reference is made to Chinese, German, French, Polish, English, and American sources, some of which are being publicized for the first time. The time scope is purposely broad, encompassing the prehistoric period to the present time. Social and cultural as well as political and economic topics receive attention. Using the most recent Soviet publications, an attempt is made to give the first up-to-date account of Sakhalin's past and present published outside of the U.S.S.R.

My interest in Sakhalin dates from 1964. The island's historical role as a frontier between China, Russia, and Japan and its present-day strategic and economic significance had attracted little attention outside of Russia and Japan. I decided to attempt the reconstruction of Sakhalin's history through a comprehensive investigation of available materials. As the important sources are scattered, it has been necessary to consult libraries and archives in the U.S.A., Great Britain, the U.S.S.R., and Japan. Unfortunately, I have been unable to travel to Sakhalin itself. The Soviet government does not at present allow foreign tourists there,[1] and efforts to obtain special

[1] From 1965, Soviet authorities permitted one visit each summer by a limited group of Japanese who wanted to pay homage at the graves of relatives buried in Sakhalin. A Japanese television team spent five days in Sakhalin in 1964. Some Japanese trade union officials made a tour there at the invitation of their Russian counterparts in 1965.

permission to visit Sakhalin through application to the Soviet Embassy in London, the U.S.S.R. Academy of Sciences, the Sakhalin Joint Scientific Research Institute in Novosibirsk, and to individual Soviet officials met with polite but firm refusals.

That access to Sakhalin is highly restricted is not surprising. It is a frontier area. Sino-Soviet border tensions, American bases in near-by Hokkaido, and Japan's claim to the 'northern territories' lost to the U.S.S.R. in the last moments of the Second World War all make Sakhalin a highly sensitive area. The island is honeycombed with military airfields and boasts a naval base at Korsakov facing the La Pérouse Strait. As a keystone of Soviet maritime communications between Far Eastern naval bases and the Pacific Ocean, Sakhalin may well remain sealed off to foreigners for some time.

In writing this book, I owe a particular debt of gratitude to three individuals. Professor John A. White of the University of Hawaii introduced me to Sakhalin's neglected significance in his lectures on Russia in Asia. Professor W. G. Beasley of the School of Oriental and African Studies, University of London, opened up new perspectives on Sakhalin through suggestions and criticisms of my doctoral dissertation which treated Japan's northern frontier policy in the early nineteenth century. Professor Hora Tomio of Waseda University has influenced me profoundly through his studies of Japanese exploration, of China's historical association with Sakhalin, and of the territorial issue between Japan and the U.S.S.R. His generous assistance in gaining access to rare material is deeply appreciated.

As former teachers, Professor Albert M. Craig and Dr. Itasaka Gen of Harvard University, Professor Iriye Akira of the University of Chicago, and Professors George Akita and Uyehara Yukuo of the University of Hawaii have been an inspiration to study the history and language of Japan.

Several acknowledged experts of the Northeast Asia area and Russo-Japanese relations have kindly made valuable suggestions. Professor Chester S. Chard and Dr. Emiko Ohnuki-Tierney of the University of Wisconsin, Professor John A. Harrison of the University of Miami, and the late Dr. F. C. Jones of the University of Bristol have introduced me to various aspects of Sakhalin's past. Dr. Leonid N. Kutakov, formerly attached to the Soviet Embassy in Tokyo and at present serving in the United Nations

Secretariat, has offered sound advice on source material and methodology. Professor George A. Lensen of Florida State University has helped me with bibliographical suggestions and has generously allowed me to use the page proofs of a forthcoming history of Soviet-Japanese relations.

Interviews with former residents and visitors to Sakhalin provided a unique channel to gain an impression of the island, especially as I could not personally travel in that part of the Soviet Union. In this connection, I would like to acknowledge the kindness of Dr. Fosco Maraini of Florence, Italy, and Professor Martin Schwind of the Ost Asiens Institut in Bochum, German Federal Republic (both of whom travelled to Japanese Karafuto in the 1930s); Miyatake Shōzō of the Nihon Hōsō Kyōkai (who visited Sakhalin in 1964 as a journalist); Okuyama Ryō of Sapporo, Hokkaido (who was a schoolteacher in Maoka in Japanese Karafuto and lived under the Soviet occupation); Ogata Masakuni of the Zenkoku Karafuto Renmei in Tokyo (who was Karafuto's chief of police, 1939–45); and Takahashi Morizō of Tokyo (formerly of the Ōji Paper Company in Karafuto).

As collecting material for this study involved using a number of public libraries and private collections, I am deeply indebted to librarians and other individuals who not only made access possible but brought forth items of considerable interest that otherwise would have escaped my attention. Thanks are due to Matsui Masato of the East-West Center Library, University of Hawaii; A. N. Maslova and Mikhail S. Masiuk of the Khabarovsk Territorial Library; Miyamoto Shōsaburō of the library of the School of Oriental and African Studies and Laura Gurdikyan of the library of the School of Slavonic and East European Studies (both of the University of London); E. Ceadel of the Cambridge University Library; Miss Anne Abley and Mrs. Susan Chapman of the library at St. Antony's College, Oxford; Kenneth Gardner of the Oriental Books and Manuscripts Room of the British Museum; Takano Akira of the Waseda University Library; Kanai Madoka of the Shiryō Hensanjo, Tokyo University; Fukuda Isao and Okada Hiroko of the Hakodate Municipal Library; Fujimoto Hideo of the Sapporo City Library; Abe Shōtarō, Nagata Tomisato, Iwamatsu Yoshihiro, Kaiho Mineo, and Kaiho Yōko of the Hokkaido Prefectural Office: Kubota

Yoshirō of the Nanpō Dōho Engokai; Yamada Hidezō of Sapporo; and Kitagamae Yasuo of Nemuro.

I would like to thank the Fulbright Committee of the United States Education Commission in Japan for financial support to carry out research there during 1967–8.

Throughout the preparation of this study, there have been individuals who have shown abiding interest and have offered candid advice, not only on specific issues but also regarding the role of Sakhalin in Far Eastern history. The warm encouragement of Dr. Richard Storry of St. Antony's College, Oxford, Professor Hilary Conroy of the University of Pennsylvania, and Professor Sakurai Kiyohiko of Waseda University in this respect is deeply appreciated.

Finally, my parents and wife have given unstinting support. Their enthusiasm and uncanny resourcefulness in locating rare books have been a source of deep gratification.

While many individuals have contributed to this study of Sakhalin, the author holds the sole responsibility for its contents.

Tokyo
17 January 1970

CONTENTS

LIST OF PLATES

between pp. 106–7

LIST OF MAPS

NOTE

Japanese personal names are given in the Japanese fashion. The surname precedes the given name.

Transliteration of Russian names and words is according to the system employed by the United States Library of Congress, with two exceptions: (1) the apostrophe (') denoting the Russian soft sign has been omitted; (2) 'g' has been replaced by 'v' in the endings 'ovo' and 'evo' to facilitate pronunciation for the non-specialist.

All dates, unless otherwise indicated, are given according to the Gregorian calendar.

On the use of the place names 'Sakhalin' and 'Karafuto': Russians have used 'Sakhalin' to designate the entire island of Sakhalin. Japanese have used the term 'Karafuto' to refer to (1) the entire island of Sakhalin, or (2) just the southern half of Sakhalin between 1905 and 1945. This study tries to employ the appellation appropriate to the historical period and to the user.

‘I have seen Ceylon, which is paradise, and Sakhalin, which is hell.’

Anton Chekhov (1895)

INTRODUCTION

SAKHALIN is a long, narrow, sturgeon-shaped island, roughly equal in area to Ireland, lying north of Japan along the coast of Northeast Asia. For centuries it was a frontier, first between China and various indigenous tribes, and later between Russia and Japan. At present Sakhalin, together with the Kurile Islands, is an administrative district (*oblast*) in the Far Eastern region of the Russian Soviet Federated Socialist Republic.

Sakhalin's past and present significance is keenly appreciated by many Russians and Japanese but relatively neglected in the United States and Europe. The island's remote location and rigorous climate have long discouraged travellers. As a Tsarist penal colony (1881–1906), Sakhalin gained a morbid notoriety as the land of the damned. Anton Chekhov, Vasilii Doroshevich, and a few convicts with literary inclinations each testified with varying eloquence but equal fervour that Sakhalin was hell on earth.

As inhibiting as the abrasive climate and the cruel social environment were the restrictions which fettered foreign visitors. The Japanese authorities allowed foreigners to travel to Karafuto (the southern half of the island which Japan ruled from 1905 to 1945) only under strict surveillance. In the 1930s, security precautions surrounding foreign tourists grew so tight that the hapless traveller found himself escorted literally twenty-four hours a day by a succession of tireless detectives. Consequently, very few non-Japanese visited Karafuto.

Ironically, the Tsarist régime seems to have permitted more travellers to inspect Sakhalin when it was a deplorable penal colony than has the Soviet government which has allegedly transformed the island into a productive economic base with modern social and cultural amenities. To my knowledge, the only non-communist foreigners to have set foot on Sakhalin in recent years have been three Japanese reporters, a party of Japanese trade union officials, and a handful of ex-residents paying their respects to ancestral graves on stringently controlled annual tours (which began in 1965). Until these restrictions are relaxed, Sakhalin will remain a remote, inaccessible island for the Western traveller.

If climate, location, reputation, and red tape have sealed off the island from the world's eyes, Russian and Japanese scholars and writers have devoted considerable efforts towards illuminating Sakhalin's rich and varied past. Unfortunately, their works have not been available to English language readers. Furthermore, there has yet to appear a study of Sakhalin that incorporates the material found not only in Russian and Japanese but in Chinese, German, French, and English sources. Japanese works (nearly all prewar) refer only to a small fraction of Russian writings or do not use them at all. Soviet historians have taken pains to minimize the Japanese (let alone the Chinese) role in Sakhalin's past for obvious political reasons. Chinese and Japanese works are thus almost entirely absent in Soviet studies on this region. Sakhalin's historiography, like its history, is characterized by division and controversy.

A comprehensively based history of Sakhalin can be useful in several ways. First, it can define Sakhalin's role in Far Eastern history. Far from being the 'end of the world', Sakhalin's location made the island a geographical crossroads of northern and southern, continental and maritime cultural spheres in the prehistoric period and a meeting point of the Chinese, Japanese, and Russian empires in more recent times. As each of these great powers once exercised sovereignty over Sakhalin, the island might be called East Asia's 'Alsace-Lorraine'.

Secondly, a comprehensive history of Sakhalin introduces the hitherto little-known evolution of Chinese influence there from the Yüan to the mid Ch'ing period (1279–1809). The Chinese association with Sakhalin suggests that the influence of the 'Middle Kingdom' penetrated further into Northeast Asia than has generally been believed. Furthermore, Sakhalin played an important role in the small but remarkable flow of Chinese products from Manchuria to Japan in the seventeenth to nineteenth centuries.

Thirdly, Sakhalin posed one of the most baffling cartographical problems in the history of exploration. Since Russian Cossacks, Japanese surveyors, and a Dutch captain in search of 'Golden Islands' reached Sakhalin in the third and fourth decades of the seventeenth century, this often fog-enshrouded island eluded successive attempts to define its relationship to the continent. European cartographers considered it an island, a peninsula, and then an island again. Prestigious explorers such as the Frenchman La Pérouse, the Englishman Broughton, and the Russian Krusenstern subscribed to the peninsular theory only to be proven wrong by a relatively unknown (in the West) Japanese named Mamiya Rinzō.[1] As late as 1855, during the Crimean War, the English China Squadron confidently blocked a fleeing Russian convoy in what the pursuers considered to be the 'Bay of Tartary'. After weeks of waiting for their prey to emerge, the English realized to their own mortification that the 'bay' on their charts was in fact a strait through which the 'trapped' quarry neatly escaped.

Fourthly, it is instructive to study Japan's colonial administration of Karafuto. Karafuto was Japan's first overseas colony, antedating Formosa (Taiwan) by nearly ninety years.[2] The island was noteworthy as Japan's northernmost frontier. Pioneers struggled with the harsh climate, the dense virgin forests, and the inevitable loneliness of colonial Karafuto much as early settlers had done in the American West, Australia, and Siberia. Unlike Korea and Formosa, Karafuto made the transition from colony to an integral part of the homeland (in 1943).

Fifthly, Sakhalin played an important role in the development of Russo-Japanese relations. Russians and Japanese both reached the island at roughly the same time in the mid-seventeenth century, but neither side took a serious interest in exercising sovereignty there until after 1785. During the 160 years from 1785 to 1945, Sakhalin proved to be a source of friction and occasionally a battleground between these two powers. The island or parts of it passed back and forth between Russia and Japan, reflecting shifts in their relative power: joint occupation (1855–75), Russian rule (1875–1905), Japanese rule in the southern half or Karafuto (1905–45), Japanese occupation of the northern half (1920–5), and Soviet rule of all Sakhalin

[1] Soviet historians refuse to recognize Mamiya as the discoverer of Sakhalin's insularity in 1809. Instead, they accord the honour to a Russian, Captain Gennadii Nevelskoi, who duplicated Mamiya's feat forty years later (1849).

[2] It is arguable that the oldest Japanese colony was the protectorate of Mimana (*c.* A.D. 200–600) located on the southern tip of the Korean peninsula.

(since 1945). Although Japan abandoned all territorial claims to southern Sakhalin in the San Francisco Peace Treaty (1951), the problem of repatriating former settlers complicated Russo-Japanese relations for over two decades after the end of World War II. The Japanese government considers southern Sakhalin's (formerly Karafuto) legal status still unresolved. With the reversion of Okinawa scheduled for 1972, there are voices insisting that southern Sakhalin too is Japanese territory.

Starting in the late 1960s, however, both the Soviet Union and Japan have shown an interest in economic co-operation in Sakhalin. The accelerated exploitation of the island's oil and natural gas deposits together with the possibility of joint ventures to transport these fuels to refineries and industrial centres on the Amur and in Japan suggest that the island may be assuming a new international role.

Finally, Sakhalin occupies a vital role as part of the Soviet Far East. Rich natural resources (coal, oil, gas, timber, fish) have provided the basis for rapidly expanding extractive and manufacturing industries. Sakhalin's oil is the only major deposit in the Soviet Far East and as such plays a particularly significant part in fuelling the industrial complexes in Khabarovsk and Komsomolsk on the Amur River.

Sakhalin's strategic importance to the Soviet Union can be gauged from reference to a map. Lying at the mouth of the Amur and extending southwards parallel to the coast of the Soviet Maritime Region, it not only presides over this vital river communication route but controls the only two outlets from the Sea of Japan to the Sea of Okhotsk, the straits of Tatary and La Pérouse. The island's proximity to Japan's northernmost island of Hokkaido (twenty-five miles) makes Sakhalin an eminently suitable area for tactical air bases, naval bases, and radar stations. As long as the United States and her allies control both shores of the Tsushima and Tsugaru straits, the Soviet Union's Far Eastern Fleet relies on possession of Sakhalin to ensure that it will not be 'trapped' in the Sea of Japan. A recent editorial in the Soviet press appropriately characterized Sakhalin as 'the forepost of the Soviet nation on the Pacific Ocean'.[3]

These six topics indicate the main themes treated in this

[3] *Pravda*, 13 March 1969.

history of Sakhalin. It is hoped that this study might be used not only as a guide to Sakhalin's past but also as a source for hitherto widely scattered information for the traveller (if Sakhalin is ever opened to foreign visitors) and for those interested in the relations of the world's second and third greatest economic powers—the Soviet Union and Japan.

Map 1. Sakhalin in Northeast Asia

I

GEOGRAPHY AND PREHISTORY

'Nature created this island in a moment of wrath.'
VASILII DOROSHEVICH (1903)

THE island of Sakhalin lies between 45°54′ and 54°24′ north latitude and between 141°38′ and 144°55′ east longitude. It extends for 593 miles in length from Cape Elizaveta in the north to Cape Krilon in the south. The width varies from 100 miles to 16 miles. Sakhalin is separated from the continent by a narrow, shallow Nevelskoi Strait (4½ miles wide at Cape Pogibi) and from Hokkaido by the 25-mile wide La Pérouse Strait. Sakhalin's area, 30,500 square miles (78,000 square kilometres) is a fraction smaller than that of Hokkaido.[1]

Sakhalin's topography falls roughly into two sections: the low-lying, gently undulating taiga of the north and the heavily forested mountainous south. The south is divided by two mountain chains which run lengthwise along the island, the Western Sakhalin Range which follows the coast of the Straits of Tatary and the less extensive but higher Eastern Sakhalin Range which faces the Sea of Okhotsk. The Eastern Range is crowned by Mt. Lopatin (5,279 feet) while the highest peak in the Western Range is Mt. Onor (4,250 feet). These mountains consist largely of slate, sandstone, and limestone. They differ little in composition from the ranges in the Soviet Maritime Region to the west. Between Sakhalin's Eastern and Western ranges lies a long, narrow valley drained in the north by the Tym River and in the south by the Poronai River. The Poronai Valley is covered with a clay floor of moderate fertility and enjoys a warmer climate because of the protection from winds afforded by the surrounding mountains. In the wooded valleys of the south, pine, larch and birch are joined by the Manchurian oak, elm, the Korean willow, and even wild bamboo.[2]

[1] Akademiia nauk SSSR, Sakhalinskii kompleksnyi nauchno-issledovatelskii institut, *Atlas Sakhalinskoi oblasti* (Moscow, 1967), p. 1.

[2] For a detailed discussion of Sakhalin's topography and climate, see A. I.

The northern section of Sakhalin is characterized by low hills in the centre and marshy plains covered with tundra vegetation towards the coasts. The northern reaches of the Eastern and Western ranges recede from the coast and dwindle to low hills covered with pines and larches. At the extreme north of the island, the Schmidt Peninsula juts out into the Okhotsk Sea, tipped by the formidable rocks of Cape Elizaveta. The peninsula's geological structure repeats that of the southern half of the island with two parallel ranges bracketing a rift valley. The isthmus joining the Schmidt Peninsula with the main part of the island contains a considerable portion of Sakhalin's oil reserves.

Sakhalin's coasts offer no suitable natural harbours. Most of the western coast facing the continent lacks indentations and presents a sheer façade of sandstone, clay and shale cliffs rising in places to 400 feet. North of the Nevelskoi Straits, these cliffs give way to a low, sandy marshland equally unsuitable for harbours. Sakhalin's east coast is laced with barrier beaches sheltering shallow lagoons. These lagoons can reach a length of 100 miles, but their usefulness as navigation routes is impaired by frequent spits and bars. The numerous river mouths on this coast have shores of thick layers of peat covered by moss. The eastern coast, south of the Poronai River, becomes steep and rugged. Only around Aniwa Bay in the extreme south of Sakhalin does the coast assume a more hospitable aspect with gentler inclines and an occasional inlet.

Anton Chekhov was told during his visit to Sakhalin in 1890 that the island had no climate but only 'bad weather'.[3] Sakhalin's climate is severe, humid, and capricious. Raw winters and damp summers have a depressing effect on most visitors. In the north, the average temperature in January is −10°F. and in July is 59°F. The south is warmer with an average of 17°F. in January and 63°F. in July. The low-lying northern section of the island is exposed to icy winds that permit only grasses and scrubby bushes to thrive. The east coast facing the Sea of Okhotsk

---

Zemtsova, *Klimat Sakhalina* (Leningrad, 1968); *Atlas Sakhalinskoi oblasti*, pp. 1–4; Erich Thiel, *The Soviet Far East* (London, 1957), pp. 326–33; Great Britain, Foreign Office, Historical Section, ed., *Sakhalin* (London, 1920), pp. 1–5.

[3] Anton Chekhov, 'Ostrov Sakhalin', *A. P. Chekhov: sobranie sochinenii*, X (Moscow, 1963), 117.

remains frozen for six months of the year. Ice floes can be seen as late as July. The west coast is influenced by a warm ocean current coming from the Sea of Japan and has a milder climate, but the Tatary Straits are still frozen over from November to March. The sheltered Poronai and Susui river valleys in southern Sakhalin offer the most habitable conditions. Protected by mountain ranges from the relentless winds that buffet the north and coastal areas, these valleys have deciduous trees and even wild bamboo (unknown elsewhere in the Soviet Union). The entire island is plagued by thick fogs during the summer that render navigation treacherous. Any visitor to Sakhalin will testify to the virulent swarms of gnats, mosquitoes, and horse flies that make the warm humid months an ordeal only slightly less trying than the winter.

As if to compensate for its abrasive climate, Sakhalin is richer in a diversity of natural resources than any comparable area in the Soviet Far East. The abundance of salmon, herring, cod, and king crab have led it to be called a rival to Newfoundland as a fishing ground.[4] When the Russian explorer Krusenstern entered Aniwa Bay in 1805, he hesitated to send longboats ashore for fear that they would be overturned by masses of whales that were churning up the waters of the bay.[5] Forests of larch, fir, spruce, and birch cover 60 per cent of the island and provide raw materials for paper and cellulose. Rich deposits of oil and natural gas in the north and along the east coast are the only reserves of any significance in the Soviet Far East. High quality coal seams run along the cliffs of the west coast. Total coal reserves have been estimated in 1967 at over 19,000,000,000 metric tons.[6] Peat, clay, and phosphorus exist in large quantities. Iron, gold, silver, copper, tungsten, mercury, and chromatic ores have been found in the Eastern and Western mountain ranges and on the Schmidt Peninsula. Sakhalin has been called a 'treasure'[7] with good reason.

Sakhalin's geological history contains large gaps that can only be filled by conjecture. In the absence of Palaeozoic period

[4] A. A. Panov, *Shokuminchi to shite no Sagaren* (Tokyo, 1942), p. 2. This is a Japanese translation of Panov's *Sakhalin kak koloniia* (Moscow, 1905).

[5] A. J. von Krusenstern, *Voyage Round the World in the Years 1803, 1804, 1805, 1806*, II (London, 1813), 50.

[6] *Atlas Sakhalinskoi oblasti*, p. 36.

[7] G. Gor and V. Leshkevich, *Sakhalin* (Moscow, 1949), p. 3.

data, the formation of Sakhalin is generally dated from the early Cretaceous period. In quaternary times, Sakhalin is said to have undergone several transformations through rising and falling water levels.[8] At one time, water flooded over the low-lying parts of Sakhalin leaving two islands formed by the main mountain ranges. Judging from comparative flora, fauna, and geological structures, Sakhalin was united with both the continent and Hokkaido during the end of the Neocene period making it a link in a continuous land bridge extending through Japan to Korea. From the early Pleistocene until approximately 65,000 years ago, Sakhalin existed as an island. From around 65,000 to 40,000 years ago, the changing water level led it to be connected again with Hokkaido. The island state resumed from 40,000 to 22,000 years ago. For the ensuing 12,000 years, land links with Hokkaido and the continent were re-established for the third time. These shifts have been traced by examining the terracing of Sakhalin's coasts and contrasting the remains of marine life found within them. Although Sakhalin has been an island for the past 10,000 to 12,000 years, geological movement still continues as anyone who has experienced an earthquake there will readily testify.[9]

Prehistory

When Europeans and Japanese first reached Sakhalin in the seventeenth century, they found the island inhabited by three distinct groups of people: Gilyak (Nivkhi) in the north, Oroki around the central east coast, and Ainu in the south. The Gilyak and Ainu are generally classified as 'Palaeoasiatics' (a heterogeneous label which includes Kamchadal, Aleut, Chukche, Koryat, and Eskimo) to distinguish them from the various Mongol and Tungus tribes that once occupied the banks of the Amur and Ussuri rivers. The Oroki are related to the Olchi tribes of the lower Amur and are a Tungus people.

Who were Sakhalin's earliest human inhabitants and from where did they come? This question has been debated for over a century, yet a definitive answer has still to be discovered. Soviet

[8] S. D. Galtsev-Beziuk, 'O soedinionii Sakhalina c materikom i o. Khokkaido v chetvertichnoe vremia', Akademiia nauk, SSSR, *Izvestiia. Seriia geograficheskaia*, I (Jan.—Feb. 1964), 56–62.

[9] L. S. Oskorbin, A. A. Poplavskii, V. N. Zaniukov, *Noglikskoe zemletriasenie 2 oktiabria 1964 goda* (Iuzhno-Sakhalinsk, 1967), pp. 73–83.

archaeological expeditions have recently carried out systematic excavations on Sakhalin and their findings throw new light on this problem. But before discussing the latest discoveries, it is instructive to recapitulate some of the older theories.

No Palaeolithic remains have been uncovered in Sakhalin although numerous such sites exist in Western and Central Siberia including the area around Lake Baikal.[10] The earliest of Sakhalin's excavated sites are classified as late Neolithic and are dated from the end of the third millenium B.C. The island's earliest settlers, whatever their racial identity, apparently arrived about four thousand years ago.

Until recently most scholars were convinced that the Ainu were Sakhalin's earliest inhabitants. The Ainu, whose origin remains a riddle, have been linked variously with Gilyak, Tungus, Mongol, Japanese, Korean, Chinese, Malayo-Polynesian and Australoid origins. One imaginative theory even identifies them with the lost tribes of Israel.[11] Europeans generally considered the Ainu to be Sakhalin's earliest settlers simply because these people with their Caucasian-like features left an indelible impression upon the first explorers to reach the island's shores. The accounts of Sakhalin by Moskvitin (1640), Vries (1643), Witsen (1687), La Pérouse (1787), Broughton (1796), and Krusenstern (1805) make special mention of the Ainu. These testimonials stimulated a series of systematic studies beginning in the mid-nineteenth century which with minor exceptions propounded the theory that the Ainu were Sakhalin's earliest inhabitants.

Leopold von Schrenk led the first scientific expedition to Sakhalin in 1854–6 under the joint auspices of the Imperial Academy of Sciences and the Russian Geographical Society. Schrenk classified the Ainu as 'Palaeoasiatics' from Mongolia who had reached Sakhalin via Korea, Honshu, and Hokkaido. He doubted that these Ainu migrations to Sakhalin were preceded by any other people.[12]

[10] R. V. Kozyreva, *Drevneishee proshloe Sakhalina* (Iuzhno-Sakhalinsk, 1960), p. 28. Ivan A. Lopatin, *The Cult of the Dead among the Natives of the Amur Basin* (The Hague, 1960), p. 19.

[11] Carl Etter, *Ainu Folklore* (Chicago, 1949), p. 210, referring to the Hebraic hypothesis of Oyabe Zenichirō.

[12] Leopold von Schrenk, *Ob inorodtsakh Amurskovo kraia*, I (St. Petersburg, 1883), 70–3, 286.

In the succeeding twenty years, Russian archaeologists such as M. M. Dobrotvorsky, I. Lopatin, and I. S. Poliakov carried out excavations at Aleksandrovsk and along the Susui River near Aniwa Bay. Prehistoric settlements containing stone tools and pottery were unearthed. Nevertheless, Schrenk's basic ideas remained unchallenged.

In 1889 a young man by the name of Lev Iakovlevich Shternberg was exiled to Sakhalin for 'participating in revolutionary movements'. Shternberg spent his time studying the local indigenous population and produced a work highly praised by Friedrich Engels.[13] Shternberg revisited Sakhalin in 1910 and again in 1926 collecting material for a definitive exposition of its aboriginal population. He noted Gilyak and Ainu legends of an ancient, extinct people called 'tonchi' who had lived on Sakhalin before being driven off by the Ainu. Dismissing this legend as baseless, he argued that the Ainu were 'Austronesians' from Sumatra, Borneo, and Mindanao who migrated northwards through Formosa and Japan to settle in uninhabited Sakhalin. He cited linguistic, archaeological, and anthropological data to support this theory.[14]

Another exile of this period who took the opportunity to examine linguistic and archaeological data on the Ainu was the Pole, Bronislaw Pilsudski. Pilsudski's sojourn from 1887 to 1905 afforded him ample time to collect material for a distinguished work on Sakhalin's Ainu.[15] Unlike Shternberg, Pilsudski gave credence to the 'tonchi' legend and remained sceptical about his colleague's diagnosis of Sakhalin's prehistory.

While Japanese scholars are divided on the question of the Ainu's origin, there seems to be a consensus that the Ainu preceded all other men to Sakhalin. Some theories follow the lead of Schrenk and Shternberg and suggest that the Ainu reached Sakhalin from Hokkaido. Kindaiichi Kyōsuke advanced an argument by which the Ainu came to Sakhalin from Northern Europe in an arctic odyssey that led through Iceland, Greenland, North America, Alaska, the Aleutian Islands, and the Kurile

[13] Kozyreva, *Drevneishee proshloe Sakhalina*, p. 13.

[14] L. Ia. Shternberg, *Giliaki, orochi, goldy, negidaltsy, ainy* (Khabarovsk, 1933), pp. 558–67.

[15] Bronislaw Pilsudski, *Materials for the Study of the Ainu Language and Folklore* (Cracow, 1912).

Islands.[16] Shiratori Kurakichi, working from Chinese sources of the T'ang period (A.D. 618–907), concluded that the Ainu crossed the Tatary Straits from the continent.[17]

Between 1905 and the outbreak of the Second World War, Japanese archaeologists carried out a series of excavations in several sites in Karafuto (southern Sakhalin). The results tended to emphasize the antiquity of Ainu settlement there. Kiyono Kenji postulated in 1925 that the Sakhalin Ainu culture showed a close affinity to the prehistoric shell mounds on the island. The comparisons of Sakhalin and Hokkaido prehistoric ceramic designs by Kōno Hiromichi (1932) and the chronological system developed by Itō Nobuo (1937–42) both linked Sakhalin's prehistory with that of the Japanese islands.[18]

Japanese scholars were handicapped in that they could not carry out excavations in Sakhalin before 1905. After 1905 a national frontier along the 50th parallel restricted the Russians to the northern and the Japanese to the southern part of the island. Linguistic as well as political barriers inhibited the exchange of information and ideas. During the disorders of the Russian Civil War and the Japanese occupation of northern Sakhalin (1918–25), the anthropologist Torii Ryūzō availed himself of the opportunity to survey Neolithic sites on Russian territory. His findings, however, offered no breakthrough in identifying Sakhalin's earliest inhabitants.[19]

After the Second World War, the Institute of Material Cultures of the Soviet Academy of Sciences organized a series of archaeological expeditions to a newly reunited Sakhalin. These expeditions represented an extension of the work pioneered by A. P. Okladnikov in Western and Central Siberia during the inter-war years. Before the results of the postwar Sakhalin expeditions were published, Soviet archaeologists were divided on the question of Sakhalin's earliest inhabitants. M. V. Vorobev supported Shternberg's theory on the priority of the Ainu while N. V. Kiuner felt that the pre-Ainu 'tonchi' people had a basis

[16] Kindaiichi Kyōsuke, *Ainu no kenkyū* (Tokyo, 1925), pp. 363–5.

[17] Shiratori Kurakichi, 'Tō jidai no Karafuto ni tsuite', *Rekishi chiri*, IX (1907), 336.

[18] Yoshizaki Masakazu, 'Prehistoric Culture in Southern Sakhalin in the Light of Japanese Research', *Arctic Anthropology*, I, 2 (1963), 131–58.

[19] Torii Ryūzō, *Kokuryūkō to kita Karafuto* (Tokyo, 1943).

in fact.[20] The subsequent excavations appear to have confirmed Kiuner's ideas—that the Ainu were preceded in Sakhalin by a still earlier migration.

From 1952 to 1959, the Institute of Material Cultures carried out excavations throughout Sakhalin. The most important Neolithic yields came from Aleksandrovsk and Nogliki in the north and from Nevelsk, Kholmsk, Promyslovaia (Poronaisk district), and Starodubskoe (Dolinsk district) in the south. The teams found ornaments, pottery fragments, stone weapons and tools (chipped, polished, drilled), and the remains of boats. The richest deposits came from shell mounds or middens along river beds and coastal terraces. Analysis of these unearthed objects revealed close associations with similar Neolithic sites in the Amur and Maritime regions and with sites in the Kurile Islands and Kamchatka. In southern Sakhalin, excavators unearthed Neolithic artifacts of a type found in Japan but also objects related to arctic maritime cultures in the Aleutians and southwestern Alaska. On this basis, the following general hypotheses have been advanced.[21]

First, Sakhalin's earliest settlers were a Neolithic people who came from the continent around 2000 B.C. They settled in the south of the island along the coasts and rivers. A second migration of Neolithic hunters crossed from the continent to northern Sakhalin around 1000 B.C. Both groups maintained close ties with Neolithic cultures of the Amur and Maritime regions whence they originated. Nevertheless, these people used flat-bottomed boats and bone harpoon tips characteristic of Eskimo cultures of the Chukhota Peninsula and the Aleutian Islands. This suggests either that continental tribes 'spontaneously' developed a maritime culture on Sakhalin (Okladnikov), or that there was an influx of an arctic population from the north or north-east (Chard).[22] What few specimens of proto-Jōmon pottery have been found in southern Sakhalin give the impression that any link with the Japanese islands was tenuous.

[20] For a discussion of the Vorobev and Kiuner theories, Kozyreva, *Drevneishee proshloe Sakhalina*, pp. 23–5; R. V. Kozyreva, *Drevnii Sakhalin* (Moscow, 1967), pp. 17–18.

[21] R. V. Chubarova, 'K istorii drevneishevo naseleniia Sakhalina', *Sovetskaia etnografiia*, IV (1957), 60–75. Kozyreva, *Drevnii Sakhalin*, pp. 109–18.

[22] Chester S. Chard, 'Time Depth and Culture Process in Maritime Northeast Asia', *Asian Perspectives*, V (Winter, 1961), 213–16.

Secondly, from approximately 1000 B.C. to A.D. 1000, these diverse groups on Sakhalin gradually fused, adopting new cultural patterns better suited to a maritime environment. Larger and more sophisticated boats reflect a development of a fishing economy. Toggle harpoons, bone knives, and adzes bear witness to enduring cultural influences from Chukhota and Kamchatka. Primitive metallurgical techniques appeared. There was still no appreciable contact with the Jōmon culture of Japan until towards the end of the period.

Thirdly, from A.D. 1000 Sakhalin's Neolithic culture began to show divergent tendencies. The inhabitants of the north strengthened cultural ties with maritime cultures of Kamchatka, Chukhota, and the Aleutian Islands. In the south, a growing influence from Japan is discerned in the form of metallurgy, stone polishing techniques, and pottery design.

Fourthly, the Ainu appear to have crossed over to Sakhalin from Hokkaidō sometime after A.D. 1000.[23] These Ainu met, intermingled, and occasionally fought with the Neolithic population already on the island. The Ainu called these people 'tonchi'. These 'tonchi' taught the Ainu new fishing techniques (such as the use of the flat-bottomed boat). Furthermore, 'tonchi' influence is detected in the Sakhalin Ainu ornaments, ceramics (the spiral design), and pottery (the absence of handles). Ainu legends state that these 'tonchi' were eventually pushed out of Sakhalin to the north.

Who were the 'tonchi'? Their boats closely resemble those of the Gilyak which suggests that the Gilyak may be descendants of Sakhalin's Neolithic population. Yet Sakhalin's Neolithic inhabitants shared characteristics with Eskimo cultures, especially Aleut artifacts excavated in Unalaska. The Ainu word for Aleut is 'tonchi'. Moreover, Aleut legends describe their tribe's eviction from an island in the west which could well refer to Sakhalin. It is a strong possibility that the distant Aleuts of the northern Kuriles, Kamchatka, and the Aleutian Islands may provide the key to solving the remaining problems of Sakhalin's prehistory.

[23] Japanese scholars may disagree with this 'late' date of the Ainu arrival in Sakhalin. The Soviet hypothesis has support from Chester Chard who estimates the Ainu dispersion from north-east Hokkaidō to southern Sakhalin as occurring around A.D. 1300. Chard, 'A New Look at the Ainu Problem', (mimeograph) (University of Wisconsin, 1969), p. 6.

These hypotheses by Soviet archaeologists suggest that the 'tonchi' mentioned in Ainu and Gilyak legends were the descendants of Neolithic hunters who reached Sakhalin from the Amur and Maritime regions 3,000 to 4,000 years ago. The fate of the 'tonchi' is still unclear. They may have been absorbed by the Ainu, Gilyak, and Oroki immigrants or possibly were pushed northwards and eastwards to Kamchatka, Chukhota, and the Aleutian Islands where they settled as the ancestors of the Aleuts.

The American archaeologist Chester Chard has advanced some important reservations concerning the Soviet hypotheses on Sakhalin's prehistory. Chard agrees with Soviet scholars that mainland Neolithic tribes probably crossed over to Sakhalin from the lower Amur River and Maritime Region. However, he doubts that these inland-oriented river tribes spontaneously acquired the maritime culture that has been discovered in excavations in southern Sakhalin's shell middens. Sakhalin's maritime culture (toggle harpoons and flat-bottomed boats of a sea-oriented economy) may have originated from the influx of arctic or sub-arctic peoples in the last centuries B.C. who later spread via northeastern Hokkaido to the Kurile Islands. This intrusion, Chard feels, possibly had its roots in south-west Alaska where a similar maritime culture of proven antiquity existed.[24]

These archaeological discoveries have raised intriguing questions on Sakhalin's role in prehistoric Northeast Asia. Geography made the island a meeting and dispersal point for several distinct groups of peoples and cultures which are now associated with Hokkaido, Eastern Siberia, Kamchatka, the Kurile and Aleutian islands, and Alaska. Future research in this field may bring to light significant insights and perspectives on the prehistoric migrations in north-east Asia and north-west America.

[24] Chard, 'Time Depth and Culture Process in Maritime Northeast Asia', pp. 213–16.

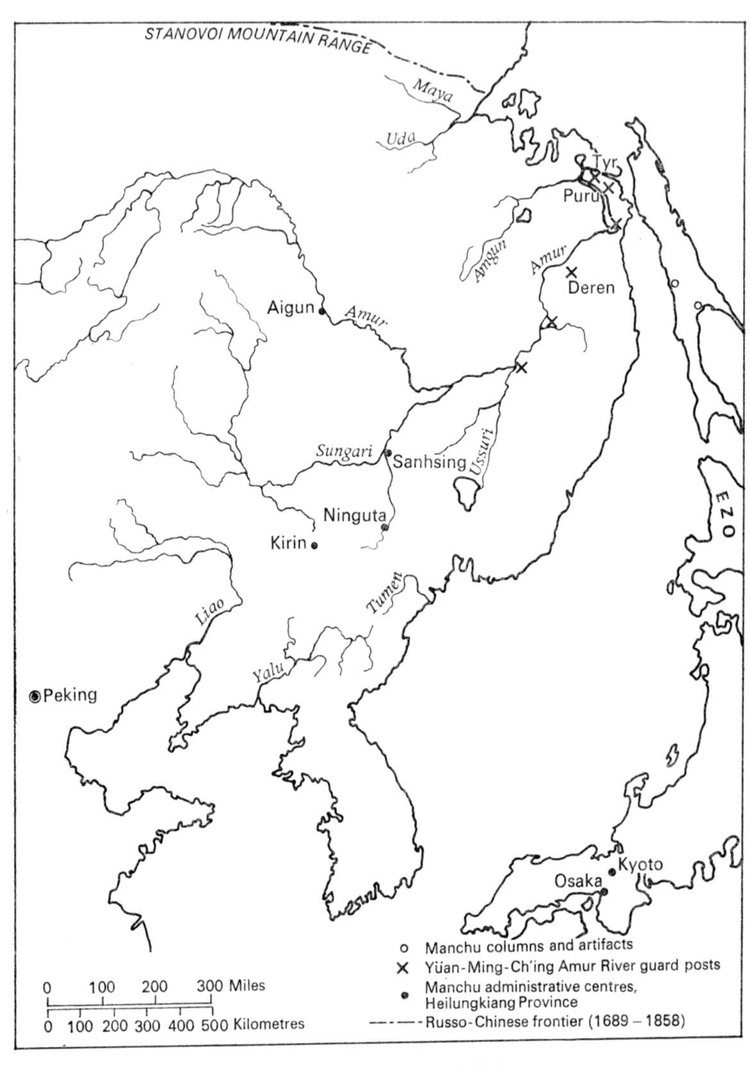

MAP II. Sakhalin and China

II

SAKHALIN AND CHINA

'If the rights of sovereignty fell to the discoverer, then it is clear that Sakhalin or at least northern Sakhalin would belong to China.'

HORA TOMIO (1956)

MOST people who are familiar with Sakhalin have the impression that the island was a historical frontier between Russia and Japan. Few are aware that from the thirteenth century China also played an important role in Sakhalin's past. Soviet historians of Sakhalin have avoided referring to China's association with the island. Their sensitivity to this topic is understandable. As the Chinese reached Sakhalin at least four centuries before any Russians, it is hard to support the Soviet claim that 'the entire island of Sakhalin belongs to our motherland by right of first discovery, first settlement, first exploration, and first unification'.[1]

By the treaties of Aigun (1858) and Peking (1860), China formally handed over to Russia the lands on the left (north) bank of the Amur River and the entire Maritime Region between the Ussuri River and the Sea of Japan. That these treaties failed to mention Sakhalin should not obscure the fact that China once exercised a loose sovereignty over that island. This chapter examines the development of China's relationship with Sakhalin and evaluates the impact of the Heavenly Kingdom on this remote island's history.

The borders of China's Heilungkiang Province approach to within 350 miles of southern Sakhalin. The distance from Peking to Sakhalin (1,500 miles) is considerably longer, yet there are natural routes of communication (the Sungari, Ussuri, and Amur rivers) by which the traveller could reach Sakhalin with less

[1] A. N. Ryzhkov, 'Iz istorii otkrytiia, issledovaniia, i osvoeniia Sakhalina i Kurilskikh ostrovov', in K. I. Kniazev, ed., *Sakhalinskaia oblast* (Iuzhno-Sakhalinsk, 1960), p. 43.

pains than such a distance would suggest. The importance of river communications cannot be overestimated when treating China's association with Sakhalin. Availability of river transport has led one Japanese to note that Sakhalin was actually 'closer' to China than to Japan, for it was easier to travel to Peking from there than it was to Kyoto.[2]

Two types of evidence suggest that Chinese influence reached Sakhalin at a very early date. First, Sui (A.D. 581–618), T'ang (618–907), and Sung (960–1279) period glass beads and earrings have been excavated in Sakhalin.[3] Liao (907–1123) and Chin (1114–1234) period copper bells have also been uncovered. These articles were traded by Sakhalin's inhabitants and mainland tribes who in turn had obtained them from China.

Secondly, there is tentative evidence that the Chinese were aware of Sakhalin's early inhabitants in the beginning of the first millenium A.D. Han period (202 B.C.–A.D. 220) written sources such as the *Shan hai ching*, the *San kuo chih*, and the *Huai nan tzu* make references to natives in the extreme north-east who wore fish skins and others who were covered with hair.[4] These 'hairy people' (*mao min*) mentioned in Han period sources may have been the ancestors of the Ainu. The accompanying geographical descriptions appear to refer to the vicinity of the lower Amur River.

The T'ang dynasty extended its frontiers westward deep into Central Asia and north-eastward down the Sungari River towards the Amur. Two T'ang period sources, the *Hsin T'ang shu* and the *T'ung tien* describe a distant island in the north-east called 'Liu kuei kuo' (literally 'country of vagrant devils') that the Japanese scholar Shiratori believed to be a reference to Sakhalin.[5] It is not clear whether Chinese travellers at this time actually set foot on Sakhalin. However, the dynasty did construct a tribute-collecting post at the junction of the Amur and Sungari rivers. At these posts, Chinese officials received delegations

[2] Kikuchi Kieji, *Kita Nihon no hanashi* (Tokyo, 1944), p. 152.

[3] Hora Tomio, *Karafuto shi kenkyū* (Tokyo, 1956), p. 60.

[4] Ibid., p. 98. Wada Kiyoshi, 'Shina no kisai ni arawaretaru Kokuryūkō karyū iki no genjumin', *Tōa shi ronsō* (Tokyo, 1942), pp. 457–8 (cited hereafter as Wada, 'Shina no kisai').

[5] Shiratori Kurakichi, 'Tō jidai no Karafuto ni tsuite', *Rekishi chiri*, IX (1907), 329. Shiratori used the *T'ung tien* (vol. 200) and the *Hsin T'ang shu* (vol. 220) for this inference.

of natives from the lower Amur and possibly from Sakhalin.

The Mongol conquests of the thirteenth century signalled a new era in China's relationship with Sakhalin. It was after the Mongols established the Yüan dynasty in China (1279–1368) that Sakhalin first came under a form of sovereignty imposed from without. Moreover, starting in this period, Chinese written references to Sakhalin increased in frequency and in detail.

In 1263 Mongol forces reached the mouth of the Amur River and erected a fortification and administrative post at Tyr at the junction of the Amur and Amgun rivers.[6] While the Gilyak population inhabiting the region of the Amur mouth and northern Sakhalin submitted to Mongol suzerainty, the Sakhalin Ainu stubbornly refused to yield. For the next forty years, the Ainu engaged in sporadic warfare with the Yüan dynasty. A Mongol expedition was launched against Sakhalin in 1264, but it seems to have foundered. A more ambitious campaign was conducted in 1284, but an Ainu counter-attack obliged the Mongols to call for reinforcements of 10,000 men in 1286. By 1287, the Yüan dynasty had stationed garrisons in Sakhalin that included Han Chinese foot soldiers. Undeterred, the Ainu responded with a daring assault across the Tatary Straits to the mainland in 1297. Only in 1308 did the last of the Ainu chiefs submit to Yüan sovereignty and agree to pay tribute at Tyr. During the height of Yüan power in this area (1280–1320), the Mongols established and maintained forty-five guard posts on the lower Amur and Ussuri rivers. After 1320, however, the Mongols left Sakhalin and retired up the Amur River.

The Ming dynasty (1368–1644) resumed China's contact with Sakhalin, but the relationship differed from that created by the Mongols. While the Yüan advance was characterized by conquest, the Ming expansion penetrated the lower Amur and Sakhalin without resort to arms. The Chinese collected a tribute of furs in exchange for beads and silk products. Ming sources reveal that soon after the Yüan collapse, the emperor T'ai Tsu ordered the re-occupation of the guard posts on the lower Amur (1387).[7] In 1409, the Yung lo emperor established

[6] Hora, *Karafuto shi kenkyū*, pp. 99, 120–1. Wada, 'Shina no kisai', pp. 465–6. Both Hora and Wada quote the Yüan dynasty annals, *Yüan shih* (vols. 5, 8, 11, 13, 30, 91) and the Ming period work, *Liao tung chih* (vol. 9).

[7] *Ta Ming i t'ung chih* and *Liao tung chih* (vol. 9) as quoted by Hora, *Karafuto shi kenkyū*, pp. 103–5, and Wada, 'Shina no kisai', pp. 466–84.

the Nurkan administrative district (lower Amur and Sakhalin) and constructed a large temple on the ruins of Tyr. The remains of this temple could be seen as recently as 1918, after which its fate is unclear.[8]

Despite its destruction by Gilyaks in 1412, Tyr was rebuilt and continued to operate as a symbol of Ming prestige until the middle of the fifteenth century. No expeditions were sent to Sakhalin but the Ainu were either persuaded or overawed into sending regular tribute missions. The traveller Hsing Shu toured the Nurkan district in 1409, and it is thought likely that he visited Sakhalin.[9]

From the middle of the fifteenth century, the Ming administration withdrew from the lower Amur, inaugurating almost two centuries during which Chinese influence was attenuated if not eclipsed.

The approach of Manchu power to fill the vacuum left by the retreat of the Ming from the lower Amur and Sakhalin dates from the early seventeenth century. Pushing northwards along the Ussuri and Sungari rivers from bases in Kirin and Ninguta, the Manchus established a military base at San Hsing in 1607 and reached the north bank of the Amur in 1616. While the main thrust of the Manchu expansion was directed southward towards the Liao Valley and north China during the 1620s, other groups of Manchus subjugated the Tungus tribes on the lower Amur and reoccupied the old Mongol/Ming posts there.

The investment of the lower Amur was completed in 1644 when the Tungus, Gilyak, and Ainu submitted and entered into tributary relations with the newly established Ch'ing dynasty (1644–1912). It is interesting to note that 1644 is the year in which a band of Cossacks under Vasilii Poiarkov descended the Amur and spent the winter at the river's mouth, just across the Tatary Straits from Sakhalin. The Manchu's northern advance preceded the Russians by only two or three decades. Nevertheless, the Ch'ing rulers were able to check Russian incursions in a series of military expeditions. The Manchu success on the north-eastern frontier was codified by the Treaty of Nerchinsk

[8] The Yüan and Ming monuments on the lower Amur have been described, sketched, and photographed. See Perry McDonough Collins, *A Voyage Down the Amoor* (New York, 1860), pp. 293–300, and Torii Ryūzō, *Kokuryūkō to kita Karafuto* (Tokyo, 1943), frontispiece photographs nos. 1–4, pp. 146–52, 390–2.

[9] Hora, *Karafuto shi kenkyū*, p. 104.

(1689) which excluded the Russians from the Amur River valley and designated the Sino-Russian frontier as following the crest of the Stanovoi Mountain Range. The Nerchinsk Treaty made no mention of Sakhalin, an omission which the Russians would later exploit.

The Soviet historian B. P. Polevoi has advanced an ingenious argument explaining the absence of any mention of Sakhalin in the Treaty of Nerchinsk.[10] According to Polevoi, the Russian plenipotentiary at the treaty negotiations was clearly aware that Russian Cossacks had occupied the island, that the Manchus were under the false impression that Sakhalin was an 'independent Ainu kingdom', and that Russia did not have the power to defend Sakhalin in the event of a Manchu attack. In view of these circumstances, the Russian plenipotentiary purposely avoided any reference to Sakhalin in his negotiations with the Manchus in order to perpetuate their delusion. Consequently, Polevoi argues, the Nerchinsk Treaty omitted any mention of Sakhalin, and the island consistently remained Russian territory. Polevoi's explanations leave several questions unanswered. First, there is no evidence that any Cossacks actually occupied Sakhalin in the seventeenth century. The available documents merely suggest that some members of Poiarkov's expedition *saw* a large island across the Tatary Straits in 1644. Secondly, when the Governor-General of Eastern Siberia, Count Muraviev, advanced a claim to Sakhalin in 1859 *vis-à-vis* the Japanese, he cited the Aigun Treaty (1858) which transferred Manchu territory on the north bank of the Amur to Russia. Muraviev's association of the lower Amur and Sakhalin strongly implies that he regarded the latter to be within the jurisdiction of the Manchu Empire before 1858. Thirdly, it is debatable whether the Manchus were as ignorant about Sakhalin as Polevoi has suggested.

The Manchu interest in Sakhalin dated from the early years of the seventeenth century. The noted scholar Wei Yuan (1794–1856) wrote that the Manchus dispatched an expedition to Sakhalin in 1617.[11] Manchu craft sailed along the coast of the Maritime Region from present-day Vladivostok to the Amur estuary and traded with the indigenous Tungus tribes.

[10] B. P. Polevoi, *Pervootkryvateli Sakhalina* (Iuzhno-Sakhalinsk, 1959), pp. 68–9.
[11] Wei Yuan, *Sheng wu chih* (vol. I), cited by Hora, *Karafuto shi kenkyū*, pp. 125, 142.

In 1709, the emperor K'ang-Hsi dispatched a surveying mission accompanied by three Jesuits down the Amur River.[12] The Jesuits did not reach Sakhalin, but they were told by natives on the Amur that a large island existed at the mouth of the river. They called this island 'Saghalien anga hata' which meant 'cliffs at the mouth of the black river'. 'Saghalien' (black) was the Manchu appellation for the Amur River. The Jesuits learned that the inhabitants of this island traded with the Manchus and raised reindeer (which Sakhalin's Oroki natives still do today).

After the Jesuits returned to Peking, K'ang-Hsi sent out a second mission consisting entirely of Manchus which descended the Amur and succeeded in crossing the straits to Sakhalin. It may have been this expedition which erected the wood and stone columns with Manchu inscriptions that were later discovered by Japanese explorers around Terpenie Bay on Sakhalin's eastern coast.[13]

From about 1700 to 1820, Sakhalin's Ainu, Gilyak, and Oroki natives sent tribute missions to Manchu posts on the Amur River. Some of the native chiefs travelled as far as Ninguta and Kirin, and there are indications that tribute missions from Sakhalin may have reached Peking. These longer voyages resulted from a Manchu policy of encouraging the chiefs to take Chinese wives.

These tribute missions stimulated a flow of Chinese goods (brocade, beads, fans, clothing, pipes, needles) into Japan. Natives visiting the Manchu posts received Chinese products in return for furs. They in turn traded with Japanese merchants in southern Sakhalin or northern Hokkaido. The merchants brought these Chinese articles to Osaka and Edo where they were highly valued. This multi-stage exchange was called the 'Santan trade', the word 'Santan' being an Ainu term referring to the Goldi tribe of the lower Amur River.[14]

The Japanese explorer Mamiya Rinzō (1776–1844) provided valuable information on Sakhalin's relationship to China during the early nineteenth century. Mamiya made two trips to Sakhalin

[12] J. B. Du Halde, *Description de l'Empire de la Chine*, IV (Paris, 1735), 12–14.

[13] Itō Tasaburō, 'Nihonjin no tankenteki seishin', *Nihon bunka kenkyū*, VII (1959), 45. Hora Tomio, *Mamiya Rinzō* (Tokyo, 1960), p. 131.

[14] Hora, *Karafuto shi kenkyū*, pp. 59–78, 135. John Harrison, 'The Saghalien Trade: a Contribution to Ainu Studies', *Southwestern Journal of Anthropology*, X (Autumn, 1954), 278–93.

(1808, 1809) at the order of the Japanese government which sought to clarify the island's geography and political status. The Japanese had long suspected that northern Sakhalin was under the sovereignty of China. The Japanese appellation of Sakhalin, 'Karafuto', is said to have denoted originally 'Chinese people'.[15] The influx of Chinese products through the Santan trade indicated to some observers that there even may have been Chinese living on the northern half of the island. Mamiya's mission was to investigate at first hand the source of these speculations.

Mamiya exceeded his instructions. Not only did he explore northern Sakhalin, but he accompanied a group of Gilyaks to the continent on a tribute mission to Deren, a Manchu post on the Amur River located near present-day Novoilinovka. His description of this trip in *Tōdatsu kikō* (an account of travels in Eastern Tartary) gives a unique glimpse into the Manchu tribute system in operation.[16]

According to Mamiya, Sakhalin's Gilyak headmen visited Deren annually bearing marten furs. They prostrated themselves before three Manchu officials seated upon a platform inside a wooden stockade. In return, the chiefs received glass beads and highly decorated brocade which symbolized both the link with the Ch'ing dynasty and confirmed their own prestige inside Sakhalin. To formalize their position of leadership, these chiefs were awarded titles: *harada*, denoting 'village headman', and *kashinta*, 'district chief'. These titles passed from generation to generation. Mamiya later met a Sakhalin Ainu chief who possessed a bundle of documents in Manchu script. When translated, these turned out to be credentials for tribute voyages and a set of injunctions concerning marriages and successions.[17]

Mamiya Rinzō witnessed the tribute system in Sakhalin and on the lower Amur in the twilight of the Manchu presence in these places. Already in the last decade of the eighteenth century, the southern part of Sakhalin was falling increasingly under the

[15] Taking the then commonly used characters for Karafuto (唐太), the cartographer Takahashi Kageyasu (1785–1829) argued that the character for 'kara' meant 'Chinese'. 'Futo' was a dialect term in northern Japan for 'hito' or 'man' (人). Thus, Japan's northern inhabitants originally referred to Sakhalin as 'an island where Chinese are'. Karafuto chō, ed., *Karafuto sōsho*, VI (Toyohara, 1941), 4. Miyazaki Raihachi, *Karafuto shi monogatari* (Tokyo, 1944), p. 18.

[16] Mamiya Rinzō, *Tōdatsu kikō*, ed., Mantetsu kōhōka (Dairen, 1938).

[17] Mamiya, *Tōdatsu kikō*, p. 26. Hora, *Karafuto shi kenkyū*, pp. 135–40.

economic influence of Japanese merchants, although the Manchus reportedly kept guard-boats at the mouth of the Amur as late as 1790.[18] The Manchu retreat from Sakhalin and the lower Amur began almost simultaneously with the acceleration of Japan's northern expansion after 1785. The frontier posts at the Amur estuary were abandoned in the 1790s. Deren was closed down in 1826. The Manchus gradually pulled in their outposts and withdrew further and further up the Amur. Sakhalin's natives crossed to the continent less frequently. The tribute system fell into disuse. Chinese and Manchu traders continued to operate on the lower Amur until the 1860s, but the actual power of the Ch'ing dynasty in Sakhalin was moribund.

Why did the Manchus fail to develop the lower Amur and Sakhalin, thus assimilating these areas into the empire? Partial answers lie in the suffocating restrictions imposed by Manchu administrative, immigration, and trade policies on their north-east frontier.

The Manchus did not erect a permanent administrative apparatus on the lower Amur or Sakhalin.[19] These areas were administered as part of the military district of Heilungkiang from Ninguta (until 1676), Kirin (1676–1735), and San Hsing (after 1735). Each of these centres proved to be too remote from Sakhalin for effective control. The guard and tribute-collecting posts strung out along the Amur River were staffed only during the summer months. Only very rarely did a Manchu official travel to Sakhalin.

Secondly, the Manchus failed to retain this region because they restricted the immigration of Han Chinese. During the reigns of the Shun-chih, K'ang-Hsi, and Yung-cheng emperors (1644–1736), the immigration of Han Chinese into southern Manchuria was not obstructed. Han Chinese participated in the civil bureaucracy of the three northern provinces. This policy continued during the first fifteen years of the Ch'ien-lung emperor's reign, but the year 1751 signalled a turning point towards exclusion. Anxious to preserve the 'purity' of their homeland, the Manchus banned Han Chinese from the administration

[18] A. J. von Krusenstern, *Voyage Round the World in the Years, 1803, 1804, 1805, 1806*, II (London, 1813), 175.

[19] Agnes Fang-chih Ch'en, 'Chinese Frontier Diplomacy: the Eclipse of Manchuria', *Yenching Journal of Social Studies*, V (July, 1950), 81–4. Also see R. H. G. Lee, *The Manchurian Frontier in Ch'ing History* (Cambridge, Mass., 1970).

of the northern provinces and severely restricted immigration. Even travellers, Chinese or Manchu, were forbidden to proceed down the Sungari River beyond San Hsing.

Thirdly, although the Manchus accepted tribute brought to them from Sakhalin, they discouraged private trade. In 1846 only ten monopoly merchants who had received special permission to gather the ginseng root were allowed to descend the Ussuri and Sungari rivers.[20] Of course secret trade, the bribery of officials, and other devious stratagems prevented the total insulation of the lower Amur from Chinese contacts. Nevertheless, the Manchu garrisons and patrol boats discouraged frequent evasion of the exclusion laws. By preserving the pristine state of the 'Great Northeast' (Sakhalin, the Amur Valley, the Maritime Region), the Manchus ironically facilitated the incorporation of these lands into the Russian Empire by a handful of determined men in the 1850s.

The treaties of Aigun (1858) and Peking (1860) by which Russia gained over 400,000 square miles of Chinese territory made no mention of Sakhalin. Sakhalin's status before the 1850s remained ambiguous, although some European observers (Russians among them) considered at least the northern part of the island to be Chinese.[21] Unfortunately, I have been unable to find sources that throw light on the question of how Sakhalin affected (if at all) Manchu leaders during 1858–60. The Russo-Japanese Treaty of Shimoda (1855) stipulated that Sakhalin be held jointly by Russia and Japan. This was the first mention of the island in an international treaty. There is no evidence that the Manchus protested or were even aware of this treaty's implications. After approximately 1790, Sakhalin quietly slipped

[20] E. G. Ravenstein, *The Russians on the Amur* (London, 1861), p. 82, quoting from a letter dated 5 April 1846 from the French missionary, de la Brunière, just before the latter's death at the hands of Gilyak natives on the lower Amur.

[21] A. W. Habersham, *The North Pacific Surveying and Exploring Expedition* (Philadelphia, 1858). Habersham visited Sakhalin in 1855 and noted that 'it is said to be divided between Chinese and Japanese', p. 305. The famous Russian surveyor of the Kuriles, V. M. Golovnin, considered Sakhalin to be divided between China and Japan, V. M. Golovnin, *Zapiski Vasiliia Mikhailovicha Golovnina v plenu u Iapontsev v 1811, 1812, i 1813 godakh*, III (St. Petersburg, 1851), 119–20, as cited by George A. Lensen, *The Russian Push toward Japan: Russo-Japanese Relations, 1697–1875* (Princeton, 1959), p. 272n. The French scholar Paul Labbé asserted that all of Sakhalin was Chinese until 1800. Labbé, 'Sakhaline', *Questions diplomatiques et coloniales*, XX (Oct. 1905), 424. Mamiya Rinzō also believed northern Sakhalin to be Chinese. Hora, *Karafuto shi kenkyū*, p. 51.

out of China's sphere of influence and for the next 150 years became a contested frontier between Russia and Japan.

China showed no particular interest in the Russo-Japanese rivalry over Sakhalin between 1806 and 1945. In 1950, Premier Chou En-lai publicly supported the Soviet Union's claim to all Sakhalin.[22] With the aggravation of the Sino-Soviet rift in the 1960s, however, there appeared faint indications that Sakhalin is not yet a closed issue, at least as a propaganda instrument.

The publication of Liu Pei-hua's *Brief History of Modern China* in 1952 indicated that even in the People's Republic of China, there existed a consciousness of lands lost to Russia in 1858 and 1860.[23] Liu's history noted the extent of the lost territories and illustrated the area with a map of China's frontiers as they had existed in 1840. Sakhalin was clearly included inside China. In itself, this book was not extraordinary, for both Communist and Nationalist historical studies freely refer to China's former boundaries as being unjustly violated by 'unequal treaties'. It is significant, however, that Liu's map of the 1840 boundaries was reissued in 1962 and widely distributed at a trade fair in Mexico in 1964. Moreover, in the new edition of Liu's map, the Outer Mongolian and Central Asian territorial claims were dropped, but the lost lands of the 'Great Northeast' were prominently displayed.

In March 1969 a series of armed confrontations on Damansky (Chenpao) Island in the Ussuri River aroused world interest in the Sino-Soviet frontier along Heilungkiang Province and the Soviet Maritime Region. It would be dangerously misleading to infer that China is about to make territorial claims on the Russians to revise the 'unequal treaties' of 1858 and 1860. Moreover, Sakhalin lies well beyond the Amur and Ussuri islands in question and was not specifically mentioned in the 'unequal treaties'. Nevertheless, in the sense that the Chinese remain conscious of their 1840 boundaries, this island will remain part of the broader frontier issues between the Soviet Union and the People's Republic of China.[24]

[22] *New York Times*, 5 December 1950

[23] Francis Watson, *The Frontiers of China* (London, 1966), pp. 26, 190–1.

[24] A 1969 Peking publication depicts Sakhalin (called 'K'u Yeh-tao') as historically Chinese territory, confirmed by the Treaty of Nerchinsk (1689). *Shin tsua o datō seyo! Kokuryūkō to Usurikō de no Soshū no han Chūgoku no bōgyaku kōi* [Strike Down the New Tsars! Anti-Chinese Atrocities of Soviet Revisionists on the Amur and Ussuri Rivers] (Peking, 1969), p. 19.

On 25 May 1969 the New China News Agency announced that 'China has no territorial claims against any of her neighbouring countries'.[25] Sakhalin is not at present claimed by China, nor is it likely to be at any time in the near future. The fact that China's historical connection with Sakhalin antedated that of Russia, however, should lend weight to the Chinese moral argument that the 1858 and 1860 treaties were territorial brigandage cunningly imposed at the moment of China's weakness. Of course, China's own advance down the Amur after the thirteenth century can be represented as a form of imperialism imposed upon the Tungus and Paleosiberian indigenes of the region.

China's seven-century association with Sakhalin left no lasting influence. Successive expeditions and tribute missions had only a local significance except for a trickle of Chinese goods into Japan, a cartographical expedition, and scattered monuments attesting to a long-dead sovereignty. But, there is one important fact that has been overlooked by the Russian and Japanese patriots who have advanced claims to Sakhalin based upon 'historical rights' of 'prior discovery' and 'prior sovereignty'. Neither Russia nor Japan was the first foreign power to reach and excercise suzerainty over Sakhalin. The honour must go to the Mongol Yüan dynasty and its Chinese successor, the Ming.

[25] Quoted in *The Times* [London], 26 May 1969.

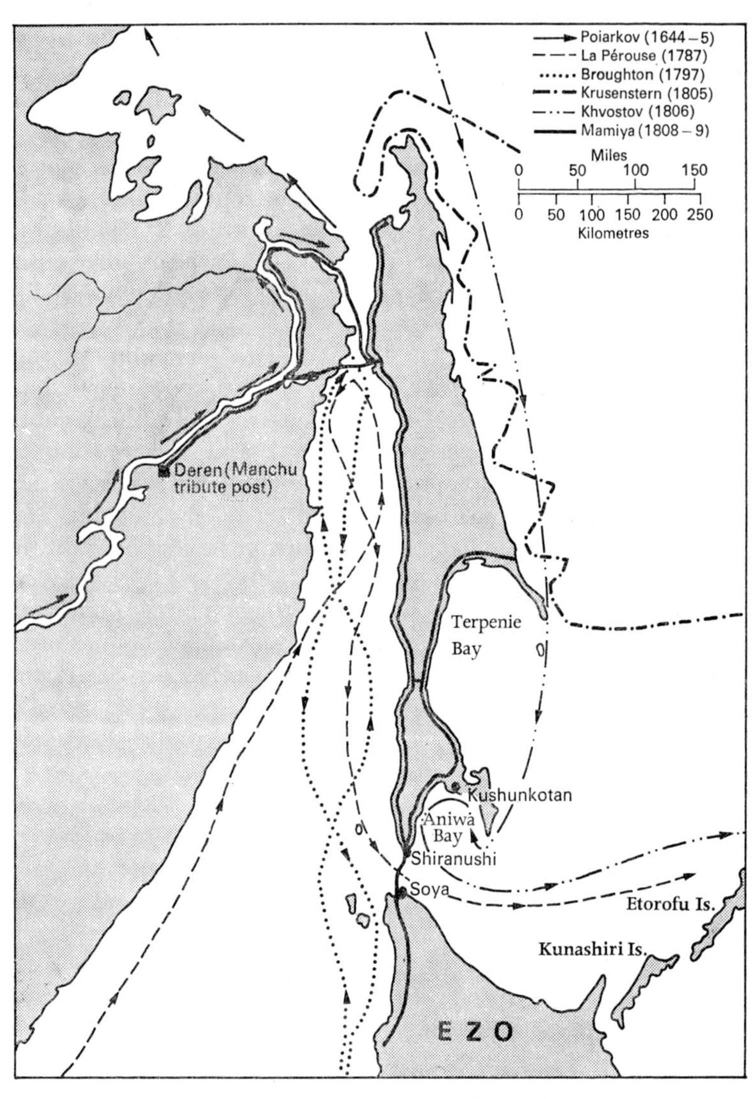

MAP III. The exploration of Sakhalin

III

DISCOVERY AND EXPLORATION

'The history of Sakhalin's discovery, exploration, development, and defence is the history of the feats of the Russian people.'

A. N. Ryzhkov (1960)

'Undoubtedly, the right of first exploration belongs to the Japanese, and the Japanese were the first to occupy southern Sakhalin.'

Anton Chekhov (1895)

NOTWITHSTANDING its long association with China, Sakhalin remained unknown by the rest of the world until the middle of the seventeenth century. Even after its 'discovery' by Russians, Japanese, and Dutchmen, the island attracted little attention for over a century. Then two interrelated developments transformed Sakhalin from a forgotten backwater into an object of international attention. First, the riddle of the island's cartography lured a succession of explorers. Secondly, the expanding frontiers of Russia and Japan met in Sakhalin and turned it into a scene of friction. Sakhalin's cartography was conclusively clarified by 1855, but the frontier issue continued with minor interruptions to exacerbate Russo-Japanese relations until the present day.

Who first discovered Sakhalin is a matter of dispute fuelled by political polemic and complicated by confusion surrounding dates and documents. Soviet historians unanimously claim the honour for Russia by citing the roving Cossack bands which descended the Amur River in the 1640s. The Japanese claims vary according to the patriotism of the spokesman. Even the most modest Japanese claims, however, allude to events that antedate the coming of the Cossacks. Finally, the well-documented voyage of the Dutch explorer Maerten Gerritszoon Vries who reached Aniwa Bay on 15 July 1643 has its adherents. All these claims are, strictly speaking, irrelevant, for the Chinese clearly 'discovered' Sakhalin before anyone save the aborigines. Discounting China, the evidence points to the Japanese as having reached Sakhalin before either the Cossacks or Vries.

Patriotic Japanese historians have asserted that Sakhalin was part of Japan since the second century B.C., that General Abe Hirafu fought the *mishihase* tribes there in A.D. 659, that the Buddhist monk Nichiji of the Nichiren sect prosyletized there in 1295, and that the lord Takeda received Sakhalin as part of his fief of Ezo (Hokkaido) in the 1450s.[1] These claims are colourful, imaginative, unfounded, and probably false. Some Western (including pre-revolutionary Russian) historians date the earliest Japanese contacts with Sakhalin from 1613, which is an error based on a misreading of Japanese sources.[2] The first reliably documented Japanese landing on Sakhalin was made in 1635 by a surveying expedition dispatched by the lord of Matsumae (southern Hokkaidō).[3] A second Japanese mission penetrated as far north as Terpenie Bay in 1636 and collected information which formed the basis of Japan's first map of Sakhalin published in 1639.[4] The lord of Matsumae sent further missions in 1650, 1689, and 1700 and opened seasonal fishing villages there in 1679.[5]

The first Russians approached Sakhalin from the north and west less than a decade after the Japanese had begun their surveys. Vasilii Poiarkov descended the Amur River with a small band of Cossacks in 1644 and spent the winter somewhere near the mouth of the river. Although there is no evidence that he

[1] Miyazaki Raihachi, *Karafuto shi monogatari* (Tokyo, 1944), pp. 1, 8, 37. Oka Sakae, *Kita Karafuto* (Tokyo, 1942), p. 9. Yamashita Ryūmon, *Karafuto ron* (Tokyo, 1929), pp. 2–3. Nishizuru Sadayoshi, *Karafuto shi no shiori*, Vol. VI of *Karafuto sōsho*, ed., Karafuto chō (Toyohara, 1941), 15–22.

[2] Anton Chekhov, 'Ostrov Sakhalin', in *A. P. Chekhov, sobranie sochinenii*, X (Moscow, 1963), 52. F. A. Golder, *Russian Expansion on the Pacific*, 1641–1850 (Cleveland, 1914), p. 256. Great Britain, Foreign Office, Historical Section, *Sakhalin* (London, 1920), p. 7. Philipp Franz von Siebold, *Nippon. Archiv zur Beschreibung von Japan*, I (Leyden, 1832), 260–1. Siebold seems to have misread the Japanese year period date Kan'ei 12 (1635) as 1613. Chekhov, Golder, and others took their dates from Siebold and perpetuated the error.

[3] Hokkaido chō, ed., *Shinsen Hokkaido shi*, II (Sapporo, 1936), 111–12. Abe Makoto, 'Edo makki ni okeru Karafuto tanken', *Chiri shigaku*, LXIII (1934), 51–2.

[4] Takakura Shinichirō and Shibata Sadakichi, 'Waga kuni ni okeru Karafuto chizu sakusei shi', *Hokuhō bunka kenkyū hōkoku*, II (Oct. 1939), 276 (hereafter cited as Takakura, 'Karafuto chizu sakusei shi').

[5] A survey of 1700 listed twenty-one settlements in Sakhalin. 'Matsumae shima no kyōchō', *Zoku zoku gunsho ruijū*, IX (Tokyo, 1906), 323–5.

crossed the straits and set foot on Sakhalin, he has been called the 'first to discover Sakhalin'.[6] Even if Poiarkov had reached the island, his discovery came a year later than that of the Dutch explorer Vries. The Soviet historian B. P. Polevoi has recently advanced new evidence that two of Poiarkov's companions, Ivan Moskvitin and Ivan Kolobov, actually caught sight of Sakhalin in 1640.[7] Soviet historians insist that the Japanese did not reach Sakhalin until 1786 (as opposed to 1635), which conveniently leaves the distinction of discovering the island to Moskvitin and Kolobov who preceded Vries by three years.

The Soviet claims to prior discovery are designed to reinforce the political argument that Sakhalin's territorial sovereignty belongs historically to Russia. To uphold this position, Soviet historians have omitted all mention of Japan's association with Sakhalin before 1786. This omission of data to justify nationalistic claims reminds one of the prewar Japanese patriots solemnly describing the mythical exploits of Abe Hirafu and the monk Nichiji in Sakhalin.

Cartography

Sakhalin has a singularly complex cartographical history for such a comparatively small island. Discovered in the seventeenth century, its true shape, size, and relationship to the continent were not correctly grasped by a vast majority of map-makers until after 1855. Remoteness, fogs, sandbars, and winds conspired to frustrate maritime surveys. When the Japanese and Russians finally did draw up moderately accurate maps, they spared no effort to keep these charts a state secret. It was only the outbreak of the Crimean War (1854) and an embarrassing gaffe of the English China Squadron that provoked a thorough survey of the island's position.

The first extant European map to depict Sakhalin was published by Nicolaes Witsen in 1687.[8] His map of north-east

[6] A. N. Ryzhkov, 'Iz istorii otkrytiia, issledovaniia i osvoeniia Sakhalina i Kurilskikh ostrovov', in K. I. Kniazev, ed., *Sakhalinskaia oblast* (Iuzhno-Sakhalinsk, 1960), p. 51. Semion Buitovoi, *Sadi i okeana* (Leningrad, 1957), p. 127.

[7] B. P. Polevoi, *Pervootkryvateli Sakhalina* (Iuzhno-Sakhalinsk, 1959), pp. 7–22. P. T. Iakovleva, 'Pervootkryvateli Sakhalina', *Istoriia SSSR*, VIII (Mar.–Apr. 1964), 181–2.

[8] Nicolaes Witsen, *Noord en Oost Tartaren* (Amsterdam, 1705), p. 968, depicting a map dated 1687.

Tartary described a small island labelled 'Amoerse Eylandt' at the mouth of a large river which is apparently the Amur. Witsen seems to have derived his information from an account of Mikul Timofiev, one of Poiarkov's companions who wintered at the mouth of the Amur River in 1644–5.[9]

Witsen's 'Amoerse Eylandt' remained the standard map of Sakhalin until 1735 when J. B. Du Halde brought out a history of China that carried J. B. B. D'Anville's charts of the Amur region based largely on the Jesuit survey of 1709.[10] D'Anville resorted to his imagination when drawing Sakhalin's shape and size. He placed the entire island north of the 50th parallel (which should bisect it). He did, however, faithfully transcribe the native appellation and dubbed the island 'Saghalien anga hata' or 'cliffs at the mouth of the black river'. The present name of the island was thus first introduced into European parlance.

Sakhalin continued to be considered an island until three prestigious European explorers convinced scholars that it was actually connected with the continent by an isthmus. In the summer of 1787, Jean Francois Galoup de la Pérouse tried in vain to discover a passage between Sakhalin and the mainland by approaching them from the south. After advancing partially through the straits, La Pérouse judged the path ahead impassable and concluded that Sakhalin was a peninsula.[11]

The next attempt was made by the English surveyor William Broughton in 1797. Broughton, like his predecessor, approached the straits from the south. Taking frequent fathom measurements, he pushed fifteen miles further north than had La Pérouse. He then entered what appeared to be a bay. To be doubly sure, he lowered a small boat and surveyed the area until satisfied that no straits existed.[12]

Following the expeditions of La Pérouse and Broughton, the Russian explorer, Captain Ivan Fedorovich Krusenstern, en-

[9] B. P. Polevoi, 'Zabytye svedeniia sputnikov V. D. Poiarkova o Sakhaline (1644–1645 gg.)', *Geograficheskoe obshchestvo SSSR. Izvestiia*, XC (Nov.–Dec. 1958), 547–51.

[10] J. B. Du Halde, *Description de l'Empire de la Chine* IV (Paris, 1735). Engelbert Kaempfer's map of Japan published in 1727 depicted 'Okujeso' (a Japanese term for Sakhalin) as the southern tip of Kamchatka which extended across the Pacific Ocean to America. Kaempfer, *The History of Japan together with a Description of the Kingdom of Siam 1690–92* (Glasgow, 1906), I, 108; III, 387

[11] J. F. G. de la Pérouse, *Voyage de la Pérouse autour du monde*, II (Paris, 1798), 418.

[12] W. R. Broughton, *Voyage of Discovery in the North Pacific Ocean* (London, 1804), vii.

deavoured to determine Sakhalin's relation to the continent by approaching the straits from the north in 1805. Like his two predecessors, however, Krusenstern found his advance obstructed by sand bars. Still separated by over 200 miles from the point of Broughton's most northerly position, he called off the attempt. Krusenstern concluded that the Amur River emptied into a wide shallow sand bed. Accumulated alluvial soil and sand rendered navigation from the river to the ocean impracticable. Reading Broughton's published account of his explorations, Krusenstern expressed deep satisfaction that his prognosis of Sakhalin's geography was confirmed.[13]

European geographers felt serenely convinced that Sakhalin was an extension of the Asiatic continent. In 1812, a German geographer eloquently celebrated the superiority of European science after recapitulating the voyages that had 'proved' Sakhalin to be a peninsula.[14] When an English cartographer named Arrowsmith published a map of Asia in 1822 which showed Sakhalin as an island (following D'Anville's model), he was cavalierly dismissed by the famous orientalist H. J. Klaproth as 'the most ignorant of those whose occupation is cartography'.[15]

The history of Japanese cartography of Sakhalin showed some similarities with that of the evolution of European opinion on the island. There appeared a 'peninsula theory' which misled Japanese scholars as much as their European contemporaries. However, one important event intervened which changed the direction of Japanese thinking on Sakhalin. A Japanese explorer conclusively proved Sakhalin's island status in 1809, forty years before Captain Gennadii Nevelskoi of the Russian Navy duplicated the feat.

The earliest extant Japanese map of Sakhalin (which the Japanese called 'Karafuto', 'Kita Ezo', or 'Oku Ezo') was presented to the shogun by the lord of Matsumae in 1700.[16] The

[13] A. J. von Krusenstern, *Voyage Round the World in the Years 1803, 1804, 1805, 1806*, II (London, 1813), 178–82.

[14] Ludwig Lindner, 'Entdeckungsgeschichte der Insel Jesso und der Halbinsel Sagalien', *Allgemeine Geographische Ephemeriden*, XXXVIII (July, 1812), 424–5.

[15] H. J. Klaproth, *Observations sur la Carte de l'Asie Publiée en 1822 par M. Arrowsmith* (Paris, 1826), p. 3.

[16] Takakura, 'Karafuto chizu sakusei shi', p. 274. Japanese maps of Sakhalin are recorded to have been made in 1593 and 1636 but they have been lost or destroyed. Minagawa Shinsaku, 'Karafuto hantō setsu to Sagarin hantō setsu', *Denki*, X (March 1943), 13.

map clearly shows Sakhalin as an island, but only the southern extremity bears any resemblance to its actual shape. For the next eighty years, Japanese maps continued to portray Sakhalin as a small island north of Ezo (Hokkaido).

Confusion arose in the 1780s when two different versions of D'Anville's map of Asia reached Japan. The first (1735 edition) depicted an island called 'Saghalien' at the mouth of the Amur River. South of this lay two other islands. From this, the Japanese erroneously inferred that 'Saghalien' was not the land that lay immediately north of Ezo. 'Saghalien', they concluded, was not Karafuto but another island further to the north, beyond Karafuto. At this point a revised D'Anville map (1752 edition) appeared in Japan in which one of the two islands south of 'Saghalien' disappeared. In its place a narrow peninsula labelled 'Cape Aniwa' stretched south-eastwards from the Asiatic continent. 'Cape Aniwa' was the Japanese appellation for the southern tip of Karafuto. The Japanese naturally concluded that Karafuto was a peninsula and 'Saghalien' an island somewhere further north. Of course, there was no suspicion that 'Saghalien' and Karafuto were identical.

The revised D'Anville map was soon adopted as the basis for the 'peninsular theory' of Karafuto by most of the country's leading scholars.[17] The famous geographer and polemicist Hayashi Shihei propounded the peninsular character of Karafuto in a map published in 1785. When the shogunate dispatched the explorer Ōishi Ippei to Karafuto in 1786, it learned that Karafuto might be an island, but a second expedition of 1792 returned with the opposite opinion. After 1792 such influential individuals as Matsudaira Sadanobu,[18] Honda Toshiaki,[19] and Kondō Jūzō[20] all publicly supported the 'peninsular theory'.

[17] Hora Tomio, *Karafuto shi kenkyū* (Tokyo, 1956), pp. 29–31. Minagawa, 'Karafuto hantō setsu', pp. 9–12.

[18] Matsudaira Sadanobu was a dominant figure in the shogunate from 1787 to 1793. In 'Ezo osonae ikken' (1792), he asserted that 'old theories have it that Karafuto is an island, but they have been proven false'. Quoted in Minagawa, 'Karafuto hantō setsu', p. 13.

[19] Honda Toshiaki (1744–1821), a gifted and far-seeing polymath of 'Dutch learning', derived his opinions on Karafuto from one of his disciples, Mogami Tokunai, who was an explorer and cartographer of Ezo and Karafuto. Hora Tomio, *Mamiya Rinzō* (Tokyo, 1960), p. 112.

[20] Kondō Jūzō (1771–1829), a prominent explorer and geographer who in 1798 claimed Etorofu Island for Japan. He later became the shogun's chief librarian. Kondō, 'Henyo bunkai zukō', *Kondō seisai zenshū*, I (Tokyo, 1905), 78–80.

By 1808, the Japanese government had sent three expeditions to Karafuto (1786, 1792, 1801) in order to ascertain the size and shape of that land. None had proceeded further north than the 50th parallel or could testify accurately to what lay beyond.

In 1806 and 1807, Karafuto and the southern Kurile island of Etorofu were suddenly raided by two idealistic but misguided Russian lieutenants.[21] Some Japanese were killed and considerable damage was suffered by the local garrisons. Galvanized into an awareness of the potential menace on the northern frontier, the shogunate dispatched a fourth mission in 1808 whose task was to clarify definitively the geography of Karafuto.

The two men selected for the job, Mamiya Rinzō and Matsuda Denjūrō, set out in the spring of 1808 and proceeded, separately, northwards along Karafuto's east and west coasts.[22] Mamiya followed the eastern coast up to Cape Terpenie and then retraced his steps to the neck of the island, crossed to the west coast, and set out to find Matsuda. Matsuda meanwhile had passed Cape Pogibi (the narrowest point in the straits between Sakhalin and the mainland) and had been struck by the widening gulf of water ahead. After Mamiya caught up with him, they decided tentatively that Karafuto was an island. Mamiya favoured continuing the push northwards but was overridden by Matsuda's arguments to return to Ezo before winter set in.

Mamiya was ordered back to Karafuto in 1809 with directions to survey the east coast facing the Sea of Okhotsk. A wilful man, he followed his own inclination to determine Karafuto's relationship to the mainland and went instead northwards along the west coast.[23] On this second attempt, Mamiya pushed well beyond the narrowest point in the straits and reached Nanio (near present-day Rybnovsk). From the expanse of the waters ahead, from the receding shore across the straits, and from the strong northward flowing current, he concluded that Karafuto must be an island. After Mamiya had crossed the straits, visited the Manchu post of Deren, and descended the Amur River to its

[21] See Chapter IV for the details of the Khvostov-Davydov raids.

[22] For details of this expedition, see Hora, *Mamiya Rinzō*, pp. 128–38; Matsuda Denjūrō, 'Hokui dan', in Ōtomo Kisaku, ed., *Hokumon sōsho*, V (Tokyo, 1944), 117–276.

[23] For Mamiya's own account of this voyage, see Mamiya Rinzō, *Tōdatsu kikō*, ed., Mantetsu kōhōka (Dairen, 1938).

junction with the Straits of Tatary, he knew that Karafuto and the 'Saghalien' of D'Anville's maps were the same island. By his single-minded determination, even to the extent of disobeying his government's orders, Mamiya not only established Sakhalin's island status but mapped the lower reaches of the Amur River forty years before the much-vaunted expedition of Captain Nevelskoi.

It took almost thirty years before Mamiya's discoveries were made known in Europe.[24] This was accomplished largely through the efforts of the German physician Philipp Franz von Siebold (1796–1866). Siebold, posing as a Dutch doctor, visited the Japanese capital of Edo in 1826. Siebold's very presence in Japan was illegal. The strictly enforced exclusion laws allowed only a handful of Dutchmen to reside on a small island in Nagasaki harbour. Siebold managed to travel to Edo in the train of a Dutch official. Determined to exploit the successful deception that had brought him to the very heart of the closed country, Siebold made careful preparations to seek out a variety of intellectuals. His insatiable appetite for geographical information led to a meeting with the cartographer Takahashi Kageyasu and the explorers Mogami Tokunai and Mamiya Rinzō. In return for some European charts, Takahashi defied the laws on divulging information to foreigners and secretly gave Siebold copies of Mamiya's new map of Karafuto (Sakhalin). The German only managed to smuggle these maps out of Japan after undergoing considerable hardships. His first attempt to leave the country ended in the exposure of his transactions. Takahashi died in prison and Siebold barely escaped execution. Expelled from Japan, Siebold returned to Europe and lived in Leyden starting in 1831. In 1832, he began the publication of a monumental work—*Nippon.* In the first volume of *Nippon* Siebold credited Mamiya with the discovery of the straits between Sakhalin and the mainland. To prove the point, he included a map of the area which depicted the straits and the mouth of the Amur River.[25]

[24] The Russian surveyor, Captain V. M. Golovnin, met Mamiya in 1812 but disliked him as an individual. He did nothing to disseminate Mamiya's discoveries inside Russia. Vasilii Mikhailovich Golovnin, *Memoirs of a Captivity in Japan During the Years 1811, 1812, and 1813; with Observations on the Country and the People,* I (London, 1824, 2nd ed.), 285, 300–1.

[25] Siebold, *Nippon*, I, 26–7.

Siebold visited St. Petersburg in 1834 and paid a call upon the Russian explorer Captain Krusenstern who in 1805 had concluded that Sakhalin was a peninsula. He showed Krusenstern a copy of Mamiya's charts which clearly revealed a narrow strait between Sakhalin and the mainland. According to Siebold, the Russian stared at the charts and finally exclaimed: 'Les japonais m'ont vaincu!'[26]

Strangely, although Krusenstern knew of Mamiya's discoveries as early as 1834, Russian leaders of the 1840s continued to view Sakhalin as a peninsula. In 1846, Captain Gavrilov of the Russian American Company made an unsuccessful attempt to locate the mouth of the Amur River and reported that no navigable route existed from the Amur to the ocean or between Sakhalin and the mainland.[27]

On 20 February 1849, after repeated pleas by the Governor-General of Eastern Siberia, Nikolai Muraviev, the Emperor Nicholas I sanctioned the exploration of the lower Amur River (then officially Chinese territory) with the object of discovering its outlet to the sea, if such an outlet existed. On 3 August 1849 an expedition led by Captain Gennadii Nevelskoi entered the straits from the north and discovered a passage four miles wide between Sakhalin and the mainland. Nevelskoi's discovery was kept a close secret by Muraviev and the Russian government. They keenly realized the strategic importance of the Amur River as a communications and supply route between Siberia and the Pacific Ocean. As the guardian of the Amur, the island of Sakhalin came to assume a new significance in Russian eyes.

Nevelskoi's discovery proved to be of critical value during the Crimean War (1854–6) when Russia used the Amur river as a supply artery for its garrisons in Mariinsk, Aian, and Petropavlovsk (Kamchatka). In May 1855 a squadron of British warships under the command of Commodore J. G. B. Elliot pursued a Russian force northwards to Castries Bay which is an inlet on the Asiatic mainland just south of the narrowest point in the Nevelskoi Straits. When the Russians sailed out of Castries Bay and headed northward, Elliot believed that he had

[26] Philipp Franz von Siebold, *Geographical and Ethnographical Elucidations to the Discoveries of Maerten Gerrits Vries, A.D. 1643 in the East and North of Japan* (Amsterdam, 1859), pp. 77–8.

[27] F. A. Golder, *Russian Expansion on the Pacific*, 1641–1850 (Cleveland, 1914), p. 262

them trapped in the 'Bay of Tartary'. Consequently, he ordered a blockade of the 'bay'. Only after weeks of bewildering and fruitless searching did he learn that the Russians had made good their escape by passing through the straits and ascending the Amur to safety. This embarrassing episode impressed upon the English an appreciation of Sakhalin's geographical importance.[28]

The mystery of Sakhalin's cartography was solved by 1855; nevertheless, much of the island's interior had yet to be explored. Both Russian and Japanese surveyors visited Sakhalin in increasing numbers after 1840. Between 1840 and 1870, N. K. Boshniak, D. I. Orlov, V. A. Rimskii-Korsakov, N. V. Rudanovsky, D. I. Samarin, Okamoto Kansuke, Matsuura Takeshirō, and Matsukawa Bennosuke crossed and re-crossed the island, traced the coastline, and tracked the rivers to their sources. Although their work[29] was important, it mainly filled in the details into the broad outlines supplied by Mamiya, Nevelskoi, Krusenstern, and La Pérouse.

Who should be credited with proving Sakhalin's island status and thus solving almost two centuries of speculation and controversy—Mamiya Rinzō or Gennadii Nevelskoi? The Japanese and Siebold opt for Mamiya. Pre-1917 Russian accounts (including that of the writer Anton Chekhov) are nearly unanimous in recognizing that this Japanese explorer was the first to prove Sakhalin an island.[30]

Soviet scholars, however, have taken considerable pains to expunge the Japanese from the history of Sakhalin's exploration.

[28] John J. Stephan, 'The Crimean War in the Far East', *Modern Asian Studies*, III (July 1969), 268–74.

[29] For the Russian explorers, see N. K. Boshniak, 'Ekspeditsiia v Priamurskom krae', *Morskoi sbornik*, XXXVIII (Dec. 1858), 179–94; XXXIX (Jan. 1859), 111–31; V. Rimskii-Korsakov, 'Sluchai i zametki na shkune Vostok', *Morskoi sbornik*, XXXV (Sept. 1858), 1–45; I. A. Senchenko, ed., *Issledovateli Sakhalina i Kuril* (Iuzhno-Sakhalinsk, 1961). For Japanese explorers, see Nishizuru Sadayoshi, *Karafuto tanken no hitobito*, Vol. I of *Karafuto sōsho*, ed., Karafuto chō (Toyohara, 1939); Yoshida Takezō, *Matsuura Takeshirō* (Tokyo, 1967), Itō Tasaburō, 'Nihonjin no tankenteki seishin', *Nihon bunka kenkyū*, VII (Tokyo, 1959).

[30] Chekhov, 'Ostrov Sakhalin', pp. 52, 239n. Dimitri M. Pozdneev, *Materiali po istorii severnoi Iaponii i eia otnoshenii k materiku Azii i Rossii*, II (Tokyo, 1909), 87–95. P. I. Polevoi, 'Materiali po issledovaniiu Russkovo Sakhalina', *Trudi geologicheskovo komiteta*, New Series, XCVII (1914), 2. S. Patkanov, *Glavnishiia danniia po statistik naselienia krainovo vostoka Sibiri: Primorskaia i Amurskaia oblasti i ostrov Sakhalin* (St. Petersburg, 1903), p. 2. One pre-revolutionary account does credit Nevelskoi while omitting Mamiya's name: N. Novombergskii, *Ostrov Sakhalin* (St. Petersburg, 1903), pp. 6–7.

The studies of S. L. Lutskii, Aleksandr I. Alekseev, and Iuri Zhukov denigrate Mamiya's achievements, while the works of V. I. Kantorovich, I. Osipov, I. Vinokurov, F. Florich, A. N. Ryzhkov, and B. P. Polevoi do not even mention his name.[31]

The banishment of Japanese figures from the history of Sakhalin's exploration is not limited to books. A visitor to the Museum of Regional Studies in Iuzhno-Sakhalinsk in 1964 noticed that not a single Japanese name was mentioned in connection with the island's discovery and exploration.[32] When I visited the Khabarovsk Historical Museum in 1966, there was an exhibition on Sakhalin's discovery and exploration that stated simply that Nevelskoi was 'the first man to prove that Sakhalin was an island'. The museum curator professed never to have heard the name Mamiya Rinzō. In an atlas of Sakhalin published by the U.S.S.R. Academy of Sciences in 1967, a chart entitled 'Most Important Discoveries and Explorations' carefully lists forty-nine land and sea routes of past explorers. All forty-nine are Russian. The Mongol, Chinese, and Japanese expeditions, not to mention those of Vries, La Pérouse, and Broughton are omitted as if they had never taken place.[33]

Perhaps this is a natural by-product of Sakhalin's confused and divided history as eastern Asia's 'Alsace-Lorraine'.

[31] S. L. Lutskii maintains, apparently forgetting Siebold, that Mamiya's writings were never translated from the Japanese and hence did not reach Europe. *Ostrov Sakhalin* (Moscow, 1946), p. 4. Alekseev and Zhukov dismiss Mamiya's discoveries as of no importance. Aleksandr I. Alekseev, *Po taezhnim tropam Sakhalina* (Iuzhno-Sakhalinsk, 1959), pp. 5–6. Iuri Zhukov, *Russkie i Iaponiia* (Moscow, 1945) pp. 101–2. I. Osipov, *Sakhalinskie zapisi* (Moscow, 1945). I. Vinokurov and F. Florich, *Po iuzhnomu Sakhalinu* (Moscow, 1950). Vinokurov and Florich, *Podvig Admirala Nevelskovo* (Moscow, 1951). V. I. Kantorovich, *Soviet Sakhalin* (Moscow, 1933). V. I. Kantorovich, *Sakhalinskie tetradi* (Moscow, 1965). A. N. Ryzhkov, 'Iz istorii otkrytiia, issledovaniia i osvoeniia Sakhalina i Kurilskikh ostrovov', *Sakhalinskaia oblast*, pp. 43–90. B. P. Polevoi, *Pervootkryvateli Sakhalina* (Iuzhno-Sakhalinsk, 1959).

[32] Miyatake Shōzō, *Shiberia* (Tokyo, 1965), pp. 214–15.

[33] Sakhalinskii kompleksnyi nauchno-issledovatelskii institut, Sibirskovo otdeleniia, AN SSSR, *Atlas Sakhalinskoi oblasti* (Moscow, 1967), pp. 6–7.

IV

THE ADVENT OF RUSSO-JAPANESE RIVALRY, 1785–1875

'Sakhalin is the Orient's Alsace-Lorraine.'
PAUL LABBÉ (1905)

RUSSO-JAPANESE rivalry in Sakhalin differed in character from Japan's rivalry with England and the United States in China or other parts of eastern Asia. Whereas the latter grew primarily from commercial competition, the former revolved about the vital issue of national frontiers. When the expanding frontiers of Russia and Japan met in Sakhalin and in the Kurile Islands at the beginning of the nineteenth century, the 'island country' Japan faced the problem of a contiguous land frontier with a foreign power (moreover a European power) for the first time in her history. The gravity of this challenge evoked a dynamic response from Japan during the years 1785–1813 that involved the exploration, colonization, and economic development of parts of Hokkaido, the southern Kuriles, and southern Sakhalin. The Russian stimulus and the Japanese response created a situation that transformed Sakhalin from a neglected, barren buffer state into disputed territory. With minor interruptions, possession of Sakhalin continued to be an abrasive issue between Russia and Japan until the cataclysm of 1945.[1]

In the seventeenth and eighteenth centuries, Sakhalin constituted a buffer between Russia and Japan. The Treaty of Nerchinsk (1689) with China excluded Russians from the Amur region (and by implication from Sakhalin) and kept them north of the Stanovoi Mountain Range. Without access to or from the Amur, Sakhalin had little significance to Russia. Until the late eighteenth century, the Russians concentrated their activities further eastward, in Kamchatka and in the northern Kuriles.

[1] For a good general survey of this topic, see W. C. Amidon, 'The Issue of Sakhalin in Russo-Japanese Relations', University of Michigan, Center of Japanese Studies, ed., *Occasional Papers*, VII (Ann Arbor, 1957), 60–9.

Between Poiarkov's sighting of Sakhalin in 1644 and Krusenstern's survey in 1805, only a handful of Russians managed to reach the island. It is possible that individual Cossacks visited Sakhalin from Okhotsk in search of furs during the last half of the seventeenth century, but no reliable records have come to light which confirm this conjecture. Soviet historians who argue that all Sakhalin is Russian territory because some Cossacks collected the *yasak* (tribute in furs) from a group of Sakhalin Gilyak natives that they had met on the Amur in 1655 are producing rather tenuous evidence to support a claim to sovereignty.[2]

Nevertheless, by the eighteenth century, there appeared authentic indications of Russian contacts with the island. A member of the Bering expedition, Aleksei Shelting, sailed along the east coast of Sakhalin in 1742 and mistook it for Hokkaido. In 1789, L. F. Terentiev stopped briefly at Terpenie Bay while sailing from Okhotsk to Japan. The Japanese explorer Mogami Tokunai met a Russian called Ivanov on southern Sakhalin in 1792. Ivanov apparently was the sole survivor of five Russians who had been stranded on Sakhalin since 1790 after an abortive attempt to reach Kamchatka from Okhotsk. Four had been killed by local tribes. Ivanov's ultimate fate remains unknown.[3]

The first Russian to show interest in acquiring Sakhalin as a possession was the surveyor Captain Krusenstern. Visiting Aniwa Bay at the southern extremity of the island in May 1805 he was deeply impressed by the potential of the area for a strategic depot for the Russians to open trade with Japan, Korea, and China.[4]

Krusenstern boldly suggested seizing the area from Japan. He reasoned that the Japanese were too weak to put up serious resistance. Moreover, the Japanese government did not dare to risk its reputation on the issue of a struggle with Russia. If the Japanese did resist the Russian occupation, Krusenstern asserted

[2] B. P. Polevoi, *Pervootkryvateli Sakhalina* (Iuzhno-Sakhalinsk, 1959), pp. 58–65. B. P. Polevoi, 'Istoriia Russkikh issledovaniia', *Atlas Sakhalinskoi oblasti* (Moscow, 1967), p. 5. P. T. Iakovleva, 'Pervootkryvateli Sakhalina', *Istoriia SSSR*, VIII (Mar.–Apr. 1964), 182.

[3] Mogami Tokunai, 'Ezo sōshi gohen', in Yoshida Tsunekichi, ed., *Ezo sōs* (Tokyo, 1965), pp. 185–6.

[4] A. J. von Krusenstern, *Voyage Round the World in the Years 1803, 1804, 1805, 1806*, II (London, 1813), 65.

that 'Two cutters of sixteen guns and sixty men would be sufficient, with moderate air of wind, to sink the whole Japanese fleet, had it even ten thousand men on board.'[5]

Krusenstern conceded that it could be considered unjust to seize Sakhalin from Japan, but he rationalized that if Russia did not do it some other European power would.

> As such an event as a European establishment in the island of Sachalin (perhaps the only means of partaking in the Japanese trade) is probably at no great distance, I have merely mentioned in a few words the possibility of such an undertaking. To the English from the East Indes, or Spaniards from the Philippines, it would be extremely easy, but particularly so to the Russians from Kamchatka or the northern parts of Siberia.

Krusenstern's proposals were frank and realistic. By chance, they were acted upon (without his knowledge) by two lieutenants in 1806 in a quixotic raid on Japanese settlements in southern Sakhalin. Nothing came of these exploits, but Krusenstern's words were both prophetic and ironic. They were prophetic in the sense that Russia did occupy southern Sakhalin in 1853 and overawed the Japanese there. At the same time, Krusenstern's words were ironic in that his disparagement of the Japanese fleet in May 1805 was followed, exactly one hundred years later in May 1905 by the Battle of Tsushima at which the Imperial Japanese Navy won one of the most crushing naval victories ever recorded by annihilating the Russian Baltic Squadron.

Growing Japanese Alarm

The approach of Russian surveying and trading expeditions to Japan in the eighteenth century gradually elicited voices of alarm, first among certain sensitive and astute Japanese scholars and eventually in the central government. Although the earliest Russo-Japanese encounters date back at least to 1697,[6] it was only in the second half of the eighteenth century that the Japanese began to view these foreigners with unease. This sense of disquiet grew out of two related impressions: that Russia was encroaching upon Japanese territory, and that its envoys were attempting to

[5] A. J. von Krusenstern, *Voyage Round the World in the Years 1803, 1804, 1805, 1806*, II (London, 1813), pp. 66–7.

[6] George A. Lensen, *The Russian Push toward Japan; Russo-Japanese Relations, 1697–1875* (Princeton, 1959), p. 26.

break the 'closed country' laws that had sealed off Japan from all but a tenuous contact with the outside world through the Dutch and Chinese at Nagasaki.

The Japanese first learned of Russia's approach from the north in 1756.[7] During the next three decades, reports of Russians moving southward along the Kurile Islands and even onto Hokkaido evoked a growing sense of urgency. Scholars such as Kudō Heisuke, Hayashi Shihei, and Honda Toshiaki published alarmist tracts between 1781 and 1801 warning about the danger of 'Aka Ezo' ('Red Ainu') and calling for the strengthening of national defences. The shogunal government eventually took cognizance of these warnings and sent exploratory missions to southern Sakhalin in 1786, 1792, and 1798. After the Laxman mission with its trade proposals in 1792–3, an Ainu rebellion with rumoured Russian backing in 1789, and after persistent reports that the lord of Matsumae was indulging in secret trade with the Russians, the shogunal government decided to assume provisional direct rule over southern Hokkaido, Kunashiri, and Etorofu (1799). Moderate economic success accrued from the first seven years of direct rule and the government extended the sphere of its authority to all of Hokkaido and Sakhalin in 1807.[8]

Japanese authority in Sakhalin before 1807 had only a fragile foothold and was wielded by a vassal of the shogun, the lord of Matsumae, whose seat of power was in southern Hokkaido. Matsumae clan retainers explored the coasts of southern Sakhalin in 1635, 1636, 1650, 1689, and 1700, but no one cared to spend the winter there. Indeed, those who survived a Sakhalin winter were viewed with admiration and incredulity. Seasonal fishing settlements grew up around Aniwa Bay after 1679, and itinerant merchants carried on trade with the Sakhalin Ainu. In 1790, the lord of Matsumae constructed guard posts along the southern coast and set up a permanent trading centre at Shiranushi on Cape Krilon. Until 1807, however, neither the shogunal government nor the lord of Matsumae made any claim to Sakhalin.

In the autumn of 1806, five months before the shogunate announced the extension of direct rule to Sakhalin, Russians

[7] Suematsu Yasukazu, *Kinsei ni okeru hoppō mondai no shinten* (Tokyo, 1928), p. 104.

[8] For an analysis of direct rule, John J. Stephan, 'Ezo under the Tokugawa Bakufu, 1799–1821: an Aspect of Japan's Frontier History', (Unpublished Ph.D. dissertation, University of London, 1969), pp. 75–140.

and Japanese clashed for the first time on the island. A young idealistic lieutenant, Nikolai Khvostov, raided and burned Japanese settlements in Aniwa Bay.[9] The incident had a comic-opera air, but some Japanese have taken a serious view of it. One historian called it 'the first Russo-Japanese war',[10] and another termed it 'the first Russian invasion of our territory'.[11]

It is now clear that the raid was not ordered by the Russian government but was an instrument of revenge of a director of the Russian-American Company, Nikolai Rezanov. Rezanov spent six months in Nagasaki (October 1804–April 1805) fruitlessly attempting to open trade with Japan. Frustrated by the Japanese refusal to his proposals, Rezanov returned to Kamchatka via Aniwa Bay, reconnoitring the fishing settlements there. He communicated his burning indignation against the Japanese to two young lieutenants, Khvostov and Davydov, while travelling to California later in 1805. Rezanov urged them to take retaliatory action. In 1806, Rezanov returned to Moscow (he died en route) leaving only vague written instructions regarding the Japanese with these two lieutenants. After some hesitation, Khvostov and Davydov decided to carry out the raids on Sakhalin and Etorofu. They reasoned with a curious logic that the destruction of Japan's frontier settlements would force them to agree to open trade with Russia.

Khvostov's appearance at the Japanese settlement of Kushunkotan in southern Sakhalin's Aniwa Bay (19 October 1806) came as an absolute surprise to the small garrison of Matsumae retainers stationed there. He landed a party of armed men, read a proclamation to the astounded and uncomprehending Japanese, and began looting storehouses. Before departing, the sailors handed a note to some Ainu informing them that they were henceforth under the protection of the Tsar, carried away four protesting guards, and posted a copper plaque on a local temple.[12]

Because Khvostov had burned all the garrison's boats, news

[9] W. G. Aston, 'Russian Descents into Saghalien and Itorup', *Transactions of the Asiatic Society of Japan*, First Series, I (1882), 78–86. Lensen, *The Russian Push toward Japan*, pp. 158–76. Suematsu, *Kinsei ni okeru hoppō mondai no shinten*, pp. 310–36.

[10] Shinkawa Kōzō, *Hokkaido e no shōtai* (Tokyo, 1965), p. 117.

[11] Adachi Kinnosuke, 'Sakhalin: What it means to Japan', *Independent*, LIX (14 September 1905), 619.

[12] The plaque read as follows:

(1) It is unjust of the Japanese to hinder trade of the Russians on Sakhalin Island.

of this incident did not reach the Japanese capital until June of 1807. By that time, northern Japan was gripped with anger and consternation, for Khvostov and Davydov had in the meantime inflicted damage to life and property in an attack on Etorofu and again at Kushunkotan in southern Sakhalin.

These raids were the acts of idealistic but misinformed individuals. Krusenstern, after whose proposals cited earlier the operation seemed to be patterned, knew nothing of the action until he heard about it in Moscow. He curtly noted, 'this expedition had no permanent object, being merely intended to destroy the Japanese establishments in Aniwa Bay and on the north side of Jeso'.[13] When the Japanese captured a Russian surveyor and some of his companions in retaliation (1811), the Russian Governor of Okhotsk officially disowned the attack and apologized (1813).

The Khvostov-Davydov episode cast a shadow over Russo-Japanese relations in Sakhalin. Many Russians gained an impression of the Japanese as effeminate poltroons.[14] This underestimation had tragic results in 1904. The Japanese smarted under the humiliation and instituted a purge of officials involved in the incident. Japanese historians have generally considered the affair the product of Rezanov's spleen and Khvostov's credulity. Anton Chekhov laconically described it as 'piracy'.[15]

Soviet historians of Sakhalin interpret the Khvostov-Davydov incident in a radically different manner. Zhukov characterizes Khvostov's mission as one of peaceful intent until the Japanese started shooting. Ryzhkov describes the Russian lieutenants as 'patriots', 'young heroes' carrying out their duty of reclaiming Russian land illegally seized and plundered by the Japanese.

---

(2) If the Japanese should change their decision and wish to trade they can send notification thereof to Sakhalin Island or to Etorofu Island.

(3) If the Japanese will persist for long in denying the just demand, the Russians will lay waste to the northern part of Japan.

Quoted in Aston, 'Russian Descents into Saghalien', p. 79. The text was written in Russian. For an analysis of the documents left by Khvostov, Takano Akira, 'Fubuosutofu bunsho kō', *Waseda daigaku toshokan kiyō*, VI (Dec. 1964), 1–28.

[13] Krusenstern, *Voyage Round the World*, II, 69–70.

[14] N. V. Busse, *Ostrov Sakhalin: Ekspeditsiia 1853–54 gg* (St. Petersburg, 1872), p. 79. A. A. Panov, *Shokuminchi to shite no Sagaren* (Tokyo, 1942), p. 5. Lensen, *The Russian Push toward Japan*, pp. 196, 343–4, 464.

[15] Chekhov, 'Ostrov Sakhalin', p. 236.

Osipov notes that they liberated the Ainu from Japanese oppression by destroying the facilities of the exploiters and distributing fish and salt to the grateful natives. All of these sources agree that the significant point of the affair was Khvostov's raising the Russian flag over Sakhalin thus officially sealing the island's ownership. Khvostov then landed five sailors elsewhere in Aniwa Bay. These men died on the island without ever regaining contact with their countrymen. They are hailed as Sakhalin's first settlers.[16]

The 1806–7 episode has thus been transformed from an embarrassing gaffe into a glorious chapter of the establishment of Russian sovereignty on Sakhalin.

Sakhalin lapsed into forty years of relative placidity after the events of 1806–7. Having secured an official apology from the Russians in 1813, the shogunate gradually lost interest in the northern frontier. Japanese garrisons were withdrawn from southern Sakhalin in 1814. The abolition of direct rule in 1821 left the island a ward of the hopelessly inadequate lord of Matsumae who could hardly administer his own domain of Ezo (Hokkaido) let alone be expected to care for Sakhalin. Consequently, Japanese contacts with Sakhalin after 1821 consisted of private merchants and fishermen who visited coastal Ainu settlements in the warm summer months. Matsuura Takeshirō's explorations in 1846 were an isolated example of energy in a general atmosphere of torpidity and indifference.

Russia also seemed to have lost interest in Sakhalin after 1813. The successors of Rezanov in the Russian-American Company directed their attention to Alaska while government leaders in St. Petersburg devoted their energies to European, Balkan, and Caucasian problems. In 1813, the governor of Irkutsk ordered Sakhalin to be left untouched in order to avoid either a confrontation with Japan or the arousal of Manchu suspicions—eventualities which might adversely affect Russo-Chinese trade. When the Russian-American Company finally sent an expedition to locate the mouth of the Amur in 1846, its results were so

[16] Iuri Zhukov, *Russkie i Iaponiia* (Moscow, 1945), pp. 54–78; I. Osipov, *Sakhalinskie zapisi* (Moscow, 1946), pp. 9–10; A. N. Ryzhkov, 'Iz istorii otkrytiia, issledovaniia i osvoeniia Sakhalina i Kurilskikh ostrovov', K. I. Kniazev, ed., *Sakhalinskaia oblast* (Iuzhno-Sakhalinsk, 1960), pp. 61–3; G. Gor and V. Leshkevich, *Sakhalin* (Moscow, 1949), pp. 26–7; E. Ia. Fainberg, *Russko-iaponskie otnosheniia v 1697–1875 gg* (Moscow, 1960), pp. 97–101.

disappointing that the Foreign Minister Count Nesselrode declared the question closed for ever.[17]

From 1853 to 1875, Russia and Japan once again disputed the possession of Sakhalin. Actual hostilities erupted only in isolated instances, but the extent of mutual territorial claims carried ominous implications. Repeating the pattern of fifty years earlier, the initial thrust came from Russia. This time, however, the Japanese suffered from grave weaknesses. Foreign pressures and internal disorders were undermining the authority of the Tokugawa shogunate. Meanwhile, under the energetic leadership of the Governor-General of Eastern Siberia, Count Muraviev, Russia built up a superior position in Sakhalin. Overwhelmed by immigrants and overawed by the military forces, Japan eventually decided to abandon her claim to Sakhalin in exchange for the Kurile Islands north of Etorofu in 1875.

The years 1849–54 marked the first stage of the Russian occupation of Sakhalin.[18] Two figures played a leading role in this occupation: the Governor-General of Eastern Siberia, Nikolai Muraviev and a young impetuous naval captain, Gennadii Nevelskoi. Muraviev recognized Sakhalin's strategic importance in relation to the Amur River and steadily pressed the sluggish Tsarist government to support an active Far Eastern policy. The governor-general entertained persisting suspicions against England after the Opium War radically altered the situation on the China coast. England, he feared, might occupy Sakhalin or the lower reaches of the Amur River, leaving Eastern Siberia in a strategically vulnerable position. Gennadii Nevelskoi's motives derived from simple patriotism. The two men shared the conviction that Sakhalin must be occupied and incorporated into the Russian Empire notwithstanding the Manchus, the Japanese or the timorous caution of the Foreign Minister, Count Nesselrode, and the Chief of Naval Staff, Prince Menshikov.

After some hesitation (it was after all Chinese territory) the Tsar Nicholas I sanctioned a circumspect exploration of the lower Amur in February, 1849. Nevelskoi exceeded his

[17] Lensen, *The Russian Push toward Japan*, pp. 259, 264–5.

[18] Ibid., pp. 271–307; Busse, *Ostrov Sakhalin*; Ivan Barsukov, *Graf Nikolai Nikolaevich Muraviev-Amurskii*, I (Moscow, 1891), 191–6; Vera Vend, *L'Amiral Nevelskoi et la Conquête définitive du fleuve Amour* (Paris, 1894).

instructions. After ascertaining that Sakhalin was an island in August, he proceeded to establish a post at the mouth of the Amur (Nikolaevsk) and issued proclamations to groups of natives stating that they were henceforth subjects of the Tsar. Nevelskoi's precipitous actions outraged Nesselrode, but the Tsar Nicholas reacted differently, uttering the famous phrase that 'where once the Russian flag has flown, it must not be lowered again'.

Nevelskoi's attention was attracted to Sakhalin late in 1851 when some Gilyak natives told him that five Russians had been living on the island, the last of whom had just died.[19] Moreover, one of the Gilyaks had a button consisting of a piece of coal. Intrigued, Nevelskoi sent a Lieutenant Boshniak in February 1852 to survey the island for coal deposits. Boshniak returned after a month's trek, bringing back data on the location of coal beds at Dué and Viakhty along the western coast. A second mission was then sent under Lieutenant Voronin to determine suitable areas for Russian settlements and to inform any foreigners (English, Americans, or Japanese) that Sakhalin was Russian territory.

There is little evidence that suggests that any foreigners other than the Russians were interested in staking a claim to Sakhalin. A. N. Ryzhkov, however, has uncovered an alleged plot in 1848 where the American Aaron Haight Palmer, director of the American and Foreign Agency (an agent to steamship lines), presented to President Polk a plan to 'plunder' Sakhalin.[20] Palmer was an enterprising New York businessman who entertained bright visions of trade with Russia and Japan, but there is no suggestion in his letter to Polk that the United States should seize or plunder Sakhalin.[21] It is true that in the 1840s and 1850s American whalers made occasional visits to Sakhalin. American seal hunters are known to have landed on Tiulenii Island at the end of Cape Terpenie on Sakhalin's east coast. Soviet historians take a cold view of these whaling activities. According to

[19] L. Lutskii, *Ostrov Sakhalin* (Moscow, 1946), p. 5. N. K. Boshniak, 'Ekspeditsiia v Priamurskom krae', *Morskoi sbornik*, XXXVIII (Dec. 1858), 192–4.

[20] Ryzhkov, 'Iz istorii otkrytiia, issledovaniia i osvoeniia Sakhalina', p. 74.

[21] For the full text of Palmer's letter to Polk, see United States Senate, Miscellaneous Documents No. 80, 30th Congress, 1st Session, 8 March 1848. pp. 1–76. For a discussion of Palmer's plans, Claude S. Phillips, Jr., 'Some Forces Behind the Opening of Japan', *Contemporary Japan*, XXIV (1956), 431–59.

Ryzhkov, 'American pirates not only burned the forests but robbed the population and raped and carried off the women'.

While Boshniak prepared the groundwork for a Russian occupation of Sakhalin, Governor-General Muraviev maintained steady pressure on the government in St. Petersburg to authorize further expeditions and territorial acquisitions. His efforts were rewarded on 23 April 1853 when the government issued instructions to the Russian-American Company to occupy Sakhalin immediately.[22] These orders also stated that the government would provide troops for defence, that foreign settlements must not be allowed, that the government could freely mine the island's coal, and that the company would appoint a governor of Sakhalin to be responsible to the governor-general of Eastern Siberia. In forwarding these instructions to Nevelskoi, Muraviev added that Russian settlements should be established as far south as possible but that the Japanese fishermen should be left alone. Nevelskoi received these orders on 23 July 1853 and rapidly proceeded with their implementation.

In August 1853, Nevelskoi transported D. I. Orlov to Sakhalin to establish a post on the 50th parallel of the west coast. Orlov founded Ilinskii Post, the first *bona fide* Russian settlement on Sakhalin. The alacrity with which Nevelskoi moved to occupy Sakhalin derived from his anxiety that an American expedition under Commodore Matthew Perry would attempt to land on the island.

Nevelskoi returned to Sakhalin in October with a Major Busse to establish a second settlement in the southern part of the island. They landed at Aniwa Bay, explaining to the bewildered and startled Japanese that they were occupying Sakhalin to defend it from the Americans. After surveying the bay for a suitable location to build a fort, Nevelskoi decided on a spot close to the Japanese settlement of Kushunkotan that Khvostov had burned in 1806. They named it Muravievskii Post. Today, it is known as Korsakov.

The proximity of the Japanese and Russian settlements around Aniwa Bay created the conditions from which misunderstandings and suspicions flourished. Busse, commander of Muravievskii Post after Nevelskoi's departure, felt keenly the ambiguity of

[22] For the complete text of these orders, Lensen, *The Russian Push toward Japan*, pp. 280–1.

Russia's position.[23] Busse felt contempt for the fighting ability of the Japanese, but he recognized that the occupation of Aniwa Bay posed a direct threat not only to the resident fishermen but to Japan's entire northern frontier. He spent the winter of 1853–4 in Muravievskii Post gradually extending friendly contacts with the fishermen and Ainu who had at first fled in consternation. With the coming of spring, groups of Japanese officials began arriving with inquiries about what the Russians were intending to do there. Before these exchanges reached any conclusion, Busse and the garrison were suddenly ordered to evacuate the island (May 1854).

The Russian evacuation of Sakhalin in the spring of 1854 marked only a temporary pause in the absorption of the island into the Russian Empire. As neither Nevelskoi nor Muraviev favoured such a measure, it is possible that Admiral Evfimii Putiatin, then negotiating with the Japanese at Nagasaki, persuaded Muraviev to order a withdrawal for two reasons. First, Putiatin wanted negotiations for a Russo-Japanese Treaty of Friendship to proceed smoothly without arousing Japanese anxieties over Sakhalin. Secondly, the outbreak of the Crimean War (30 March 1854) left Sakhalin exposed to the attacks of superior English and French sea power. Muraviev and Putiatin agreed that untenable outposts should be temporarily abandoned in order to consolidate Russia's defensive strength around Petropavlovsk in Kamchatka and Mariinsk and Nikolaevsk on the lower Amur River.

If one prong of the Russian advance on Sakhalin was the establishment of garrisoned outposts in 1853–4, the other thrust came in the form of a diplomatic offensive. Admiral Putiatin's visits to Japan between 1853 and 1855 sought not only to conclude treaties of friendship and commerce but to delineate a frontier. On his second visit to Nagasaki (3 January to 5 February 1854), Putiatin broached the boundary question with the Japanese plenipotentiaries stating that it required clarification in Sakhalin and the Kurile Islands. The Russian offered to recognize the legality of Japanese settlements around Aniwa Bay but claimed that the rest of Sakhalin and all of the Kurile Islands belonged to Russia. The Japanese balked at this proposal, countering with the assertion that the southern Kuriles

[23] Busse, *Ostrov Sakhalin*, pp. 88–99.

(Kunashiri and Etorofu) had always been part of Japan and that Sakhalin should be divided at the 50th parallel. As no agreement could be reached on the frontier issue, Putiatin left Nagasaki with the matter still pending.[24]

Putiatin returned to Japan in October 1854 and negotiations were resumed at Shimoda. From December 1854 through January 1855 the two sides debated the frontier problem. As the Crimean War had forced the Russians out of Sakhalin, the Japanese had a slightly better bargaining position than in 1853. They did not suceed in gaining the 50th parallel as the boundary line in Sakhalin, but they managed to secure Russian recognition of Japanese rights there. According to Article 2 of the Treaty of Shimoda (signed on 7 February 1855), Sakhalin was declared a 'joint possession of Russia and Japan'. Moreover, the frontier in the Kuriles was fixed between the islands of Etorofu and Uruppu, leaving Kunashiri and Etorofu to Japan while Uruppu and islands to the north fell to Russia.[25] The treaty left the final disposition of Sakhalin to future settlement. As long as both Japanese and Russians rubbed shoulders over such vaguely defined ground, occasions for friction were rife.

The dual thrust of Nevelskoi's projects in Aniwa Bay and Putiatin's demands at Nagasaki in 1853–4 awakened the shogunal government to an acute realization of Sakhalin's importance, much as Russian movements in the southern Kuriles had done in the 1790s. The pattern of the Japanese response differed little from that of fifty years earlier, except in the 1850s and 1860s the shogunate acted against a complex background of internal unrest. Early in 1854 the shogunate dispatched a mission to investigate conditions in Aniwa Bay. Upon the recommendations of this mission, direct rule was extended to southern Hokkaido (1854), all of Hokkaido (1855), and all of Sakhalin (1856). A growing proportion of Japan's leaders

[24] For details of Putiatin's negotiations in Nagasaki on the subject of Sakhalin, see Ōta Saburō, *Nichiro Karafuto gaikō sen* (Tokyo, 1941), pp. 46–78; Maruyama Kunio, *Nihon hoppō hatten shi* (Tokyo, 1942), pp. 174–89; Peter Berton, *Nichiro ryōdo mondai: 1850–1875* (Tokyo, 1967), pp. 15–16; Lensen, *The Russian Push toward Japan*, pp. 323–9, 336–7.

[25] Ryzhkov erroneously asserts that the Treaty of Shimoda awarded all of the Kuriles to Russia. 'Iz istorii otkrytiia, issledovaniia i osvoeniia Sakhalina', p. 78. Taken at face value, Ryzhkov's statement supports the position of the present Japanese government which argues that Kunashiri and Etorofu are not part of the Kurile Islands.

realized that only through a centralized effort to populate and develop Sakhalin could the island be preserved from absorption by Russia.[26]

Notwithstanding constant pressure from individuals such as Tokugawa Nariaki, the lord of Mito, the shogunate proved incapable of supporting a sustained, vigorous economic policy on the northern frontier. From 1856 until 1867 (when the Tokugawa shogunate collapsed), Japanese colonial enterprises in Sakhalin proved haphazard, fitfully heroic, and hopelessly inadequate.

The shogunate could not draw on the organizational methods of a centralized modern state to colonize Sakhalin. Although it held legal authority over the island after the decree announcing direct rule in 1856 (the shogunate had ruled Sakhalin directly also between 1807 and 1821), the shogunate delegated military and economic responsibilities to the feudal lords and private merchants respectively. Soldiers from the northern fiefs of Sendai, Akita, Nambu, and Tsugaru performed garrison duties. When the shogunate called for the immigration of warriors and their families to Sakhalin, and promised subsidies to merchants who would open fishing enterprises along the island's coasts, it failed to follow through with adequate financial assistance or technical guidance. Consequently, Sakhalin's economic development was largely the product of independent men of means acting on their own initiative.

Matsukawa Bennosuke was one of those men like Mamiya Rinzō and Mogami Tokunai whose life eloquently contradicted the cliché that the Japanese dislike cold climates. Born the son of a wealthy peasant, he served the shogunate by directing land reclamation and road construction projects in Hokkaido. In 1855, he petitioned the shogunate for permission to develop Sakhalin's fisheries at his own expense. Accorded monopoly rights on stretches of Sakhalin's coasts, he began in 1857 to operate herring and salmon fisheries on a large scale between Aniwa Bay and the 50th parallel. Matsukawa managed these enterprises successfully until 1864 when he sold out his interests to other merchants.

[26] For Japanese policy in Sakhalin (1854–67), Maruyama, *Nihon hoppō hatten shi*, pp. 211–68; *Karafuto sōsho*, I, 105–64; VI, 167–91. Karafuto chō, ed., *Karafuto enkaku shi* (Toyohara, 1925), pp. 8–17.

Similar undertakings were carried out by other men. Some acted in the capacity of an advisor to a particular lord, and some were attracted to the northern frontier as entrepreneurs. The shogunate promoted these activities to the extent of issuing licenses and granting modest subsidies in the form of low-interest loans.

In addition to encouraging the development of fisheries, the shogunate sent a series of explorers to Sakhalin to map its northern sections. Kuriyama Tahei surveyed both the east and west coasts before he died from illness in Nikolaevsk in 1860. In 1867, Okamoto Kansuke performed the unprecedented feat of completing a full circuit round the island's coastline including the ragged Schmidt Peninsula. Japanese charts of Sakhalin made vast strides in accuracy and detail during the last decade of the shogunate's existence.

To forestall the spread of Russian political and religious influences among Sakhalin's aborigines, the Japanese attempted to win over the island's Ainu, Gilyak, and Oroki population by teaching them fishing techniques and distributing tools and nets. Opinions vary widely on how the natives viewed the Japanese and the Russians. Soviet historians predictably hold the conviction that the Japanese were hated as oppressors and the Russians welcomed as liberators. Patriotic Japanese hold similar views with the roles reversed. Original sources reveal that the Russians and Japanese showed both kindness and cruelty, and that the natives reacted with feelings of fear, gratitude, and hatred depending on the specific case. The Japanese had a long and largely unhappy historical association with the Ainu in northern Honshū and Hokkaidō. Starting in the eighteenth century, Japanese merchants resorted to dubious practices in employing the Ainu as fishermen. Deception, chicanery, and brutality left a blot on Japanese-Ainu relations that an occasional burst of official or private philanthropy could not erase. On the other hand, there are recorded instances where Russians shot Ainu for sport. Vodka as well as *saké* helped these unfortunate natives along the road to near-extinction. In the last analysis, Sakhalin's aborigines had virtually no role in deciding the island's political fate.

Japanese economic and colonial enterprises on Sakhalin continued up to and after the Meiji Restoration (1868), but they could not compete in scale or organization with the imposing influx of Russians after 1856. From 1857 until 1875, it was the Russians who accomplished the most dramatic gains on the island.

The Crimean War precipitated a temporary Russian retreat from Sakhalin. However, the war demonstrated to many Russian leaders Sakhalin's vital importance for the defence of Siberia. Wartime operations in the Far East resulted in a resounding success for Governor-General Muraviev who engineered the repulse of an Anglo-French assault on Petropavlovsk in Kamchatka (October 1854) and confounded the Allied commanders by successfully withdrawing and preserving his few precious ships in the Amur estuary. The Amur River proved to be an invaluable supply route for the remote Russian garrisons in the Far East. Moreover, Nevelskoi's discovery of a channel between Sakhalin and the mainland left a large English squadron blocking a Russian convoy (which escaped up the Amur) in what was considered the 'Bay of Tartary' but was of course not a bay but a strait. Muraviev's successes in 1854–6 thrilled St. Petersburg where the government was suffering from pessimism occasioned by stalemates and setbacks in the Crimea. The war convinced Russian leaders that the Amur and Sakhalin must be incorporated into the empire. The vigorous diplomatic and colonial activity on Sakhalin after 1856 grew out of this new awareness.

The Russians began the re-occupation of Sakhalin shortly after the end of the Crimean War.[27] Early in 1856, St. Petersburg relieved the Russian-American Company of responsibility for the island and placed it under the direct control of the Governor-General of Eastern Siberia, Count Muraviev. Later that year, teams were sent to establish a settlement at Dué where rich coal deposits had been uncovered. Scientists, cartographers, engineers, and inevitably bureaucrats began to visit Sakhalin. L. I. Schrenk made a thorough investigation of the island's ethnography and zoology. The geologist F. B. Schmidt led an expedition of the Russian Geographical Society that included

[27] For the Russian advance into Sakhalin (1856–75): Colonel Veniukov, 'On the Island of Sakhalin', *Journal of the Royal Geographical Society*, XLII (1872), 373–88; Lutskii, *Ostrov Sakhalin*, pp. 5–7; Gor and Leshkevich, *Sakhalin*, pp. 17–18; Panov, *Shokuminchi to shite no Sagaren*, pp. 10–18; A. Keppen, *Ostrov Sakhalin* (St. Petersburg, 1875), *passim*.

Brilkin who studied the Ainu language, and Rashkov and Shebunin who conducted a cartographical survey. The mining engineer, I. A. Lopatin, trekked 1,100 miles around Sakhalin in 1867–8 locating new coal deposits. Colonel Veniukov assessed Sakhalin's strategic significance and concluded that it possessed a singular importance not only by guarding the Amur River but by controlling passages from the Sea of Japan to the Sea of Okhotsk. Finally, officials in St. Petersburg began to discuss the possibility that Sakhalin be turned into a huge penal colony where convict labour would work the island's coal deposits.

While building up their own position, the Russians exerted steady pressure to squeeze the Japanese out of Sakhalin.[28] In the summer of 1858, a Russian military detachment suddenly appeared at the Japanese settlement of Kushunkotan and began building a fort. More Russian military bases were constructed at Kushunnai and Shinnui. When asked about these problems during the negotiations for a Russo-Japanese treaty of commerce in August, Admiral Putiatin shrugged off the complaint explaining that he had no authority to discuss frontier problems.

The rapidly developing Russian presence in Sakhalin after 1856 received a strong stimulus from Muraviev's successful conclusion of the Treaty of Aigun with China on 28 May 1858. Russia acquired the left bank of the Amur by this treaty which assured legal as well as *de facto* control over that communication artery. No mention was made of Sakhalin in the treaty, presumably because of Chinese indifference and Russian reluctance to involve a third party in the rivalry for that island. Fresh from his diplomatic success in China, Muraviev turned his attention to Japan to clear up the problem of Sakhalin. Unlike Putiatin, Muraviev did not accept the concept of joint occupation, for he feared that the English would exploit this ambiguous state of affairs. Nor did he countenance a demarcation of a frontier along the 50th parallel as the Japanese had suggested. Muraviev came to Japan determined to acquire all of Sakhalin for Russia.

[28] Russo-Japanese manoeuvres over the Sakhalin problem (1856–67) are discussed in: Abe Kōzō, 'Bakumatsu ki Nichiro kankei', *Nihon gaikōshi kenkyū* (Dec. 1960), pp. 44–58; Berton, *Nichiro ryōdo mondai*, pp. 18–45; Ōta, *Nichiro Karafuto gaikō sen*, pp. 88–138; Lensen, *The Russian Push toward Japan*, pp. 425–36; Hiraoka, *Nichiro kōshō shiwa*, pp. 359–67; John Harrison, *Japan's Northern Frontier* (Gainesville, 1953), pp. 39–51.

Arriving at Shinagawa in August 1859, Muraviev presented three claims to the Japanese: (1) that Sakhalin was Russian territory, (2) that Japanese fishermen working in Sakhalin could continue to do so, and (3) that Japanese travellers might travel freely along the Amur. These overtures met with no success. The Japanese maintained their right either to half of Sakhalin or to the joint occupation prescribed in the Shimoda Treaty of 1855. Both sides used the 'threat of England' to justify their positions. Muraviev declared that England would harbour schemes against Sakhalin unless the island were occupied and defended by Russia. The Japanese retorted that to abandon their claim to Sakhalin would invite English designs on Ezo (Hokkaido). With both parties adamantly clinging to these irreconcilable arguments, the talks ended in deadlock.[29]

Muraviev's failure in 1859 spurred a growth of tension inside Sakhalin as both the Russians and the Japanese increased their forces. In October 1860, the shogunate announced that the lords of Sendai, Aizu, and Shōnai were to send garrisons to Kushunkotan, the principal Japanese base at Aniwa Bay. For their part, the Russians dispatched troops, settlers, and even a few convicts. Russian settlements sprung up along the west coast starting at Dué and spread southwards towards the Japanese posts.

Russian territorial gains were not limited to Sakhalin. In July 1860 a young officer named Ignatiev masterfully negotiated the Treaty of Peking with the Manchus (then beset by internal rebellion and foreign intervention) according to which the Tsar acquired territory stretching from the Ussuri River to the Sea of Japan and southwards to the Korean border. In March 1861 a Russian warship occupied the strategic island of Tsushima located in the straits between Japan and Korea. These developments convinced the shogunate that a frontier settlement in Sakhalin was indispensable in order to avoid a dangerous confrontation.

Between 1861 and the fall of the Tokugawa shogunate in 1868, the Japanese sent two missions to St. Petersburg in an attempt to reach an agreement on the frontier problem in Sakhalin. Both of these missions failed. The first, led by Take-

[29] Abe, 'Bakumatsu ki Nichiro kankei', p. 48. Berton, *Nichiro ryōdo mondai*, pp. 21–3. Lensen, *The Russian Push toward Japan*, p. 372.

nouchi Yasunori, negotiated with Count Nikolai Ignatiev (the author of the successful Peking Treaty of 1860 and now director of the Asiatic Department of the Foreign Ministry) in the summer of 1862. After an exchange of the usual claims, Ignatiev suggested the 48th parallel as a boundary. The Japanese were tempted to accept this offer but were constricted by their government's instructions to have the 50th parallel or nothing. Unable to compromise, the Japanese refused. The negotiations closed with an agreement to postpone a decision and to delegate plenipotentiary powers to Rear-Admiral Kazakevich, Commander-in-chief of the Pacific Fleet, to implement further discussions at a later date. The Japanese never met Kazakevich, although he notified them of his availability at Nikolaevsk.

The Japanese thus lost an opportunity in 1862 to secure Sakhalin south of the 48th parallel. By 1866 the deterioration of the shogunate's position in Sakhalin together with mounting domestic unrest forced the Japanese to dispatch a second mission to St. Petersburg which sought to establish a boundary at the 48th parallel that they had refused only four years previously. This mission was led by the Governor of Hakodate, Koide Hidesane. Acutely aware of his country's vulnerability in Sakhalin, Koide had memorialized the shogun in 1865 to accept the 48th parallel as a frontier. During February and March of 1867, Koide broached his government's new position to Petr Stremoukhov, Ignatiev's successor at the Asiatic Department. The Russian terms had hardened since 1862. Stremoukhov insisted on a frontier at the La Pérouse Strait, conceding to Japan four of the Kurile Islands and residence rights for fishermen in Sakhalin. All the evidence that Koide could muster—maps, letters, and other historical documents—fell upon deaf ears. Stremoukhov insisted that Russia could accept nothing short of complete sovereignty over all of Sakhalin. Faced with yet another breakdown, the negotiators signed on 30 March the 'Tentative Regulations Relative to the Island of Sakhalin' which merely reaffirmed the principle of joint occupation.[30]

Koide had scarcely returned to Japan when the Tokugawa shogunate collapsed, the victim of complex social, economic,

[30] For the full text, see Japan, Foreign Office, *Treaties and Conventions between the Empire of Japan and other Powers together with Universal Conventions, Regulations, and Communications since March, 1854*, rev. ed. (Tokyo, 1884), pp. 633–7.

and political forces that were transforming the country. The new imperial government faced manifold problems of foreign relations, domestic order, finance, and institutional reform. Moreover, remnants of shogunal supporters continued to fight on in northern Japan during 1868–9. The efforts of the young Meiji government to retain Sakhalin were consequently handicapped.

Okamoto Kansuke, appointed to responsibility for Sakhalin's development, spared no effort to promote the settlement of the island, even at the risk of a clash with Russia. Starting in 1868, he personally led hundreds of colonists to Aniwa Bay and planned the construction of Ōtomari (located next to Korsakov). Yet Okamoto stood out as an exception to the general official posture towards Sakhalin between 1868 and 1875. The new government lacked the unity of purpose, let alone the means, to implement a sustained development of the island. Personal feuds among the Japanese leaders and a predilection for organizational experimentation spawned a series of administrative organs (*Hakodate saibansho*, *Hakodate fu*, *Hokkaido kaitakushi*, *Karafuto kaitakucho*, *Karafuto kaitakushicho*) that succeeded each other with bewildering rapidity.[31]

While attempting to construct a colonial administration, the Japanese tried to settle the frontier problem by resorting to three tactics in succession: (1) engaging a third party to arbitrate Russo-Japanese claims, (2) purchasing the island from Russia, and (3) abandoning Sakhalin in return for concessions elsewhere.

As a rival to Russia in East Asia, England naturally took an interest in the progress of the Russo-Japanese border dispute in Sakhalin.[32] The English ambassadors Sir Rutherford Alcock and Sir Harry Parkes issued grave warnings to the Japanese on the Russian threat in Sakhalin. Parkes went so far as to supply information on Russian troop movements and deployments. He eventually counselled, however, that the Japanese abandon Sakhalin and concentrate on the development of Hokkaido. The Japanese were little comforted by Parkes's advice. It was to the

[31] The details of these changes are treated in: Maruyama, *Nihon hoppō hatten shi*, pp. 303–19; *Karafuto sōsho*, VI, 227–44; *Karafuto enkaku shi*, pp. 169–70.

[32] Berton, *Nichiro ryōdo mondai*, pp. 51–4. Ōta, *Nichiro Karafuto gaikō sen*, pp. 152–4, 167–76.

Americans that they turned in 1870 when they sought a foreign arbiter for the frontier question.

The United States seemed to be the natural choice for the role or arbiter. The country was on good terms with both Russia and Japan and had expressed in 1858 a standing arbitration offer. In 1869 the Japanese privately approached the former Secretary of State William H. Seward (then visiting Japan) who had two years previously managed the purchase of Alaska from Russia. Seward advised, predictably, that the Japanese should attempt to buy Sakhalin. In March 1870 an official request for American arbitration was made to the minister to Japan, Charles E. DeLong. When the Americans forwarded this proposal to the Russians in December, the government in St. Petersburg replied with a flat refusal.

With the failure of arbitration, the Japanese experimented with offering to buy out Russia's interests in Sakhalin as Seward had suggested in 1869. In the summer of 1872 the Japanese foreign minister Soejima Taneomi and the Russian minister in Tokyo Evgenii Biutsov engaged in discussions about Sakhalin's disposition. Soejima offered to purchase the Russian rights in Sakhalin for 2,000,000 yen. This was turned down. Biutsov countered with a proposal that the Japanese sell their own interests in Sakhalin to Russia. As neither side showed an inclination to compromise, the negotiations were called off.

When both arbitration and purchase schemes proved fruitless, the Japanese were forced to make a difficult decision: to hold on to Sakhalin at all costs or to abandon it to Russia in return for concessions elsewhere. This decision could not be put off indefinitely, for hostile incidents in Sakhalin were increasing in frequency and severity. At the same time the debate on Korea, the punitive expedition against Formosa, and the growing unrest among large segments of the warrior class combined with financial woes to render the position of the Meiji government awkward. At this juncture, two ways of thinking about Sakhalin crystallized and clashed. One advocated the retention of the island at all costs. The other urged its abandonment.[33]

[33] For details of the debate on Sakhalin (1872–5): Sata Hakubō, 'Karafuto hyōron', Yoshino Sakuzō, ed., *Meiji bunka zenshū*, XXII (Tokyo, 1929), 13–22; Ōta, *Nichiro Karafuto gaikō sen*, pp. 186–97; Iguro Yatarō, *Kuroda Kiyotaka* (Sapporo, 1965), pp. 71–3; *Karafuto sōsho*, VI, 256–7.

Okamoto Kansuke, Nabeshima Naomasa, and Maruyama Sakura stood out as the foremost spokesmen of the 'hard line' on Sakhalin. Okamoto and Nabeshima directed the colonization of southern Sakhalin through the *Karafuto kaitakushi* and stoutly upheld a determination to fight and die for the island. Maruyama used his influence as an official in the Foreign Affairs Ministry to back up their views. These men were supported until 1873 by such important figures as Saigō Takamori and Etō Shimpei, both of whom keenly felt the need for national defence and a role for the disintegrating warrior class as colonists along Japan's sensitive northern frontier.

In opposition to this group, there grew up after 1871 a manner of thinking represented by Kuroda Kiyotaka, a director of the *Hokkaido kaitakushi*. Returning from a tour of the United States in 1871, Kuroda entertained ambitious projects for the development and colonization of Hokkaido. He viewed Sakhalin's potential as a productive colony with scepticism. He considered Sakhalin to be not only a financial burden to Japan but a dangerous political liability. In a memorial to the throne in May 1873, Kuroda warned of the joint occupation of Sakhalin as a threat to Hokkaido's security, for the contested island constituted a potential source of war between Russia and Japan. He then denigrated Sakhalin's importance to Japan with the following arguments: (1) from 1870 until 1873 the government had spent over 400,000 yen with no appreciable economic results; (2) two-thirds of the 3,073 'Japanese' population on Sakhalin consisted of Ainu or Oroki natives; (3) Sakhalin's severe climate precluded successful agriculture; and (4) any exploitation of coal required a huge investment and commensurate risk. Kuroda concluded by asserting that without any palpable signs of economic growth, there was no reason to prolong a volatile situation created by the joint occupation of Sakhalin with Russia.

Kuroda's arguments prevailed over those of Okamoto, Nabeshima, and Maruyama. Early in 1874, Japan's leaders decided to exchange Sakhalin for the central and northern Kurile Islands. Several factors contributed to this decision. Russian pressure on Sakhalin in the form of immigrant settlers, convicts, and military detachments grew with each year. The outnumbered and outgunned Japanese stood helpless and overawed before this seemingly irresistible wave. Meanwhile, Japan's leading counsellors became preoccupied with developments in Korea and Formosa. Climatically, Formosa seemed to offer more suitable conditions for colonization than Sakhalin. When a fierce debate regarding the advisability of war with Korea (*seikanron*) split the senior counsellors, Saigō Takamori and Etō Shimpei reluctantly sacrificed their championship of Sakhalin in a manoeuvre to win support for a campaign against Korea.[34]

One year elapsed between the government's decision to abandon Sakhalin and the signing of the Treaty of St. Petersburg by Admiral Enomoto Buyō (a Kuroda protégé) and Prince Aleksandr Gorchakov on 7 May 1875.[35] The treaty provided for the exchange of Japanese rights to Sakhalin for Russian rights to all the Kuriles north of Etorofu. Although Japan renounced sovereignty over an island with which historical associations went back for over 200 years, the Japanese retained some important privileges there. They were allowed to open consular offices in Korsakov (Ōtomari), were to be compensated by up to 90,000 yen for immovable property, and their vessels were to enjoy duty-free access to Korsakov for ten years. In addition, Japanese fishermen were allowed to continue to operate off Sakhalin's coasts, and the Japanese were accorded most-favoured nation treatment in the rights of fishing, commerce, and navigation in the ports of the Sea of Okhotsk and Kamchatka.

Supplementary articles to this treaty were signed in Tokyo on 22 August which dealt with the new status of inhabitants of Sakhalin and the Kurile Islands.[36] In effect, Japanese then living on Sakhalin were granted noteworthy privileges. While retaining their nationality, they were allowed to continue 'in the full right of their industries' being 'protected in the full exercise of their present right of property'. Moreover, Japanese were exempted from all taxes and duties for the life of the resident. The aboriginal inhabitants did not fare so well. The Sakhalin Ainu could not retain Japanese citizenship without

[34] *Karafuto sōsho*, VI, 256. Ōta, *Nichiro Karafuto gaikō sen*, p. 187. Miyazaki Raihachi, *Karafuto shi monogatari* (Tokyo, 1944), p. 354.

[35] For the text of the treaty, see Appendix A.

[36] See Appendix A.

leaving the island. They were given three years in which to reach a decision of whether to become a subject of the Tsar of Russia or the Emperor of Japan.

In September 1875, one month after the treaty's ratification, ceremonies held in Korsakov formally marked the transfer of Sakhalin to Russian rule. Eight hundred and sixty-one Ainu applied for evacuation to Japan. They were taken to Hokkaido and resettled along the Ishikari River. Some of them lived to return to their native island in 1905.

Chauvinistic Japanese and Russians have attacked the Treaty of St. Petersburg as unjust, insulting, and even fraudulent.[37] It would be more accurate to describe the treaty as a realistic accommodation by both sides. By 1875 Russia in fact possessed Sakhalin through an overwhelming preponderance of settlers and military might. In renouncing sovereignty over Sakhalin, Japan not only deferred an expensive and explosive border problem but earned two decades of relatively good relations with Russia. These decades were crucial to Japan's internal consolidation and economic development.

Seventy years of rivalry in Sakhalin came to an apparently peaceful end in 1875, but the settlement proved only to be for a limited duration. Japan never forgot her economic and emotional ties with Sakhalin. After a lull of thirty years, the island once again became the object of mutual hostilities.

[37] Yamashita Ryūmon, *Karafuto ron* (Tokyo, 1929), p. 43. Motoyama Keisen, *Roshia Shinkan sanbyakunen* (Tokyo, 1939), p. 236. Kokuryūkai, ed., *Tōa sengaku shishi kiden* II (Tokyo, 1934), 803–4. Ōta, *Nichiro Karafuto gaikō sen*, p. 222. Hiraoka, *Nichiro kōshōshi wa*, p. 380. A. N. Ryzhkov, 'Iz istorii otkrytiia, issledovaniia i osvoeniia Sakhalina', p. 79. Zhukov, *Russkie i Iaponiia*, p. 142.

V

SAKHALIN UNDER TSARIST RULE, 1875–1905

'Everyone wants to escape from here—the convicts, the settlers, and the officials.' GENERAL KONONOVICH, Military Governor of Sakhalin (1890)

THE years 1875 to 1905 were Sakhalin's Dark Ages. During these three decades, the island stagnated as a vast penal colony, a monument to human misery. On Sakhalin, the guards were more criminal than the convicts and the free settlers suffered more than the imprisoned. On Sakhalin, free women sold their children to preserve a mockery of a family, while convict women, rationed like precious commodities, were known to murder their designated spouses in hope of a better match. On Sakhalin the aborigines enjoyed an open season on escapees with a bounty for each corpse. On Sakhalin, men and women went to the woods not in search of grapes nor to gratify their lust, but for deadly toxic wolfsbane which would bring a quick end to their tormented lives. On Sakhalin, peasants talked wistfully of that same Siberia that Muscovites dreaded. On Sakhalin, one convict murdered a perversely cruel jailer by suffocating him in fermenting bread dough. The event caused such rejoicing that the other convicts rewarded the murderer and the authorities re-named the town after the jailer. On Sakhalin, the coal-miners ate tallow candles and rotten wood while the rivers were clogged with salmon. Sakhalin infused its unfortunate residents with a special malady. Chekhov called it 'febris sachalinensis' and described it as sensations of dampness, shivering fits, severe headaches, rheumatic pains, and a sinking feeling that one would never be able to leave the island. He added that 'if only those who liked Sakhalin lived there, the island would be uninhabited'.[1]

[1] Anton Chekhov, 'Ostrov Sakhalin', in *A. P. Chekhov, sobranie sochinenii*, X (Moscow, 1963), 364.

Yet in 1875 many Russians entertained high hopes for Sakhalin's economic potential. As rich in coal as Wales, in fish as Newfoundland, and in oil as Baku, the island seemed to be the pearl of Russia's eastern possessions. Through insensitivity, lack of imagination, and inertia, these dreams evaporated in the squalor and degradation that endowed Sakhalin with an international notoriety. During this period, Sakhalin literally lived up to its Manchu name—'black'.

After the Treaty of St. Petersburg (1875) that awarded all of Sakhalin to Russia, Japan's role in the island was reduced but not extinguished. Consular authorities in Korsakov and fishermen operating in coastal areas typified the enduring ties. By 1904, the number of Japanese working in Sakhalin had grown to well over 7,000.

Convicts, guards, and fishermen were not the only visitors to Sakhalin. Attracted by the island's infamy and mystery, scientists, scholars, writers, journalists, and an assortment of Victorian dilettantes made their way across Siberia or up through Hokkaido to satisfy their curiosity. Geologists uncovered its natural wealth. Ethnographers pondered over the aborigines. Writers and journalists exposed the sordid evils of the penal system and evoked the pathos of its victims. In short, Sakhalin's début among the educated public in the West occurred during these thirty years. The images created long outlasted the period itself. As late as 1935, a patriotic Russian referred to Sakhalin as an 'island of ill repute'.[2]

When Russia acquired undisputed sovereignty over all of Sakhalin in 1875, several informed men envisioned a bright economic future for the island. Already, Captain Krusenstern (1805), Major Busse (1854), and Colonel Veniukov (1872) had pointed out that the island's location between the Amur River and Japan made it invaluable for trade as well as for defence. M. S. Mitsul visited Sakhalin in 1870 and, enchanted with the wild grapes and bamboo, dreamed of a flourishing agricultural oasis populated by reformed convicts. The mining engineer A. Keppen noted that the island's coal was as fine as the best in Wales and much better than any in Japan. With rational exploitation and marketing, he asserted, Sakhalin would provide fuel for English and American steamers in the Far East. Ia.

[2] V. Koudrey, 'Island of Ill Repute', *Asia*, XXXV (March 1935), 143.

Butkovskii claimed that the colonization of Sakhalin together with the development of coal, fishing, forestry, and iron ore would reap a success surpassing that of Sydney and Melbourne.[3]

These hopes were doomed to disappointment, largely because of one fatally erroneous calculation—that economic development could be achieved by convict labour. Convicts were first introduced into Sakhalin as early as 1859 to work the exposed coal beds around Dué on the west coast.[4] A severe manpower shortage led to a further introduction of prison labour in 1861 for the Dué mines. In 1862 small groups of convicts arrived as agricultural colonists. After 1868 the number of convicts and exiles entering the island gained momentum with a shipment of 800 arriving in 1869. Whereas the Russian population of Sakhalin in 1873 barely reached 3,000, it rose to 28,000 in 1897 and to 35,000 in 1904, swollen by the influx of exiles.[5] From 1859 until 1870, the importation of convict labour from the continent seems to have been carried out haphazardly with no overall plan other than to fill labour needs in the coal-mines and bolster the Russian population in order to overawe the Japanese.

Starting in 1870, the Russians began considering the possibility of turning the island into a penal colony. The government dispatched a mission of inquiry to Sakhalin in 1870, and one of its leaders, M. S. Mitsul, enthusiastically recommended the creation of such a colony. In enumerating its advantages, Mitsul cited the island's 'ideal' conditions for agriculture and mining. Most important, Sakhalin was 'escape proof'. Hardened criminals could be transferred from camps in Siberia to lead productive lives in a remote insular part of the empire. Two

[3] N. V. Busse, *Ostrov Sakhalin* (St. Petersburg, 1872), p. 79. Colonel Veniukov, 'On the Island of Sakhalin', *Journal of the Royal Geographical Society*, XLII (1872), 373–88. M. S. Mitsul, *Ocherk ostrova Sakhalina v selskokhoziaistvennom otnoshenii* (St. Petersburg, 1873), pp. 137–9. A. Keppen, *Ostrov Sakhalin* (St. Petersburg, 1875), pp. 120–3. Ia. Butkovskii, *O Sakhaline i evo znachenii* (St. Petersburg, 1873), pp. 1–37. A. A. Panov, *Shokuminchi to shite no Sagaren* (Tokyo, 1942), pp. 6–10.

[4] Panov, *Shokuminchi to shite no Sagaren*, p. 55.

[5] J. W. McCarthy, 'Saghalin from a Japanese Source', *The Geographical Magazine*, V (1 Aug. 1878), 208 for the 1873 figure. S. Patkanov, *Glavnishiia danniia po statistik naselieniia krainovo vostoka Sibiri Primorskaia i Amurskaia oblasti i ostrov Sakhalin* (St. Petersburg, 1903), p. 3 for the 1897 figure. Iuri Zhukov, *Russkie i Iaponiia* (Moscow, 1945), p. 142 for the 1904 figure.

purposes would be served: the liquidation of Siberian camps which would ameliorate the social climate on the continent, and the defence and development of a frontier island comfortably far from the main concentrations of population, yet too close to Japan to be left unoccupied. A second mission, sent to Sakhalin in 1880, confirmed these recommendations.

In 1881 the government created a penal administration on the island responsible jointly to a military governor at Khabarovsk and the Bureau of Prisons in the Ministry of Interior. Three years later, Sakhalin acquired its own military governor residing at Aleksandrovsk. He stood at the apex of a dual hierarchy—the military guards and civilian officials in the Bureau of Prisons. Three local administrative districts were set up: Aleksandrovsk, Tymovsk, and Korsakov.

The establishment of a penal administration spurred the influx of convicts. Each year after 1884 1,000 exiles were shipped to Sakhalin on cramped convict vessels sailing from Odessa on a two month voyage that led through the Suez Canal, the Indian Ocean, and the East China Sea. New prisons were built at Dué and Korsakov. More primitive stockades sprang up in the smaller towns. By 1888 Sakhalin had become, in the words of George Kennan, 'the largest and most important penal establishment in Siberia'.[6]

The exile population in Sakhalin varied from one or two thousand in 1875 to something over 20,000 in 1904. About 60 per cent of the exiles were Russian, followed by White Russians (10 per cent), Ukrainians (10 per cent), Poles (5 per cent), Tatars (5 per cent) and a sprinkling of Latvians, Estonians, and Germans.[7] Exiles fell into three general classes: (1) hard labour convicts, (2) convict settlers, and (3) peasants who were formerly exiles.

Hard labour convicts (in 1897 they numbered 4,220 men and 759 women) lived in the island's six prisons. Incorrigibles, hardened criminals, and those under special punishment (for attempted escape or assault) were kept in ball and chain. The rest were engaged in work gangs buildings roads and planting potatoes. Good behaviour over a period of time (usually two

[6] George Kennan, *Siberia and the Exile System*, II (London, 1891), 221.

[7] Patkanov, *Glavnishiia danniia*, pp. 14–15. Max Funke, 'Die Insel Sachalin', *Angewandte Geographie*, Serie 2, Heft 12 (Nov. 1906), 28–9.

years) made them eligible for 'graduation' into the second group—convict settlers.

Convict settlers numbered about 7,000 in 1897 of whom 900 were women. They lived in small hamlets throughout the island and engaged in fishing or agriculture. Allowed to take common-law wives (free or convict), they were supplied with a small homestead, seeds, tools, clothing, and a modest allowance for each child under eighteen years of age. If after six years as a convict settler an individual maintained good behaviour, he could move into the third class—peasants who were formerly exiles.

The peasant-formerly-exile group might be called the 'semi-free' in that the penal servitude on Sakhalin had legally ended and individuals in that category were at liberty to return to Russia provided they avoided certain cities, notably Moscow and St. Petersburg. As nearly everyone who could afford to leave Sakhalin did so, this category was numerically the smallest. In 1897, it consisted of only 1,273 men and 759 women.

Conditions of the Sakhalin exiles varied considerably depending on their status and location. Some hard labour convicts fared better than some convict settlers. The most appalling conditions prevailed at the notorious Voyevodsk Prison, in the Dué mines, and in the stockade at Aleksandrovsk. The testimonies of Chekhov, Miroliubov, and Doroshevich graphically evoked the unspeakable squalor, degradation, and hopelessness that transformed a man into a bundle of lice-infected, foul rags covering a degenerating soul.[8]

Bad as these conditions were, the island's penal system did not fail for lack of good intentions. According to Chekhov, the Rykovsk Prison was tolerably clean and well-run, and some convict settlements in the south of the island were not irredeemably depressing. Moreover, Chekhov praised the character of the governor, General Kononovich, for his sincerity, benevolence, culture, and aversion to corporal punishment. Even George Kennan who impartially exposed incompetence and cruelty in

[8] Vasilii Mikhailovich Doroshevich, *Sakhalin* (Moscow, 1903, republished in Paris, 1935), records a journalist's visit in 1898. I. P. Miroliubov, *Vosem let na Sakhalin* (St. Petersburg, 1901), is an autobiographical account by a former exile whose real name was Ivan Pavlovich Iuvachev. Anton Chekhov, 'Ostrov Sakhalin', in *A. P. Chekhov, sobranie sochinenii*, X (Moscow, 1963), 43–394, is the most famous account, originally published in 1895 and based upon a visit from July to October of 1890.

Siberia's exile system called Kononovich a 'humane, sympathetic, warm-hearted . . . fearless, intelligent, and absolutely incorruptible official'. Kennan was perhaps a trifle optimistic, however, when he wrote: 'As long as General Kononovich remains in command of the Saghalin prisons and mines there is every reason to believe that they will be intelligently, honestly, and humanely managed.'[9]

However fine a man Kononovich may have been, he could not alter human nature or the evils inherent in the penal system. The semi-criminal, underpaid, bored guards fell naturally into sadism tempered only by indifference. Chekhov captured the essence of the matter when he remarked that the treatment of convicts varied in proportion to their proximity to high officials. Sakhalin was very far from St. Petersburg, not only in miles but in centuries.

The story of Sakhalin's women is especially lamentable. Women were far outnumbered by men on the island and consequently were in great demand by officials, settlers, and convicts. They came to Sakhalin either as convicts or as free settlers who followed their convict husbands into exile. A handful worked in the prison administration, including one enterprising female jailer who organized a lucrative prostitution business by inducting women convicts.[10]

Convict women comprised only about 10 per cent of the exiles. When they arrived on steamers at Aleksandrovsk, officials scurried down to the wharf to select the healthiest and comeliest for kitchen maids and domestic servants. These were the lucky ones. Others were then set aside as prostitutes for the guards and minor clerks. The third and largest group were distributed to hamlets throughout the island as cohabitants for suitable convict settlers who had submitted an application for a woman. Local officials generally decided on who received a woman. The successful candidates were notified to appear on a given day at a given spot to pick up their new partners. By the time that the

[9] Kennan, *Siberia and the Exile System*, II, 219, 222.

[10] She was exposed and dismissed in 1902. Panov, *Shokuminchi to shite no Sagaren*, p. 119. The ensuing material on Sakhalin's women is from: Panov, pp. 189–208. Chekhov, 'Ostrov Sakhalin', pp. 263–75. N. Novombergskii, *Ostrov Sakhalin* (St. Petersburg, 1903), pp. 30–5. N. S. Lobas, *Katorga i poseleniie na O v. Sakhalin* (Pavlograd, 1903), p. 150. Ia. Iankelevich, 'Ostrov Sakhalin', *Vestnik Azii*, XLIX (1922), 170–4.

officials, clerks, and guards had skimmed off their share, the settlers were left with a rugged, bottom-of-the-barrel residue.

In 1893 the distribution of women was adopted as a reward for good behaviour. When one woman refused to live with her designated spouse and became pregnant by another man (her favourite) to prevent the match, officials none the less forced her to live with the stranger regardless of her emotional bonds and the child. One unfortunate convict woman happened to be sent to a settlement inhabited only by men and was subjected to forced sexual relations over twenty times daily.

Ironically, convict women in general lived better economically than their free counterparts. They received clothes and food from the penal administration for the duration of their terms. Those women who voluntarily followed their husbands and fathers into exile enjoyed no such security. Once in Sakhalin, they realized to their horror that there was no work for them except prostitution, or domestic service for the most attractive. Beset by despair, disillusion and hopelessness, they gradually hardened to the demands of the situation. To preserve the semblance of a family, free women sold themselves for enough money to support husbands and children. Young girls of twelve or thirteen were encouraged by their parents to earn money in this manner or were sold for a flat sum to convict settlers. Ten-year old syphilitics were not unknown. Such was the demand for women in the remote settlements that even grandmothers reportedly could earn their way provided they were hardy. It was among the children that the frightful effects of environment showed most tellingly. Few stayed on the island after they had passed the age of sixteen. Many became more hardened criminals than their parents.

Sakhalin had a population of free settlers which at the turn of the century numbered about 10,000. Most of them came in large groups like the 800 Ukrainians who arrived in 1868. A majority settled in the south along the Poronai River or around Aniwa Bay and attempted to engage in agriculture. Free immigrants were attracted to Sakhalin by promise of free land, tools, building materials, and a remission of taxation. Government policy was so inefficiently administered, however, that many of these colonists suffered terribly. Some were directed to land that was not arable or was periodically flooded. Others found themselves settled near prisons and lived in constant fear of molestation. Nearly all lacked adequate equipment and training to deal with Sakhalin's harsh environment. Chekhov passed through a few free villages in the south that presented a pleasing aspect. Even in these, however, peasants expressed a desire to move to the warmer and more fertile areas of the Ussuri River valley. Defeated by the lack of planning and a hostile climate, free settlement on Sakhalin perished like a stillborn child.

Censorship prevented Chekhov, Doroshevich, and Miroliubov from referring to political prisoners in their accounts of Sakhalin. Visitors were strictly barred from contact with political exiles. A letter of Chekhov's was uncovered in the Soviet Union in 1960 which reveals that the writer had a brief, clandestine meeting with a political exile named P. Dombrovskii who committed suicide in 1891.[11] Recent Soviet research has brought to light more information on this topic. It now appears that there were about fifty political exiles in Sakhalin between 1884 and 1906.[12] Among these were seventeen members of the Polish Proletariat Party and Edmund Plosskii who led the '1887 Incident' (a plot against the life of Tsar Alexander III) in which Lenin's elder brother died. Liudmila Volkenstein, M. N. Trigoni, and B. Ellinskii[13] survived their internments to play active roles in the Soviet state. Others like F. I. Suiderskii survived years of exile in Tsarist Sakhalin only to fall victim to Stalin's purges in the 1930s. Some of these political exiles gave secret instruction in revolutionary ideology to fellow prisoners. V. I. Brazhnikov even carried his activist work outside the penal colony by distributing tracts to the Gilyaks. A secret revolutionary organization called the 'Commune' was formed in the Aleksandrovsk prison, but its effectiveness does not seem to have been noteworthy.

Economic Development

As an economic experiment, the development of Sakhalin from

[11] M. V. Teplinskii, *Sakhalinskie puteshestviia* (Iuzhno-Sakhalinsk, 1962), p. 8.

[12] I. A. Senchenko, *Revoliutsionery Rossii na Sakhalinskoi katorge* (Iuzhno-Sakhalinsk, 1963), p. 89. I. A. Senchenko, *Ocherki istorii Sakhalina* (Iuzhno-Sakhalinsk, 1957), pp. 51–66. A. N. Ryzhkov, 'Iz istorii otkrytiia, issledovaniia, i osvoeniia Sakhalina i Kurilskikh ostrovov', K. I. Kniazev, ed., *Sakhalinskaia oblast* (Iuzhno-Sakhalinsk, 1960), pp. 84–7.

[13] Ellinskii wrote a novel about his ordeal in Sakhalin as a political prisoner. *Pod zvon tsepei: roman Sakhalinskikh politicheskikh sylnikh* (Leningrad, 1927).

1875 to 1905 was a failure. Fishing remained the uncontested province of the Japanese. The forests were only marginally exploited. Oil was first discovered in 1880, but systematic drilling began only after the Russo-Japanese War. Agriculture proved an unqualified fiasco, defeated by a ruthless climate and inefficient management. The exploitation of coal stands out as the only significant economic achievement of this period.

Coal was first discovered on Sakhalin by La Pérouse in 1787. Boshniak made a survey in 1851 which uncovered major deposits around Dué. Although Sakhalin was administered by the Russian-American Company during 1853–6, the government reserved the right to exploit the island's coal. After the island was placed under the jurisdiction of the governor-general of Eastern Siberia in 1856, the government contracted a group of entrepreneurs to mine the Dué coal seams. Convict labour worked these mines. To alleviate the labour shortage, Chinese coolies were imported from Hong Kong in 1868.

From 1857 until 1875, Dué's coal was exploited with haphazard recklessness. A convict received wages according to the amount of coal he mined daily. Consequently, individuals wandered from spot to spot, digging at surface deposits and abandoning them at will. Exposed to weathering, many deposits became unusable. Surveys by Lopatin (1867–8) and Keppen (1873) revealed that the Dué mines could easily yield 36,000 tons annually. These forecasts were not even half fulfilled.[14]

Containing little ash or sulphur, Sakhalin's coal was equal in quality to the best in Europe and was superior to the coal then mined in Japan. Many officials entertained rosy visions of the island supplying the Russian Pacific Fleet and foreign steamers throughout the Far East. St. Petersburg, however, refused to take bold action and consistently rejected attractive offers from foreign entrepreneurs to develop the mines on a large scale. Ambitious plans to build coal depots in De Castries and Nikolaevsk were dropped in 1857. An attempt to sell Dué coal in Hakodate ended in failure in 1865 because the Russians brought no samples with them. In 1859 Governor-General Muraviev and the American consul in Hakodate agreed to export 50,000 tons of Sakhalin coal annually to the United States. The Russian

[14] Keppen, *Ostrov Sakhalin*, p. 90. Panov, *Shokuminchi to shite no Sagaren*, pp. 10–38.

government vetoed these plans because American vessels would be carrying the coal. In any event, it is unlikely that Sakhalin could have supplied such a large quantity at the time. From 1867 to 1875 the Russians refused repeated American and British bids to develop Sakhalin's mines. Fear of foreign economic incursions may well have been the source of this unreceptive posture.

From 1875 until 1902, the Russian 'Sakhalin Company' mined Dué's coal under contract to the government. Careless digging, exposure to weather, and inadequate drainage damaged the deposits. Hopelessly in arrears in its payments to the government, the company lost the concession in 1902 to the Makovsky Company. Sakhalin coal production increased from 2,412 tons in 1860 to 18,000 tons in 1890. This output never became a significant factor in Russia's total coal production (6,609,000 tons in 1890).[15] Not until after the Russian Revolution and the establishment of Soviet power in northern Sakhalin (1925) did coal production on the island achieve the levels optimistically forecast in 1870.

From the Treaty of St. Petersburg (1875) until the Russo-Japanese War (1904), Sakhalin hosted an unprecedented succession of foreign and Russian visitors, not all of whom were convicts. Bronislaw Pilsudski, brother of the Polish general and statesman Józef Pilsudski, came as an exile and did important research on the Ainu before fleeing the island during the Japanese invasion. Another exile, Lev Shternberg, appointed himself director of the Aleksandrovsk Historical Museum during the 1890s while carrying out his ethnographic investigations. Anton Chekhov and Vasilii Doroshevich came especially to study the penal system. Their visits aroused particular interest from Leo Tolstoy, Vladimir Korolenko, V. I. Nemirovich-Danchenko, and Maxim Gorki.[16]

Scientists as well as writers reached Sakhalin, attracted by the unstudied fauna, flora, and geology. Noteworthy work was done by the zoologist J. S. Poliakov in inaugurating a systematic

[15] A. Keppen, *Mining and Metallurgy*, Vol. IV of *The Industries of Russia* (St. Petersburg, 1893), 54.

[16] Teplinskii, *Sakhalinskie puteshestviia*, pp. 46–9. Bronislaw Pilsudski, *Material for the Study of the Ainu Language and Folklore* (Cracow, 1912). L. Ia. Shternberg, *Giliaki, orochi, gol'dy, negidal'tsy, ainy* (Khabarovsk, 1933).

investigation of Sakhalin's archaeology. P. Iu. Schmidt (namesake of the Schmidt Peninsula) studied marine life while K. S. Staritskii and S. O. Makarov made oceanographic surveys of the waters around the island.[17]

Thanks to the efforts of peripatetic journalists, the reading public in England and France was given a grim impression of Sakhalin during the thirty years after 1875. George Kennan never reached the island in his famous tour of Siberia, but he heard that penal work there was much more arduous than in the camps that he visited on the continent. When the English traveller, B. D. Howard, came to Sakhalin in 1890, he found the island so appalling that he asserted: 'Sakhalin is the unmentionable . . . this island has been reserved chiefly as the final destination of the unshot, the unhanged, the convicts and exiles who by frequent escapes or repeated murders have graduated perhaps from other prisons'. Howard felt so terrified of being murdered by convicts that he constantly sported a loaded revolver. One night, his neurosis exploded into a shooting spree that must have caused some convicts to wonder about the docility of English gentlemen. He despised the Ainu ('as repulsive creatures as it is possible to imagine') but consoled himself with a conviction of their Hebraic origins.[18]

B. D. Howard's successors (Albert Bordeaux, Charles H. Hawes, Harry DeWindt, L. V. Dalton, and W. S. Chisholm) expressed similar sentiments of disgust, repulsion, and condescension towards the island and its inhabitants. Chisholm summed up the Victorian judgment of Tsarist Sakhalin as 'the most notorious penal settlement in the world . . . the land of moral darkness and abject misery'. This image continued to plague Sakhalin long after the penal camps had been abolished.[19]

[17] J. S. Poljakow, *Reise nach der Insel Sachalin in den Jahren 1881–1882* (Berlin, 1884). P. Iu. Shmidt, *Ostrov isgnaniia: Sakhalin* (St. Petersburg, 1905).

[18] B. D. Howard, *Life with Transsiberian Savages* (London, 1893), pp. 4–5, 30–1. B. D. Howard, *Prisoners of Russia: A Personal Study of Convict Life in Sakhalin and Siberia* (New York, 1902), pp. 57, 68, 219.

[19] W. S. Chisholm, 'Saghalien, the Isle of the Russian Banished', *Chamber's Journal*, VIII, 6th Series (Apr. 1905), 301. Other descriptions of Sakhalin by foreign visitors: Albert Bordeaux, *Siberie et Californie: Notes de Voyage et de Séjour* (Paris, 1903), pp. 153–67. Charles H. Hawes, *In the Uttermost East* (London, 1903), pp. 117–30. Harry DeWindt, 'The Island of Sakhalin', *Fortnightly Review*, New Series, LXI (Jan.–June 1897), 711–15. L. V. Dalton, 'Sakhalin or Karafto', *The Imperial and Asiatic Quarterly Review*, XX (Oct. 1905), 279–85.

By 1904 Sakhalin had become a disappointment for economists, a stigma to officials, a nightmare to its involuntary settlers a field of exploration for scientists, and an exotic if macabre news story for journalists. To the aborigines and the Japanese, Sakhalin meant something rather different. The island's indigenous population (the Ainu, Gilyak, and Oroki tribes) reeled under the sudden influx of foreign settlers that was transforming the environment. Examined by ethnographers or curious travellers, infected with smallpox, measles or syphilis, occasionally singled out for indoctrination by missionaries or revolutionaries, these people moved inevitably into the sidelines of Sakhalin's development. The Japanese, in contrast to this, assumed a larger role in the island's economy after 1875. The growing economic dynamism from the south presaged the events of 1905 when Sakhalin again became a battleground between Russia and Japan.

Article 5 of the Treaty of St. Petersburg which awarded Sakhalin to Russia stipulated the right of Japanese residents of Sakhalin to remain on the island and to continue to exercise for life the right of property and industry while retaining Japanese nationality. Moreover, Japanese nationals were granted exemption from port duties in Korsakov for ten years. Using this legal justification, the Japanese quickly built up coastal fishing operations and processing facilities to a remarkable scale. In 1875 300 Japanese worked in Sakhalin. By 1904 this number had grown to over 7,000. Only 170 Russians were engaged in fishing in 1901, although a few Russian entrepreneurs managed fishing enterprises with Japanese labour.[20]

The Russian government viewed the growing Japanese economic presence with distaste if not alarm. Starting in 1883, St. Petersburg began to apply various pressures to squeeze Japanese fishing interests off the island. In May of that year the government declared the imposition of a heavy tax on all Japanese fish exports from Sakhalin. After strong protests from Tokyo, a reduction of the tax was negotiated by Japanese consular authorities in Korsakov and the island's military governor. However, successively heavier taxes on property and fish were levied in 1884, 1890, and 1894, which forced the

[20] Karafuto chō, ed., *Karafuto sōsho,* VI (Toyohara, 1941), 275–8. Panov, *Shokuminchi to shite no Sagaren,* p. 44.

Japanese to appeal for an agreement to stabilize duty rates. These appeals went unanswered. In December 1899, Russia announced extraordinary new rules for Japanese fishing in Sakhalin and the Maritime Region. First, 145 out of 269 Japanese fishing posts were ordered to close. Secondly, hitherto lifetime fishing rights were to be renewed annually by application to the military governor. Thirdly, in selecting successful applicants for each concession or fishing district, Russian nationals were to be given preference.

The Russian decree of 1899 threw Japanese fishing interests into a state of consternation and elicited the first outright retaliatory reaction from the Japanese government. In May 1900 the Imperial Diet passed a law raising import taxes on fish products. As Sakhalin was the only area from which Japan imported large quantities of such articles, the law aimed at forcing the Russians to rescind the 1899 decree by threatening a source of their tax income. A compromise was reached in December when both parties modified their recent legislation.

Scarcely a year passed before Russia revealed an even more drastic curtailment of foreign fishing rights. A decree of November 1901 stipulated the exclusion of all foreign fishing concerns from the Maritime Province and Sakhalin except for designated spots along southern Sakhalin's coasts. Moreover, all fishermen working on coastal processing establishments were henceforth to be Russian nationals. The Japanese responded to this measure in March 1902 by amalgamating all their fishing enterprises in Sakhalin into one organization—the *Sagaren suisan kumiai* (Sakhalin Marine Products Union). This newly created union ruled that only its members could engage in fishing in Sakhalin. Consequently, Russian entrepreneurs found themselves bereft of their labour force. Once again, retaliation forced the Russian government to compromise. Both sides agreed to postpone the enforcement of exclusionist measures. At this point, the outbreak of the Russo-Japanese War in February 1904 removed the Sakhalin fisheries dispute from the conference room to the battlefield.[21]

[21] The above material on Sakhalin fisheries disputes is taken from: Senchenko, *Ocherki istorii Sakhalina*, pp. 26–32. Ōta Saburō, *Nichiro Karafuto gaikō sen* (Tokyo, 1941), pp. 228–32. Miyazaki Raihachi, *Karafuto shi monogatari* (Tokyo, 1944), pp. 371–8.

Sakhalin in the Russo-Japanese War

The Russo-Japanese War (February 1904–September 1905) arose principally out of a clash of interests in Manchuria and Korea. Japan's dramatic military victories during the eighteen months of hostilities shocked European observers into a fundamental re-evaluation of that Asian power. The war altered the balance of power in Northeast Asia by checking Russia's political and economic designs on Korea and southern Manchuria and by enhancing Japan's involvement on the continent.

The Japanese attack on Sakhalin in July 1905 has received relatively little attention. It is significant, however, that Sakhalin was the only Russian territory in the war to be invaded, occupied, and partially annexed by the enemy. Although battles in Manchuria and in the Tsushima Strait captured the world's attention, the Sakhalin campaign had the wide-ranging repercussion of exacerbating and perpetuating Russo-Japanese rivalry in Northeast Asia.

Like the Soviet invasion of southern Sakhalin in 1945, the Japanese attack of 1905 came at the final stages of the war.[22] Strategically, the manoeuvre proved of little importance, as the attack took place after the main battles had already been decided. Diplomatically, it strengthened the Japanese bargaining position at the Portsmouth peace negotiations. From Russia's (Tsarist or Soviet) point of view, the Japanese attack on Sakhalin was a cynical, opportunistic piece of territorial brigandage. A Soviet historian has hinted that the attack was actively urged by American and English imperialists, Theodore Roosevelt in particular.[23] The available evidence suggests that the Japanese were eager to avenge the 'humiliation' of 1875 and needed little prodding from outsiders once Russia's naval forces in the Sea of Japan had been destroyed.

Russia made no particular effort to fortify Sakhalin when war broke out in 1904. Governor Liapunov managed to mobilize about 6,000 troops, almost a third of whom were convict settlers who volunteered on promises of a restoration of civil liberty

[22] For details of the Sakhalin campaign: S. von Ursyn-Pruszynski, *Die Kämpfe auf der Insel Sachalin während des russisch-japanischen Krieges* (Vienna, 1910). Ryzhkov, Iz istoriia Sakhalina', pp. 87–90. *Karafuto sōsho*, VI, 278–321. *The Times* [London], 11, 12, 17, 28, 31 July. 2, 3, 5, 7, 11 Aug. 7 Sept 1905.

[23] Ryzhkov, 'Iz istorii Sakhalina', p. 87.

after the war. These forces were deployed mainly around Aleksandrovsk, Dué, and Korsakov. The attacking Japanese consisted of the specially formed 13th Infantry Division (14,000 men) led by General Haraguchi Kanenari and transported by a squadron of cruisers and destroyers under the command of Admiral Kataoka Shichirō. Although one historian[24] accuses the Japanese of massing 30,000 army veterans disguised as fishermen around Terpenie Bay who acted as fifth columnists, there actually was no opportunity for the Japanese population in Sakhalin to participate actively in the invasion. All Japanese nationals on Sakhalin had in fact been evacuated before the outbreak of the war.

The Japanese attack progressed swiftly and efficiently. On the afternoon of 7 July troops landed at Jorei, a small hamlet eight miles east of Korsakov (Ōtomari) in Aniwa Bay. Korsakov was occupied on 8 July after a brief but bitter engagement. The Russians burned the town, retreating northwards to Vladimirovka (near present-day Iuzhno-Sakhalinsk). By 11 July Haraguchi's forces had swept out of Vladimirovka and were pushing northwards meeting with little resistance.

On 24 July a second Japanese force landed on Sakhalin's west coast at Aleksandrovsk and Arkovo. To safeguard their rear against Russian reinforcements from across the Tatary Strait, they sent a flying squadron to destroy the military installations in De Castries Bay. After the occupation of Aleksandrovsk, the Japanese pushed the enemy inland, cutting the opposing forces into two isolated groups, one in Derbinskoe and the other in the Onor region. Bereft of reinforcements and supplies, Sakhalin's military governor, Lieutenant General Liapunov asked for a 'cessation of hostilities' on 30 July. The following day, he accepted the victor's terms: immediate surrender of all *matériel*, officers, men, and documents. Seventy officers and 4,318 men laid down their arms. 182 Russians died and 278 managed to escape across the straits. Some hid in the forests or held out in small pockets that were mercilessly exterminated by the end of August. I have found no evidence to support a Soviet historian's claim that the Ainu, Gilyak, and Oroki people heroically joined the Russians to fight the Japanese invader.[25]

[24] Zhukov, *Russkie i Iaponiia*, p. 143.
[25] Ryzhkov, 'Iz istorii Sakhalina', p. 88.

The Japanese were elated with their success. The Emperor Meiji sent congratulatory messages to General Haraguchi and Admiral Kataoka. Haraguchi received a hero's welcome at Ueno Station when he returned to Tokyo on 28 September. Most Japanese observers were convinced that all of Sakhalin would be incorporated in the Empire. They regarded the annexation of the island as a just restoration of Japan's historical rights violated in the humiliating treaty of 1875. When General Haraguchi proclaimed the establishment of a military administration over the island on 31 July, he noted that Sakhalin was lost to Russia 'forever'.[26] On 7 August the army held an elaborate ceremony at a hastily constructed temple in Aleksandrovsk solemnly celebrating Sakhalin's 'restoration'. On 28 August the government created a civilian administration at Aleksandrovsk (located in the northern half of the island) in preparation for formal annexation.

These sanguine expectations and euphoric celebrations proved to be premature. When Russian and Japanese delegates met in August at Portsmouth, New Hampshire, at the invitation of President Theodore Roosevelt, to negotiate an end to the war, the talks foundered in a deadlock over the question of Sakhalin and an indemnity. While Japan had compiled an impressive catalogue of military successes, both sides were financially and economically exhausted by the war. The Russian plenipotentiary, Count Witte, expertly calculated this situation and skilfully deflected the Japanese demands for the cession of all Sakhalin and the payment of an indemnity for Japan's war expenditures. When the negotiations appeared in danger of breakdown, Roosevelt advised the Japanese delegate Komura Jutarō to settle for less than his original demands in the cause of securing an honourable peace. Witte's clever tenacity, Roosevelt's pressure, and a recognition by the Japanese government that the continuation of the war would put a heavy strain on the country, led to the abandonment of claims to northern Sakhalin and the indemnity.

On 5 September 1905 the Treaty of Portsmouth was signed. Sakhalin was partitioned at the 50th parallel of latitude. The southern half (henceforth called 'Karafuto') became Japanese territory. The northern section remained in the Russian Empire.

26 *The Times* [London], 2 Aug. 1905.

Article IX prohibited military fortifications in both sections of the island.[27]

News of the territorial clauses in the treaty caused deep disappointment and bitter disillusionment inside Japan. Angry riots erupted against the government in Tokyo and other cities. To those who had dreamt of a complete recovery of the island, the 50th parallel symbolized a national shame. Needless to say, an identical sensation gripped patriots in Tsarist Russia and later in the Soviet Union.

The war and the Japanese invasion brought radical and even violent changes into the lives of Sakhalin's Russian inhabitants.[28] For some of the convicts, the chaos offered an opportunity to escape the island. The Japanese, according to their own admission, released all political prisoners, but this is contested by a Soviet historian.[29] Many thousands of convicts and convict settlers undoubtedly did cross the straits (one report put the number at 30,000),[30] and terrorized the Maritime Region for many months. There have been allegations that the prison authorities brought out groups of convicts from their cells and shot them in groups.[31]

In the rush to escape the island immediately before and after the Japanese attack, free settlers sold their houses and land for a pittance or simply abandoned their homesteads in a feverish drive for the continent. The Japanese facilitated this mass migration by providing transports for the passage. The Russian government's measures to receive refugees in Nikolaevsk proved woefully inadequate to cope with the human wave. The refugee problem came under control in September when it became known that at least northern Sakhalin was to be retained. Nevertheless, Sakhalin's Russian population dropped from 40,000 to under 7,000 during the summer of 1905.

[27] See Appendix A for articles of the Portsmouth Treaty relating to Sakhalin. For the diplomatic manoeuvers at the conference, see John A. White, *The Diplomacy of the Russo-Japanese War* (Princeton, 1964), pp. 282–309.

[28] For details of the fate of Russians on Sakhalin in 1905: Iankelevich, 'Ostrov Sakhalin', pp. 176–7. I. A. Senchenko, 'Severnyi Sakhalin v 1905–16 gg.', in K. I Kniazev, ed., *Sakhalinskaia oblast*, pp. 93–5. S. Kukunian, *Poslednie dni na Sakhaline* (Baku, 1910). I. A. Senchenko, *Ocherki istorii Sakhalina; vtoraia polovina XIX v., nachalo XX v.* (Iuzhno-Sakhalinsk, 1957), pp. 67–71.

[29] Senchenko, *Revoliutsionery Rossii na Sakhalinskoi katorge*, p. 94.

[30] Mary Gaunt, *A Broken Journey* (London, 1919), pp. 182–3.

[31] S. L. Lutskii, *Ostrov Sakhalin* (Moscow, 1946), pp. 8–9.

The Treaty of Portsmouth left Sakhalin once again divided between two powers. Unlike the joint occupation from 1855 to 1875, there existed a fixed frontier along the 50th parallel which split the island into two roughly equal sections. The northern Russian sphere (approximately 16,000 square miles in area) was slightly larger than Japanese Karafuto (approximately 14,400 square miles in area). After thirty years of Tsarist rule characterized by a betrayal of economic hopes and the dismal failure of penal colonization, Sakhalin reverted to its earlier role as a contested frontier area. Under two different administrations, northern and southern Sakhalin each followed differing paths of development. This 'dual personality' of the island persisted through forty years of revolution, intervention, and increasing tension until the cataclysmic reunion of 1945.

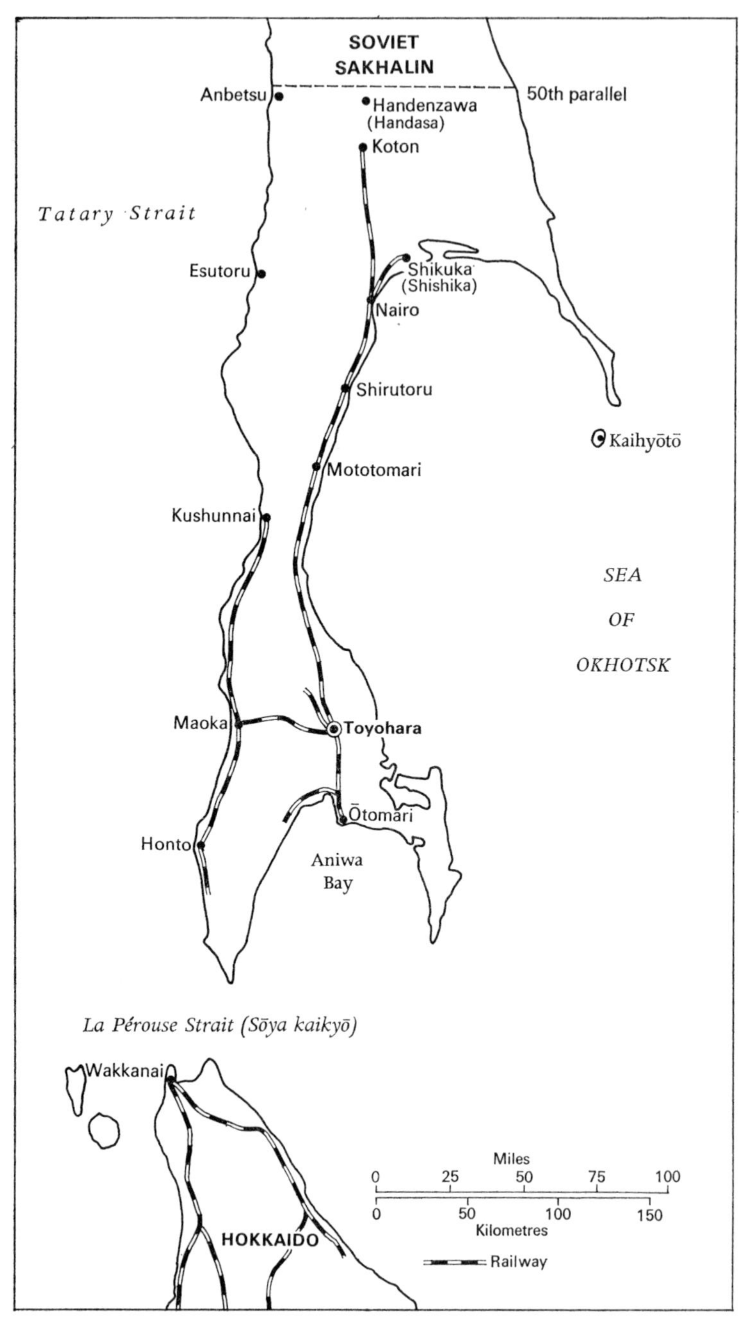

MAP IV. Japanese Karafuto

VI

YEARS OF TRANSITION AND TURBULENCE, 1905–1925

'Oh madam, how lucky you are to get away from Sakhalin!'
Governor's daughter to Mary Gaunt (1914)

IN the twenty years from 1905 to 1925, Sakhalin suffered one invasion, one intervention, and reeled from the effects of a world war, a revolution, and a civil war. As the island's economy also underwent great changes, these years might well be called ones of both transition and turbulence.

1905 to 1914 were primarily years of transition. The Russians made unprecedented efforts to build up the north, while the Japanese began to transform the south into a productive appendage of the home islands.

This state of affairs was interrupted by the First World War, the Russian Revolution and Civil War, the Allied Intervention in Siberia (1918–22), and the Japanese occupation of northern Sakhalin (1920–5). The chaotic fluidity of the years 1915–25 ended only with the establishment of Soviet-Japanese diplomatic relations by the Russo-Japanese Convention signed in Peking on 20 January 1925 and with the evacuation of Japanese military forces from northern Sakhalin on 15 May 1925. During this period Russia was beset by a succession of crises which temporarily undermined her strength. At the same time, the Japanese showed signs of using the 'threat of Bolshevism' as an excuse to exploit Russia's temporary weakness. There was even talk of rectifying the 'shame' of Portsmouth by purchasing or simply seizing northern Sakhalin.

The Japanese government, however, eventually stopped short of forceful annexation and reached a compromise with the Soviet Union in 1925. As a condition for withdrawing its forces from northern Sakhalin, Japan secured concessions to exploit precious oil and coal deposits there for forty-five years. These concessions inevitably became the source of increased tension in the 1930s.

They persisted until 1944 when Russian armies were flooding into eastern Europe and the Japanese were locked in mortal combat in China, South East Asia, and in the Western Pacific Ocean. In 1944 the tables were reversed. Russia, not Japan, was looking for an opportunity to settle old scores.

Japanese Karafuto, 1905–1925

On 1 August 1905, one day after the Russian defenders had surrendered, the Japanese declared military rule over all of Sakhalin. A temporary civil administration (*Karafuto minsei sho*) subordinate to the army was created on 28 August with its offices located at Aleksandrovsk.

The Portsmouth Treaty (5 September) reduced Japan's newly-acquired authority from the whole island to the area below the 50th parallel. The army and civil administrators were forced to move to Korsakov (renamed Ōtomari) on Aniwa Bay. From September 1905 until March 1907 Karafuto was administered by army decrees implemented by civil officials. The army paid all operating costs. The Japanese withdrew all but two regiments which were placed under the command of the 7th Division stationed in Asahikawa on the island of Hokkaido.

A Russo-Japanese team demarcated the ninety-mile boundary along the 50th parallel. The frontier area was cleared of trees and shrubs leaving a ten-metre wide path across the island punctuated by seventeen stone markers and scores of wooden posts. In accordance with Article IX of the Portsmouth Treaty, no military fortifications were to be erected by either side. Only a single road intersected the frontier. It remained unused, for from 1905 until 1945 (with brief interruptions) this boundary was sealed.

In addition to frontier demarcation, the military administration managed the repatriation of Russian residents (165 Russians still lived in Karafuto in 1909),[1] the auction of fishing concessions, the construction of a new administrative headquarters at Toyohara (formerly Vladimirovka), and the establishment of medical facilities. The exploitation of forest and coal deposits was forbidden until their extent could be evaluated.

On 31 March 1907, military rule was officially terminated with the creation of the *Karafuto chō* (Karafuto Office) which

[1] Shirani Ukichi, *Karafuto kaihatsusaku* (Ōtomari, 1909), p. 112.

continued to govern the Japanese part of the island until 1945. The governor exercised wide-ranging authority including direct control of police, defence, colonization, construction, taxation, and education. He was directly responsible to the Minister of Home Affairs (1907–10, 1912–17), to the Prime Minister (1910–12, 1917–29), and to the Minister of Colonization (1929–43). In 1943, Karafuto was incorporated into the Northern Regional Defence Area as an integral part of the home islands.[2]

The Japanese set about populating and developing their new colony with alacrity. There is no evidence, however, that they restricted immigration to army reservists or turned Karafuto into an armed base designed to threaten Russia, as some historians have maintained.[3] At this stage, the goals were economic, not strategic. Karafuto's rich fisheries, forests, coal deposits, and sheltered valleys offered promising opportunities.

Encouraging immigration was a matter of priority. Barely two weeks after the Russian surrender, the army announced that settlers from the home islands would be welcome. After 1907, the government made positive efforts to attract agrarian settlers by advertising free land, houses, tools, seeds, and exemption from taxes for able-bodied immigrants. The government-subsidized Hokkaido Colonial Bank extended long-term loans at low rates of interest to incoming settlers. The deserted Russian houses were distributed to applicants who, with characteristic attachment to Japanese ways, threw out the furniture and stoves, replacing them with mats (*tatami*) and charcoal braziers. Many regretted this precipitate action during the course of the first winter.[4]

The colonization of Karafuto followed closely the pattern of its southern neighbour, Hokkaido.[5] Surveying teams decided on suitable spots for agriculture, fishing, and forestry. Street plans were laid out for towns. Public pastures and forests were set

[2] Karafuto chō, ed., *Karafuto sōsho*, VI (Toyohara, 1941), 330–3. *Asahi nenkan 1944* (Tokyo, 1944), pp. 423–4.

[3] S. L. Lutskii, *Ostrov Sakhalin* (Moscow, 1946), pp. 9–11. Iuri Zhukov, *Russkie i Iaponiia* (Moscow, 1945), p. 156.

[4] Captain C. R. Woodroffe, 'Four Weeks in Saghalien', *Journal of the Royal Artillery*, XXXV (1908–9), 354.

[5] Takakura Shin'ichirō, *Hokkaido takushoku shi* (Sapporo, 1947), pp. 273–4. For the details of colonial policy, see Karafuto chō, ed., *Karafuto enkaku shi* (Toyohara, 1925); Karafuto chō, ed., *Karafuto shisei sanjūnen shi* (Toyohara, 1936).

aside. Roads were cut through the wilderness or were gouged out from the coastal cliffs. Because of Karafuto's relatively harsh climatic conditions, each settler received a larger parcel of land than his Hokkaido counterpart. Incoming settlers contributed their labour to the construction of schools, parks, clinics, shrines, and temples for the larger communities. By 1909 the colony had achieved a population of 41,000.

Beginning in 1911 the thrust of government policy shifted from encouraging individual farmers to making huge land grants to companies with the necessary capital to undertake large-scale forestry enterprises. Consequently, agriculture never amounted to more than 10 per cent of the colony's total valued output. Fishing, paper, wood pulp, and (after 1931) coal proved to be the mainstays of the island's economy.

Karafuto's fishing industry dates back to the early eighteenth century when Japanese came from Hokkaido in the spring and summer for herring. These visits continued during the period of Russian rule (1875–1905) despite an increasingly onerous system of taxation. After 1905, the Karafuto Office issued a fixed number of licences, published rules limiting the size of the catch and the type of nets employed, and founded fishermen's unions for self-regulation of the industry. From 1905 until 1915, Japanese fishermen flocked to Karafuto, but in the succeeding years the industry was outpaced by forestry and paper manufacturing. Fishing accounted for 64 per cent of the colony's income in 1915, but this proportion fell to 20 per cent in 1920 and to 10 per cent in 1925.[6]

Karafuto was covered with thousands of acres of pine forests that provided raw materials for pulp, turpentine, alcohol, and other wood products. Yet the colony's brightest promise at times turned large parts of the island into an inferno. The closely packed trees and thick layers of accumulated dead leaves made the forests extremely vulnerable to fires. Volcanoes, sparks from the funnels of locomotives, or simple negligence ignited blazes that raged out of control for weeks.

Equally damaging to the forests was the reckless exploitation of timber. In 1910 the government auctioned off large forest areas to corporate bidders, the Mitsui Bussan Company being

[6] Takakura, *Hokkaido takushoku shi*, p. 281. For details of the fishing industry, Sugimoto Zennosuke, *Karafuto gyosei kaikaku enkaku shi* (Maoka, 1936).

the leading buyer.[7] Mitsui built a large modern pulp factory at Ōtomari in 1913. The First World War stimulated the pulp industry in Karafuto by sharply reducing supplies available from Europe and raising pulp prices to unprecedented levels. Heavily capitalized firms opened pulp factories throughout the colony and began clearing away the forests: Karafuto Kōgyō at Tomarioru, Ōji Paper Co. at Toyohara, and Nippon Kagaku Shiryō at Ochiai. Within six years, bare hills and log-clogged rivers became a common sight.

When over-exploitation, fires, and disease had decimated Karafuto's public forests by 1920, unscrupulous companies began illegally acquiring land reserved for agriculture. Pseudo-immigration by hired 'peasants' and the outright bribery of officials enabled the paper concerns to devastate hitherto protected forests. These abuses eventually were exposed in a scandal in 1924 that involved the dismissal of many Karafuto Office officials, including the island's governor. Tokyo tightened its control over the exploitation of Karafuto's forests after 1924. During the next fifteen years the paper industry was ordered to carry out extensive forestation projects to replenish the supply of timber.

Karafuto had about 2,000,000,000 tons of coal reserves. This fell short of northern Sakhalin but proved to be an attraction to fuel-hungry Japan. From 1905 to 1912 the government allowed successful corporate bidders to mine the west coast desposits at Esutoru and Kitanayoshi. Lack of regulation led to reckless exploitation that damaged the deposits. In 1912 the government cancelled all mining licences, only to resell most of them to Mitsui interests in 1916. Coal-mining stagnated from high taxation and the lack of a suitable port until after 1931, when heavy national demand brought about a reactivation of the pits.

The Japanese invested considerable efforts in the construction of a communications system for Karafuto. In 1906, the army built a narrow-gauge railway between Ōtomari and Toyohara. During the next two decades, tracks were laid between the towns around Aniwa Bay, to Honto on the south-west coast, and to Ochiai in the north-east. Between 1925 and 1936, a line was pushed up the east coast as far north as Shikuka (now

[7] Karafuto Ringyō Shi Hensan Kai, ed., *Karafuto ringyō shi* (Tokyo, 1960), p. 53.

Poronaisk). Communications with the home islands were consolidated with the establishment of regular steamer service between Ōtomari and ports in Hokkaido (Wakkanai, Otaru, and Hakodate) in 1923. After 1920, the ice-free port of Maoka on the south-west coast of the island gradually replaced Ōtomari as Karafuto's busiest depot.

Unlike Japan's colonies of Taiwan and Korea, the island of Karafuto had only a negligible 'native' population. About 1,600 Ainu lived in designated areas set up by the government in 1907. Some 150 Russians, together with a sprinkling of Polish settlers, lived around Toyohara and Ōtomari. A hundred Chinese and Koreans, imported in the 1870s and 1880s to work the west coast coal-mines, remained on the island after 1905. These minority groups almost disappeared from sight, inundated by waves of Japanese immigrants. Karafuto's population grew from 5,000 (1905) to 20,469 (1907) to 66,280 (1916) to 189,036 (1925)—or thirty-seven times in twenty years.[8]

Despite only moderate success in agriculture and fishing, and notwithstanding the reckless exploitation of coal and timber, the Japanese succeeded in building a productive economic base in Karafuto in the twenty years after 1905. More dramatic economic developments followed in the next fifteen years (1925–40) before the Second World War intervened.

North Sakhalin, 1905–1916

The Russo-Japanese War left northern Sakhalin in a state of utter chaos. When the last of the occupying Japanese forces withdrew to south of the 50th parallel in September 1905, only 7,000 confused and embittered Russians remained out of a 1904 population of 40,000. The Japanese took with them mining machinery, livestock, and most of Shternberg's laboriously collected artifacts in the Aleksandrovsk Historical Museum.

During 1906, about 5,000 settlers returned to northern Sakhalin from the continent where they had fled during the invasion. They found their homes in ruins or occupied by squatters, their fields overgrown, and most of their possessions stolen. Litigation over property rights kept Russian authorities busy sorting out the complicated events of 1905 for years. As land titles and sales receipts deposited in Aleksandrovsk were

[8] Karafuto chō, ed., *Karafuto yōran*, 1939 (Toyohara, 1940), p. 22.

destroyed during the fighting, the returning settler found his position painfully insecure.[9]

It was clear to all that Sakhalin's convict system could not be continued. Most of the inmates had scattered during the confusion. Sakhalin, moreover, was no longer an 'island'. Russia had come to share a land frontier with Japan in Sakhalin which extinguished the 'escape-proof' conditions that had existed before 1905. Indeed, to continue sending convicts to this truncated island might endanger relations with the new southern neighbour. Sakhalin's military governor had already begun to dismantle the convict system in 1904. His successor, Governor Valuev, sent a memorial to the Minister of Interior in 1906 describing the past failures to develop Sakhalin as a product of an unhealthy social climate. Valuev recommended the abolition of the whole convict colony on the island and called for the active encouragement of free settlers to take its place. His advice was favourably received in St. Petersburg. On 10 April 1906, forty-seven years after the first convicts had set foot on the 'cursed isle', the prisons, exile settlements, and labour gangs were declared abolished.[10]

Notwithstanding the island's 'emancipation', free settlers failed to materialize. Sakhalin's infamous reputation discouraged even the most venturesome. 'All over Russia, the word "Sakhalin" was a synonym for a living hell.'[11] With such notoriety, it is not surprising that only 105 families moved there between 1908 and 1914. Governor Valuev petitioned St. Petersburg to have the island's name changed in order to give it a new image. His suit was rejected.

Given the dearth of newcomers, the administration was forced to make do with local material. In 1906, this consisted of free settlers from the prewar period (79 per cent), former exiles (20 per cent), and ex-convicts (1 per cent). These human ingredients remained fairly consistent until the outbreak of the First World War generated a sharp rise in immigration. Between 1914 and 1916, over 15,000 would-be settlers rushed across Siberia to northern Sakhalin when the government

[9] Ia. Iankelevich, 'Ostrov Sakhalin', *Vestnik Azii*, XLIX (1922), 177–8.

[10] I. A. Senchenko, 'Severnyi Sakhalin v 1905–16 gg.', K. I. Kniazev, ed., *Sakhalinskaia oblast* (Iuzhno-Sakhalinsk, 1960), pp. 94–5.

[11] V. Koudrey, 'Island of Ill Repute', *Asia*, XXXV (March 1935), 144.

announced that inhabitants of this remote isle were exempted from military service.

While the penal system officially lapsed in 1906, the restoration of full civil rights to former exiles and convicts came only gradually. In 1910 former exiles were accorded the right to participate in business concerns and to move freely about the island. If they left Sakhalin, however, these rights would be suspended. A complete restoration of civil rights came only in February 1913.[12]

Unlike their predecessors in the 1870s, the Russian officials of 1906 entertained no illusions about Sakhalin becoming self-supporting in food. They knew that agriculture could only play a subordinate role to fishing, mining, and forestry. Some moderately prosperous farms did grow up along the Tym River and around Aleksandrovsk and Rykovsk. A few rich peasants (*kulaks*) even built up sizeable land holdings.

Fishing developed rapidly in northern Sakhalin after 1905, especially around Rybnovsk in the north-west facing the Amur delta. In 1907 alone, over 3,000 tons of herring and salmon were exported to Japan.

Forestry also progressed although on a smaller scale than in Karafuto. During 1908–16, Brynner & Co., an English concern based in Hong Kong, exploited a lucrative timber concession in northern Sakhalin. Lumber exports, however, were limited by the lack of a good port.

Coal promised to be the most important single industry. Before 1904, inefficient convict labour and the absence of harbour facilities had prevented Sakhalin from becoming an important coal producer and exporter. Determined to overhaul the coal industry and to discover new sources of mineral wealth, the government sent a team of geologists under P. I. Polevoi to survey northern Sakhalin in 1908. Polevoi's expedition uncovered evidence of gold, zinc, and iron ore. Polevoi estimated northern Sakhalin's total coal reserves to be 36,000,000 tons, which seemed optimistic at the time but has since turned out to be very modest.[13] On the eve of the First World War, the

[12] Iankelevich, 'Ostrov Sakhalin', p. 182. Senchenko, 'Severnyi Sakhalin v 1905–1916 gg.', pp. 100–1.

[13] Sakhalin's coal reserves were put at 19,400,000,000 metric tons in a 1967 estimate. Akademiia nauk S.S.S.R., Sibirskoe otdelenie, Sakhalinskii kompleksnyi

government was planning the construction of a huge port to make the island's high-quality coal widely available. This project foundered during the war years and was abandoned completely during the Russian Revolution.

Oil was first thought to exist in Sakhalin in 1880 when a Nikolaevsk merchant named Ivanov heard Gilyak stories about a 'black lake of death' in north-east Sakhalin where birds perished in an inky mire which they had mistaken for pools of water. Acting on the basis of these tales, Ivanov petitioned the government for a prospecting and drilling concession in northern Sakhalin. He died before his request was answered.

Ivanov's son-in-law, a former naval captain called Grigorii Zotov, received a concession from the government in 1889 to drill around the 'black lakes' in the Okha region at the neck of the Schmidt Peninsula. Zotov drilled at Okha and Nogliki without success until 1904 when he finally struck oil. Delighted, he rushed to Harbin to raise capital for the 'Zotov Oil Association', but like his father-in-law he died before his ambitions could be fulfilled.[14]

Northern Sakhalin's oil soon attracted international interest. Surveys by L. F. Batsevich (1889) and Platonov (1902) confirmed its existence. Platonov hailed the surface deposits as surpassing those of Baku on the shores of the Caspian Sea. F. F. Klay, a German geologist, made a detailed survey of the Okha region in 1899. He then formed a syndicate in London capitalized at one million pounds sterling called the 'Sakhalin-Amur Oil Syndicate'. Klay returned to Sakhalin in 1910 but abandoned further drilling after a year for lack of capital. Meanwhile, English and American geologists began to probe the potential of this 'new Baku'. A company financed by German and Chinese capital gained access to oil-rich sites at Nutoro and Nogliki along the Okhotsk coast in 1910.[15]

The Russians responded to this interest by forming the

---

nauchno-issledovatelskii institut, *Atlas Sakhalinskoi oblasti* (Moscow, 1967), p. 36. For material on the Sakhalin coal industry (1905–16): Iankelevich, 'Ostrov Sakhalin', pp. 192–4. Senchenko, 'Severnyi Sakhalin v 1905–1916 gg.', p. 98.

[14] A. A. Panov, *Shokuminchi to shite no Sagaren* (Tokyo, 1942), pp. 40–1. Oka Sakae, *Kita Karafuto* (Tokyo, 1942), pp. 132–3.

[15] Senchenko, 'Severnyi Sakhalin v 1905–1916 gg.', p. 99. Iankelevich, 'Ostrov Sakhalin', pp. 194–5.

Petrograd Commercial Association in 1909 (the name being changed to Sakhalin Oil & Coal Co. in 1911 and finally to the Russian Far East Industrial Co. in 1914). The Russian Far East Industrial Company included among its directors an assortment of aristocrats, ministers, and Governor Grigoriev of Sakhalin. English capital played a crucial role. Half of the company's shares were held by two syndicates formed in London in 1910—the First and Second Sakhalin Syndicates.

England invested more than capital in Sakhalin's oil. In 1912, the above syndicates organized the Sakhalin Oilfields Company which sent its own engineers and equipment to Okha. Although the Russian Far East Industrial Company held a near monopoly on prospecting and exploiting oil deposits in northern Sakhalin, its lease expired in 1917. In 1916, the company petitioned the government to grant it perpetual rights to all of northern Sakhalin's oil. This request was rejected, leaving the question of oil rights in a state of confusion on the eve of the Russian Revolution.[16]

Japan's interest in northern Sakhalin's oil came relatively late but eventually carried profound implications. A member of the border demarcation commission of 1906–7 learned of the rich oil deposits and informed Tokyo, but the government remained unresponsive. Little interest was evinced until 1916 when the Russian Far East Industrial Company's bid for exclusive perpetual rights failed. That year a group of Japanese businessmen visited St. Petersburg in an attempt to take advantage of the fluid situation. Their requests for similar concessions met with firm refusals.

The March and November revolutions brought such chaos to Russia that some opportunistic Japanese shrewdly altered their tactics. In May 1918 the mining magnate Kuhara Fusanosuke signed an agreement with a private Russian firm of dubious connections (the Stakheev Company) which permitted Japanese 'oil surveys' in northern Sakhalin for four years. This ambiguously worded arrangement suited the times. In 1918 Russia had several 'governments' with foreign backers all struggling against the Bolsheviks in a confusing civil war. With Sakhalin caught between struggling Red and White Russian forces from

[16] Oka, *Kita Karafuto*, pp. 134–7.

1918 until 1925, the Japanese disregarded legal intricacies in favour of bold action.[17]

From 1905 to 1916, northern Sakhalin showed moderate economic gains, especially in the exploitation of marine and petroleum resources. Foreign capital entered the island on a substantial scale for the first time. Coal-mining and agriculture progressed slowly. The increasing numbers of prosperous peasants around Aleksandrovsk and in the Tym Valley reflected new class patterns which contrasted sharply with the previous thirty years. Judging from the civil rights legislation of 1913 and the ambitious coal and oil projects in 1914–16, northern Sakhalin might have been on the threshold of a rebirth had not war, revolution, civil war, and foreign occupation intervened.

Sakhalin and the Russian Revolution, 1917–1920

Sakhalin remained relatively isolated from the strikes that sporadically broke out from 1905 to 1917 in Vladivostok, Khabarovsk, Blagoveshchensk, and Chita. A few of the island's former political exiles participated in Bolshevik cells around the Russian Far East, and some even formed a group in Nagasaki. Unrest did erupt occasionally in two areas of northern Sakhalin: among poorer peasants in the Tym Valley and among the coal-miners at Dué. The peasant grievances generally concerned inadequate land allotments. More serious were the Dué strikes of 1905 and 1910 when hundreds of Chinese and Korean miners joined their Russian co-workers in demanding higher wages and shorter hours. The island's administration applied repressive measures only erratically, such as the wave of arrests in February 1908 of 'revolutionary suspects'.[18]

The March 1917 Revolution in Petrograd took Sakhalin by surprise. Governor von Bunge suppressed for several days the reports of the Tsar's abdication. Finally, on 20 March, the Aleksandrovsk *zemstvo* (an elective administrative assembly) met and formed a Committee of Social Security to hold executive authority on Sakhalin. A lawyer, Aleksandr T. Tsapko, was elected chairman of this committee. Tsapko's authority was

[17] Ibid., pp. 42, 135, 137–8. Ōta Saburō, *Nichiro Karafuto gaikō sen* (Tokyo, 1941), p. 276.

[18] Senchenko, 'Severnyi Sakhalin v 1905–1916 gg.', pp. 103–12.

recognized by several other *zemstvo* in Sakhalin. Nevertheless, Tsapko was soon at odds with a provincial government set up at Khabarovsk. A complex struggle ensued as the 'conservative' Khabarovsk authorities attempted to undermine Tsapko's position in Sakhalin. In September they achieved this objective by bringing about Tsapko's dismissal from the Committee of Social Security.[19]

Meanwhile, a second source of potential power appeared with the growth of soviets of workers and peasants in Russian Sakhalin led by Dr. Aleksandr M. Krivoruchko. Although riddled with factions, Sakhalin's soviets gained momentum towards the end of 1917 because of the overthrow of Kerensky's Provisional Government in Petrograd by the Bolsheviks in November, and the establishment of Soviet governments in Vladivostok, Khabarovsk, and Blagoveshchensk in November and December. In Janurary 1918 the Sakhalin soviets declared that they alone possessed authority in Russian Sakhalin. This claim was challenged by local conservative groups led by an ex-official named Ruslanov who had supplanted Tsapko as chairman of the Committee of Social Security. Ruslanov was eventually forced to recognize the soviets in March 1918 by forming a coalition government with them.

From March to May 1918 authority in Sakhalin was shared by a shaky coalition of soviets, rural *zemstvo*, and the Aleksandrovsk *duma* (council). This unstable balance was abruptly upset on 8 May when the soviets seized power in Aleksandrovsk. On 4 June, the soviets ordered the disbandment of all *zemstvo* and the *duma*.

Soviet power in northern Sakhalin proved short-lived after the Russian Civil War spread to Eastern Siberia. On 29 June part of the Czech Legion[20] and assorted White Russian forces

[19] Material on the rise of Soviet power in Sakhalin is taken from: I. A. Senchenko and P. A. Lebedev, 'Borba za ustanovlenie Sovetskoi vlasti na severnom Sakhaline: mart 1917–aprel 1920 gg.', K. I. Kniazev, ed., *Sakhalinskaia oblast*, pp. 115–20. I. A. Senchenko, *Ocherki istorii Sakhalina* (Iuzhno-Sakhalinsk, 1957), pp. 78–94. Russia, Tsentralnyi gosudarstvennyi arkhiv, Dalnevo Vostoka, Tomsk. *Pobeda Sovetskoi vlasti na severnom Sakhaline, 1917–1925 gg: sbornik dokumentov i materialov* (Iuzhno-Sakhalinsk, 1959).

[20] The Czech Legion consisted of prisoners-of-war captured on the Russian front while serving in the Austrian Army. Eager to fight the Central Powers for the liberation of their own land, they began to move along the Siberian railroad towards Vladivostok in the end of 1917 with the purpose of ultimately joining the Allies in

seized Vladivostok. The Japanese announced their intention to send troops to Vladivostok on 2 August to aid the Czechs and were soon joined by detachments from Britain, France, and the United States. The effects of foreign intervention were soon felt in Sakhalin. White forces entered Aleksandrovsk on 28 August and restored the *duma* to power. This *duma* declared its allegiance to the White government at Omsk and in November swore its loyalty to Admiral Aleksandr Kolchak when he was proclaimed 'Supreme Ruler of All Russia'.

While Kolchak's heterogeneous forces pushed the Bolsheviks westward during December of 1918, Sakhalin remained firmly controlled by conservative land holders, officers, and former Tsarist officials. However, when Kolchak's lines began to crumble under the Red Army's counter-offensive in the Ural Mountains in January 1919 the situation in Sakhalin once again moved inexorably towards chaos.

Kolchak's rout in the summer of 1919 sent ripples of tension through northern Sakhalin. Bolshevik partisan bands stepped up their activities. After the admiral's capture in Irkutsk, the Bolsheviks made a second bid to seize power in the Russian Far East. An uprising at Vladivostok (30 January 1920) miscarried because of Japanese intervention, but a similar *putsch* succeeded at Aleksandrovsk on 14 January. The conservative *duma* members and other Kolchak supporters were arrested and a Revolutionary Committee was created with Tsapko (ex-chairman of the defunct Committee of Social Security) as its chairman.

Instead of repeating the drastic measures of May 1918, the Bolsheviks retained the *duma* and *zemstvos* in a broad coalition with the soviets. The Revolutionary Committee, however, held the actual power. This state of affairs continued until May 1920 when foreign military intervention once again threw the long-suffering populace of northern Sakhalin into turmoil.

Japanese Occupation, 1920–1925

The Japanese occupied northern Sakhalin, according to the government's official announcement, in retaliation for a

---

Europe. An attempt to disarm them by the Soviet government (which had made peace with the Central Powers in March 1918) led to hostilities in which the Legion seized parts of the Trans-Siberian railroad in June 1918.

massacre of over 700 Japanese military and civilian personnel at Nikolaevsk by Bolshevik partisans on 25 May 1920.[21] Behind this widely touted explanation, there lay a complex of contributory forces: hatred of Bolshevism, suspicion of American economic penetration, fear of northern Sakhalin becoming a strategic base for attacking Japan, an opportunistic urge to exploit Russia's temporary weakness, and a visceral conviction that all of Sakhalin belonged by historical right to Japan. In addition, there was the drive for oil.

Japan was (and still is) critically dependent on petroleum imports as a source of fuel. Domestic crude oil production for 1914–18 amounted to only 400,000 tons annually, a fraction of the country's demand. Sakhalin's oil reserves were estimated in 1919 as exceeding 100,000,000 tons. Unfortunately for the Japanese, this oil was located in the northern (Russian) half of the island. Such a good source of petroleum located so close to the home islands naturally aroused considerable interest both in the fuel-conscious Imperial Navy and among enterprising industrialists. This growing concern for Sakhalin oil after 1918 contributed indirectly to the military occupation of 1920.

The Japanese first saw their opportunity to secure a lion's share of Sakhalin's oil in 1917 when the expiration of earlier Russian and English concessions invited bold initiative. Rebuffed at St. Petersburg, they deftly took advantage of the Russian Civil War in 1918 and resorted to a rather devious stratagem. In May 1918 the Kuhara Mining Company entered into an agreement with a shadowy concern called the 'Stakheev Commercial Society' to 'survey' northern Sakhalin's oilfields. Japanese geologists carried out their investigations in late 1918 and early 1919 under the benevolent eye of a conservative White Russian government in Aleksandrovsk.

On 1 April 1919 the Japanese government issued a declaration that northern Sakhalin's oil was 'absolutely necessary' to

[21] In February 1920 the town of Nikolaevsk at the mouth of the Amur River was surrounded and attacked by Bolshevik partisans. The defenders, overwhelmingly Japanese soldiers and civilians but including some Americans and Russians, eventually surrendered and agreed to leave, disarmed. They suddenly broke this agreement in March and counter-attacked, only to be defeated by the Bolsheviks. About 700 were summarily put to death. 122 were taken prisoner. Among these, the partisans executed all Japanese nationals.

solve the country's fuel problems. Moreover, the note continued, any attempt by foreign powers to intervene in northern Sakhalin's oilfields would be considered a serious threat to Japan's security.

A month later, under government auspices, a consortium of five large companies was formed to survey and exploit northern Sakhalin's oil. Called the *Hokushinkai*, the consortium included Kuhara Mining and Mitsubishi Mining companies (quarter share each), and Nippon Oil, Takada Oil, and Ōkura Mining companies (one-sixth share each). In June the Hokushinkai dispatched 200 technicians to Okha. The Navy Ministry also sent teams of geologists. By the end of 1919 Japan had secured an iron grip on the only known oil deposits in North-east Asia. At the same time, the collapse of Kolchak's forces in the west made it only a matter of time before the Japanese in northern Sakhalin would come face to face with resurgent Soviet power.[22]

When the Bolsheviks seized control of Aleksandrovsk on 14 January 1920, they presented the Japanese government with an agonizing decision: to resist or to get out. At first, it appeared as if Tokyo would avoid a conflict by withdrawing its nationals. Japanese oil technicians were evacuated to Karafuto as roving partisan bands made the raw weather even more uncomfortable by acts of sabotage. Japanese naval vessels cruised off northern Sakhalin's coasts picking up stranded compatriots.

At this point, news of the Nikolaevsk incident transformed much of Japanese public opinion into a sea of anger. The Tokyo government voiced protests on one hand and quietly moved to occupy northern Sakhalin on the other. On 21 April the cruiser *Mishima* anchored off Aleksandrovsk and landed 2,000 troops without meeting any resistance. On 14 May 5,000 soldiers disembarked at De Castries Bay just across the Tatary Strait. Two days later Tsapko and other figures allegedly sympathetic to the Bolshevik cause were summarily arrested on charges of 'partisan activities'. The Japanese Army then set up an 'Autonomous Sakhalin State' and installed as its titular head Leonid Grigorev, ex-governor of Tsarist Sakhalin and ex-director of the Russian Far East Industrial Company. In this manner, two

[22] For details of Japan's involvement in Sakhalin oil (1918–19): Oka, *Kita Karafuto*, pp. 43–4. Ōta, *Nichiro Karafuto gaikō sen*, pp. 276–7. Kobayashi Yoshio, 'Nihon no tai So shōnin to keizai mondai', *Kokusai seiji*, II (1965), 92.

months before any official announcement, the Japanese deftly occupied and seized control of Russian Sakhalin.[23]

The Japanese government officially announced the occupation of northern Sakhalin on 3 July 1920. As a justification for the action, it cited the Nikolaevsk massacre and the necessity to protect its nationals working in the oilfields. Apart from the Soviet government in Moscow and the Far Eastern Republic in Chita, the United States was the only country to lodge a protest. The Secretary of State, Bainbridge Colby, sent a note to the Japanese Foreign Ministry on 16 July which expressed doubts about the relationship of the Nikolaevsk incident and northern Sakhalin. The Japanese replied that Nikolaevsk was included in the Sakhalin administrative district created in 1914, and consequently northern Sakhalin would be held until satisfaction for the slaughter was obtained. While deploring the occupation, the American government took no further action.[24]

The Japanese lost no time in exploiting northern Sakhalin's natural wealth. On 16 July the cabinet circulated an announcement to the ministries of Foreign Affairs, Army, Navy, and Agriculture indicating that henceforth the Navy was to exercise broad control over the disposition of Sakhalin's oil and coal. The Navy thereupon turned to the Hokushinkai consortium to carry out oil-drilling operations with a special naval appropriation of 1,400,000 yen (US $700,000).

From 1920 to 1925 the Japanese took about 100,000 tons of oil annually from wells at Okha, Piltun, Nutova, Nogliki, and Katangli. During these years, the government steadily increased its subsidies to both the Hokushinkai and to the Navy in order to raise oil production. The relative importance of Sakhalin's oil output grew as domestic production fell from 400,000 tons annually (1914–18) to 270,000 tons annually (1921–4). With total domestic consumption at 840,000 tons in 1925, the country was still forced to import substantial quantities from California, Mexico, Java, and Borneo. While production in Sakhalin remained comparatively modest, quite a few company directors, shareholders, and naval officers felt optimistic about its poten-

[23] A. M. Lopachev, 'Severnyi Sakhalin v period Iaponskoi okkupatsui', in K. I. Kniazev, ed., *Sakhalinskaia oblast* (Iuzhno-Sakhalinsk, 1960), pp. 140–3.

[24] U.S. Department of State, *Foreign Relations of the United States*, 1920, III (Washington, 1936), 517–19. Japan, Gaimushō, ed., *Nisso kōshō shi* (Tokyo, 1942), p. 40.

tial. The intimate association of the Navy and private corporations in the exploitation of Sakhalin's oil persisted through the 1930s and into the Second World War. When the Hokushinkai was superseded in 1925 by the Kita Karafuto Sekiyū Kaisha (Northern Sakhalin Oil Company), Nakazato Jūji, the former chief of naval ordnance, was named its first president.[25]

Japan was not the only country with its eyes on Sakhalin's oil. During 1919 the Omsk government received a series of requests for concession rights from England, the United States, and Canada. After the fall of Kolchak and the creation of a buffer state in Eastern Siberia called the 'Far Eastern Republic', concession seekers flocked to Chita, capital of the newly formed republic. One enterprising New York millionaire secured a sixty-year monopoly for coal, oil, and fisheries in all territory east of the 160th meridian including Kamchatka. The Japanese understandably cast a cold eye on these would-be intruders. The only newcomer, however, to give the Japanese any serious trouble was the Sinclair Oil Company.

The Sinclair Oil Company could not be counted among the giants in the oil world, but what it lacked in size it made up for in aggressiveness. In the early 1920s Sinclair made a determined bid to challenge Standard Oil Company's concessions in Russia and northern Persia. The Sinclair bid for northern Sakhalin in 1921 grew out of this global rivalry for oil resources.

Sinclair representatives first approached the Japanese commercial attaché in New York (April 1921) in order to sound out his government's reaction to a joint U.S.–Japanese project to drill for oil in northern Sakhalin, Siberia, and China. The Japanese responded coldly. A second attempt by Sinclair officials to broach the subject in July met with a flat refusal. Rebuffed by Japan, Sinclair turned to the Far Eastern Republic in Chita where similar overtures were received more favourably.

Sinclair's efforts in Chita bore fruit. On 7 January 1922, the company and the Far Eastern Republic concluded a private treaty (ratified in May) which can be summarized as follows:

(1) The validity of the agreement extended until 7 January 1959 but would become automatically invalid if the

[25] For details of the Imperial Navy's role in Sakhalin oil, see Oka, *Kita Karafuto*, pp. 53–6; Kobayashi, 'Nihon no tai So shōnin to keizai mondai', p. 93.

United States government failed to recognize the Far Eastern Republic within five years.

(2) The Sinclair Oil Company undertook to advance a series of loans to the Far Eastern Republic starting at $100,000 and followed by $400,000 instalments in 1924 and 1928.

(3) The Sinclair Oil Company enjoyed exclusive rights to exploit oil on northern Sakhalin between the 51st and 52nd parallels (comprising 281,000 acres) with an annual rent of 19 cents per acre.

(4) Minimum royalties for oil were $50,000 annually.

The remaining articles specified duties on oil and stated the Far Eastern Republic's right to cancel the whole agreement unilaterally at any time without prior notice.

From Chita's (hence Moscow's) point of view, this agreement with Sinclair was a shrewd political stratagem. In fact, the Far Eastern Republic was giving away concessions in a territory that it did not control. The Russians may have envisaged using Sinclair to frustrate the Japanese in Sakhalin without cost to themselves and at the same time neatly alienate Japan from the United States. Moreover, the agreement seems to have been used as a lever to encourage the United States to extend diplomatic recognition to the Bolshevik government in Moscow (for which the Far Eastern Republic was a front). The Russians may have been particularly interested in working through the Sinclair Oil Company because of the intimate connections of its president, Harry F. Sinclair, with the United States Secretary of the Interior, Albert Fall. Indeed, when the Far Eastern Republic merged with the Moscow Bolsheviks in November 1922, the Soviet Union officially confirmed Sinclair's rights in northern Sakhalin (January 1923).

The Soviet Union's announcement of Sinclair's exclusive rights to northern Sakhalin oil set off an explosion of protests from London and Tokyo. The English indignantly brought up claims formerly held by the Sakhalin Oilfields Company and the two Sakhalin Syndicates (1909–16). Japan took a tougher stand. When a group of Sinclair geologists tried to land at Aleksandrovsk in February 1924, Japanese troops met them at the pier and politely but firmly told them to leave. Reports of this affair stirred up some patriotic declamations in the American press, but Washington had no stomach to resort to force to dislodge the Japanese army of occupation.

Sinclair's rights to northern Sakhalin fell victim to Soviet–Japanese negotiations during 1924–5 to establish diplomatic relations. At first, the Soviet delegate at the Peking negotiations, L. M. Karakhan, suggested a tripartite division of the oil between Japan, the United States, and the Soviet Union. When the Japanese adamantly rejected this proposition and insisted on a ninety-nine-year exclusive concession for themselves, the Russians changed their strategy. Sinclair's usefulness had ended.

The Russians moved to cancel Sinclair's rights by suing the American company in a Moscow court for breach of contract on the grounds that the company had failed to survey or drill. The court quickly decided in favour of the government and declared the 1921 agreement null and void on 24 March 1925. Sinclair appealed the case, stating that it could not fulfil the contract because the Japanese Army would not allow its geologists even to set foot on Sakhalin. Deaf to these cries, the Moscow court confirmed the original judgement.

The Sinclair Company then turned to the U.S. Secretary of State Charles Evans Hughes in the hope of obtaining official intervention in Tokyo and Moscow on the company's behalf. The company took the position that the 'Open Door' principle had been violated. Hughes, however, refused to plead Sinclair's case on the grounds that the United States had not extended diplomatic recognition to the Soviet Union.[26]

In justice to the Russians, it should be noted that the agreement with Sinclair contained built-in guarantees by which the Soviet government could cancel the concession unilaterally and without notice. The Sinclair Oil Company eventually licked its wounds and retired, poorer but perhaps a bit wiser.

[26] *Foreign Relations of the United States, 1924*, II (Washington, 1939), 678–81; 1925 (Washington, 1940), 697–701. Other material on the Sinclair episode: Oka, *Kita Karafuto*, pp. 249–59. Osaka Mainichi Shimbun, ed., *Kita Karafuto* (Osaka, 1925), pp. 223–7. Louis Fischer, 'Sinclair vs. Standard Oil in Russia', *The Nation*, CXIX (6 Aug. 1924), 138–40. Louis Fischer, 'The Greased Wheels of Diplomacy', *The Nation*, CXIX (8 Oct. 1924), 357–8. M. D. Kennedy, 'Japan and the Problem of Oil in the Pacific', *World Today*, XLV (June 1925), 573–82. F. J. Fithian, 'Dollars without the Flag: The Case of Sinclair and Sakhalin Oil', *Pacific Historical Review*, XXXIX (May 1970), 205–22.

The Japanese rule of northern Sakhalin from 1920 to 1925 brought little but unhappiness to the island's Russian population. Notwithstanding Tokyo's propaganda about the enthusiastic receptions, the smiling schoolchildren, and the grateful aborigines, military rule was implemented with characteristic lack of grace. According to an American woman journalist who visited Aleksandrovsk in 1924, 'high class' Polish and Russian residents accepted the Japanese as the lesser of two evils, for they had at least restored law and order.[27] It is doubtful whether this sentiment was widely entertained.

The Imperial Army seemed to interpret its mission in northern Sakhalin as consisting of three objectives: (1) to shoot Bolsheviks, (2) to prepare the land and population for annexation, and (3) to exploit local natural and human resources. The Navy occupied itself with supervising the extraction and transport of coal and oil. Japanese nationals were allowed a free hand in cutting down forests and fishing in coastal waters. 15,000 Japanese workers, officials, and military personnel joined by an assortment of archaeologists, geologists, and journalists simply overwhelmed the unfortunate Russian population.[28]

A catalogue of abuses, intended or incidental, committed by the occupiers of northern Sakhalin reflects no credit upon the Japanese. The military authorities issued strict laws against all forms of political activities. A few of the more obstreperous Bolsheviks were shot, or, like Aleksandr Tsapko, taken to sea on the cruiser *Mishima* and thrown overboard. The Judicial Department of the military government nullified all Russian laws and replaced them with Japanese statutes. The island's Russian inhabitants found themselves treated as foreigners. Towns and streets assumed Japanese names. The Japanese language was made standard in schools. Japanese merchants bought out their Russian counterparts. The Mitsubishi Company imported Korean workers for the mines at Dué, Mgachinsk, and Rogatinsk causing widespread unemployment among the

[27] Marguerite E. Harrison, 'Red Bear, Yellow Dragon, and American Lady', *Literary Digest*, LXXXI (19 Apr. 1924), 40.

[28] Some excellent Japanese studies of the lower Amur River and northern Sakhalin were made during this brief interim such as that of the archaeologist Torii Ryūzō, *Kokuryūkō to kita Karafuto* (Tokyo, 1943), and the collection of scientific and historical essays in Osaka Mainichi Shimbun, ed., *Kita Karafuto* (Osaka, 1925).

Russian population. Postal and telecommunications with the continent were severed. Perhaps most painful of all to Russian pride were the series of rules demanding respect for Japanese officers (by lifting the cap and bowing) that in later years gained notoriety in China and South-East Asia. The callousness with which many Japanese behaved in northern Sakhalin between 1920 and 1925 sowed seeds of resentment that Josef Stalin exuded in a speech justifying the Soviet attack on Japanese Karafuto in 1945.[29]

Many Japanese frankly hoped to retain northern Sakhalin either by outright annexation or through some ambiguously worded agreement with the Soviet Union. The Russians frustrated this ambition by steadfastly refusing to enter into diplomatic relations with Japan until the Sakhalin problem was disposed of in a satisfactory manner.[30]

Japan had intermittently conducted official and semi-official negotiations with the new regime in Russia, at first through meetings with representatives of the Far Eastern Republic at Dairen (July 1921–April 1922) and later at a conference at Changchun (September 1922). After these, the influential politician Gotō Shimpei held private talks with Adolf Ioffe, the Soviet minister to China, while the latter was convalescing in Japan. These probings failed to bring the two countries substantially closer to an agreement. The Japanese insisted (among other things) on compensation for the Nikolaevsk massacre and a guarantee of permanent rights in northern Sakhalin. The Russians would not retreat from their position that Japan's military withdrawal from northern Sakhalin was an absolute condition for establishing diplomatic relations.

In 1924 this deadlock broke under the pressure of forces

[29] I. V. Stalin, *O velikoi otechestvennoi voine Sovetskovo Soiuza* (Moscow, 1946), pp. 205–6. For Japanese abuses in northern Sakhalin, see: 'Japanese in Northern Sakhalin', *The Nation*, CXIII (23 Nov. 1921), 606; V. Ia. Aboltin, *Ostrov sokrovishch: severnyi Sakhalin* (Vladivostok, 1928), pp. 18–39, 154–68; Lutskii, *Ostrov Sakhalin*, pp. 11–14; Zhukov, *Russkie i Iaponiia*, p. 157; Lopachev, 'Severnyi Sakhalin v period iaponskoi okkupatsui', pp. 145–51; G. Gor and V. Leshkevich, *Sakhalin* (Moscow, 1949), p. 33. For a Japanese view of the occupation: Oka, *Kita Karafuto*, pp. 59–61; Ōta, *Nichiro Karafuto gaikō sen*, pp. 288–90. The tone of military rule can be judged from Japanese Army announcements to the Russian populace, collected in *Russkii Sakhalin kak novaia Iaponiia* (Vladivostok, 1921).

[30] The Peoples Commissar of Foreign Affairs, G. V. Chicherin in an interview with *Izvestiia* (25 Oct. 1921) in *Soviet Documents on Foreign Policy*, ed., Jane Degras, I (London, 1951), 341.

which persuaded the Japanese to modify their demands regarding the disposition of northern Sakhalin. First, the Washington Conference (1921–2) dissolved the Anglo-Japanese alliance and deprived Japan of a psychological if not physical source of support. Secondly, the anti-Japanese immigration legislation in the United States provoked a reaction that pushed Japan towards international isolation. Thirdly, the Soviet Union strengthened its position during 1924 by gaining diplomatic recognition from England, Norway, Australia, Italy, Sweden, and France. Fourthly, the Sino-Soviet Treaty of Friendship (30 May 1924) aroused Japan's concern that her 'special interests' in China might be jeopardized. Fifthly, many Japanese felt the necessity to establish diplomatic relations with the U.S.S.R. for economic reasons. There had been an active trade with Russia just before the revolution which not a few businessmen wanted to see restored. Moreover, Japan's reliance on the Kamchatka and Okhotsk Sea fisheries dictated an accommodation with the Soviet Union. The right to operate in those waters derived from the Portsmouth Treaty (1905) which the Soviet government had repudiated. Finally, groups within the Japanese civil bureaucracy (especially the Foreign Office) promoted a Soviet-Japanese treaty as a realistic step in Japan's own interest. In order to have a treaty, however, the Japanese were compelled to make concessions in northern Sakhalin.[31]

Japan and the Soviet Union formally established diplomatic relations by a convention signed in Peking on 20 January 1925. In so far as it concerned northern Sakhalin, the convention was a brilliant victory for Soviet diplomacy. The Russians succeeded in bringing about a Japanese withdrawal from the area without resorting to force, when as late as 1924 most observers were convinced that Japan would either annex or purchase the northern half of the island. By tenaciously refusing to discuss Sakhalin's sale or transfer or other substantive matters before the Japanese had promised to withdraw all military forces, the Russians obliged the Japanese to re-evaluate Sakhalin's importance in the light of other interests such as fishing rights, trade,

[31] *Nisso kōshō shi*, pp. 74–8. Kobayashi, 'Nihon no tai So shōnin to keizai mondai', p. 87. George A. Lensen, *Japanese Recognition of the U.S.S.R.; Soviet-Japanese Relations, 1921–1930* (Tokyo, 1970), pp. 40, 81, 101, 104–5. L. N. Kutakov, *Nisso gaikō kankei shi*, I (Tokyo, 1965), 74–88. K. K. Kawakami, 'Oil: the Key to Russo-Japanese Agreement', *Outlook*, CXXXIX (Feb. 1925), 180–1.

PLATES

PLATE 1

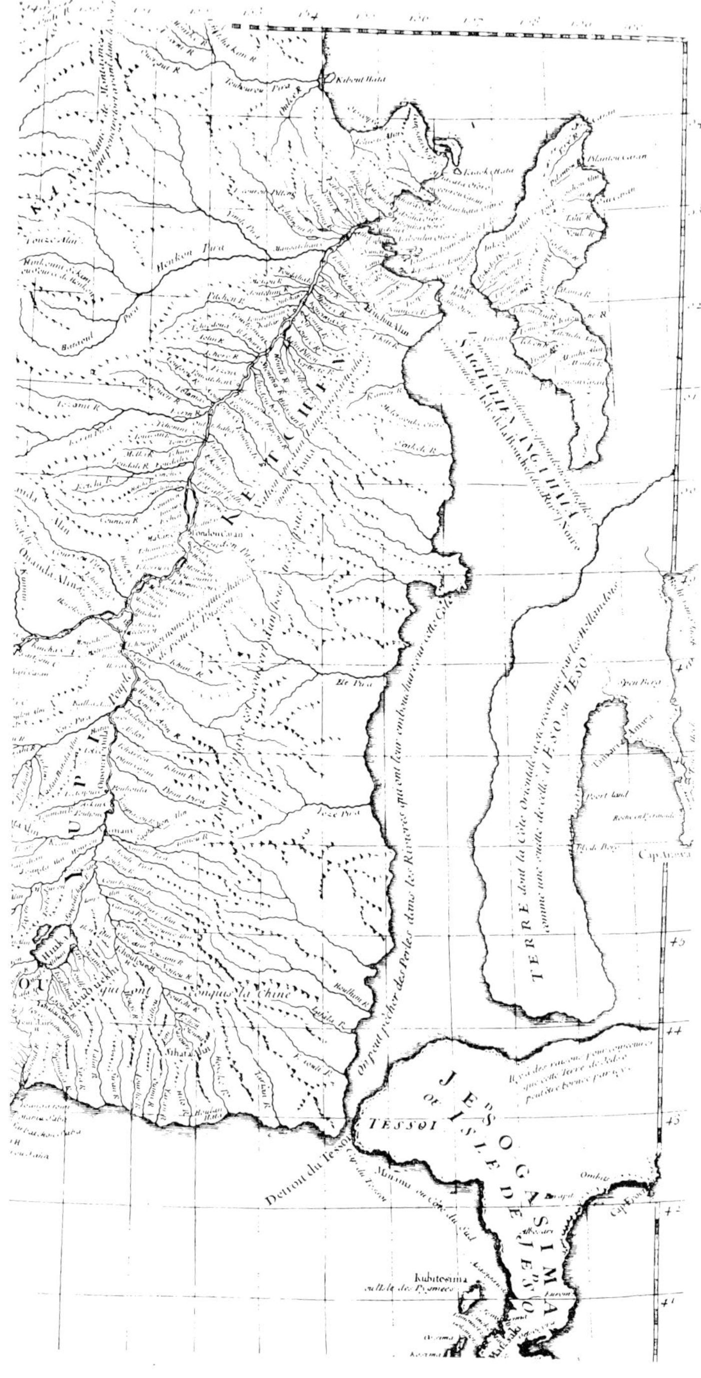

J. B. B. D'Anville Map (1735 edition). Note that Sakhalin is depicted as two islands. (Courtesy of Waseda University Library)

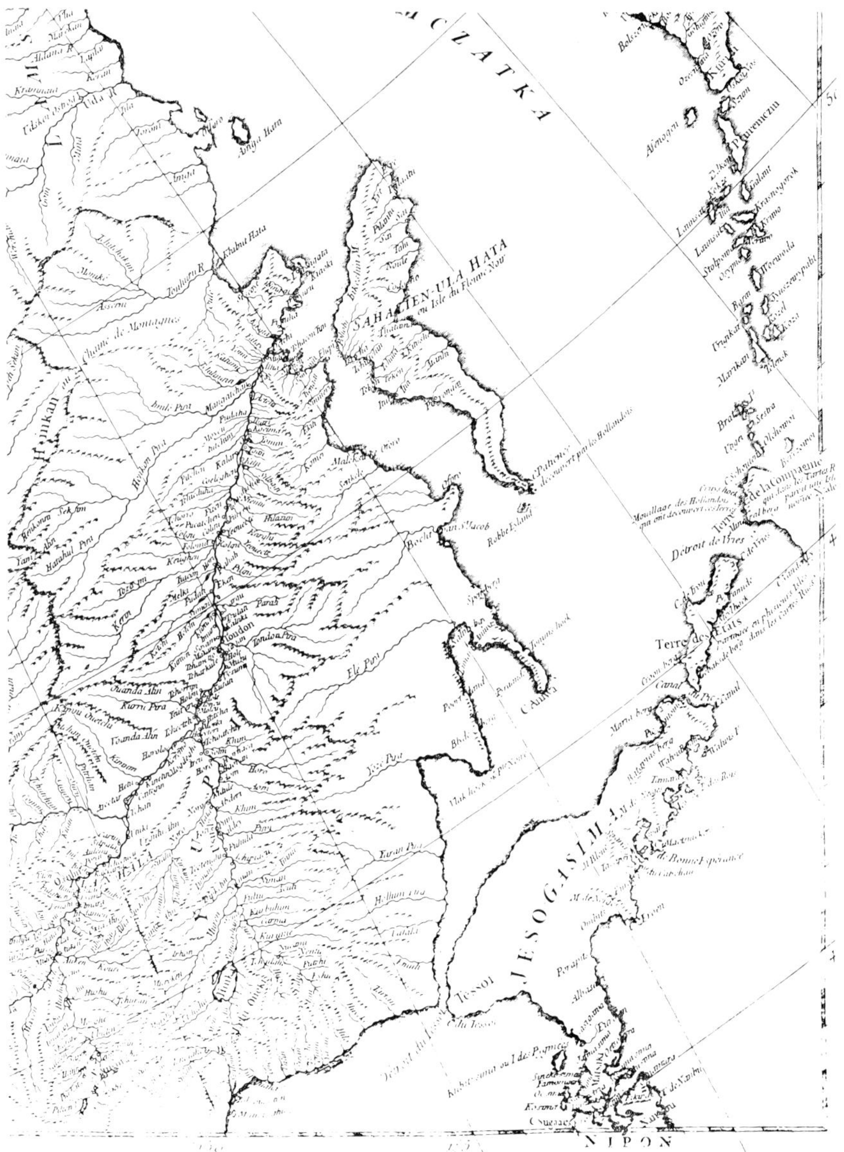

J. B. B. D'Anville Map (1752 edition). Note that northern Sakhalin is depicted as one island. Southern Sakhalin (Cape Aniwa) has been merged with the continent, forming a peninsula. (Courtesy of Waseda University Library)

PLATE 3

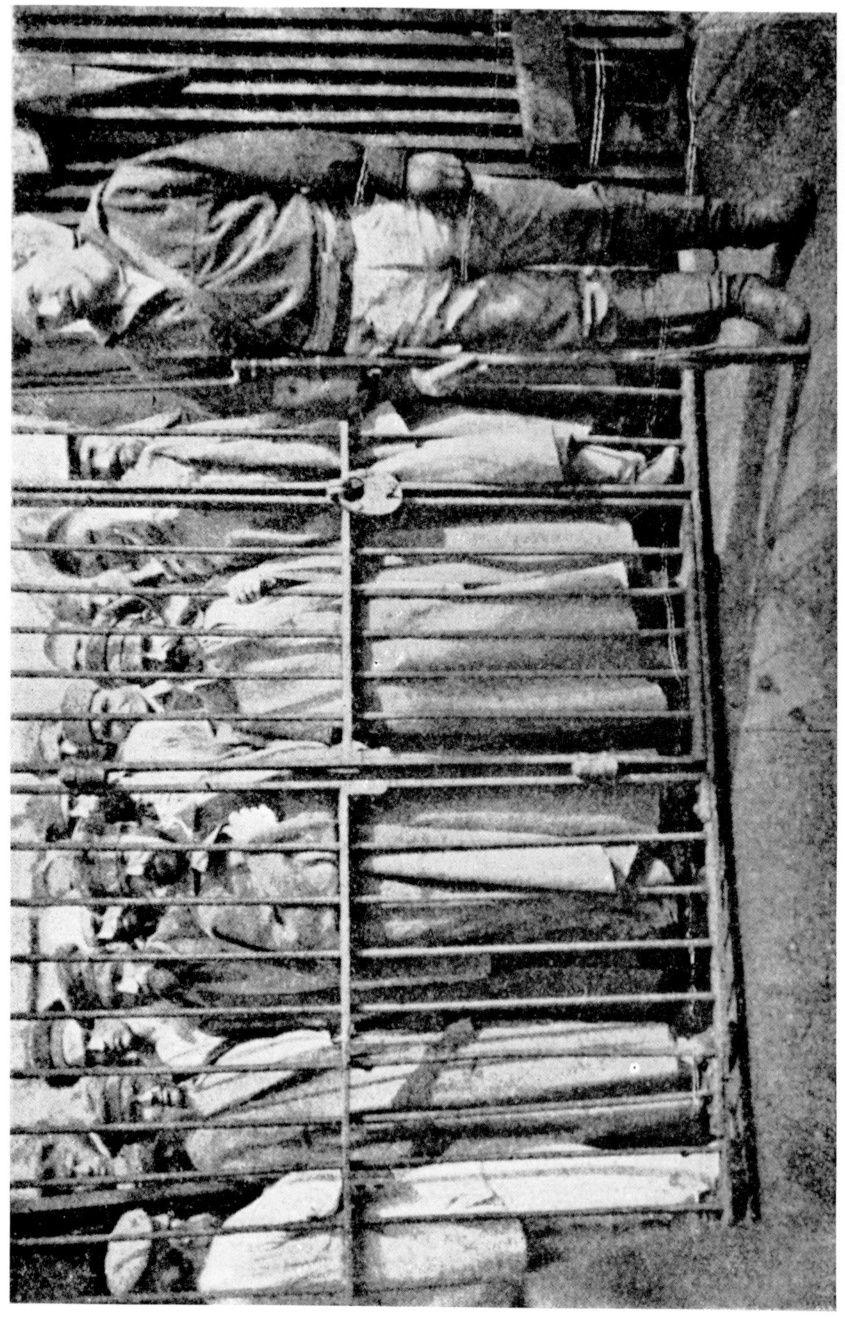

Attaching chains to a new arrival (*circa* 1900)

A Sakhalin convict in his quarters (*circa* 1900)

PLATE 5

Japanese refugees in Soviet-occupied Ōtomari (Korsakov). Ōtomari Public

Iuzhno-Sakhalinsk: Japanese temple remodelled as a Soviet planetarium

Iuzhno-Sakhalinsk Museum of Regional Studies, formerly the Karafuto Office Museum. (Note old frontier marker on bottom right)

Iuzhno-Sakhalinsk Park, formerly The Toyohara Park

View of modern Iuzhno-Sakhalinsk

and the validity of the Treaty of Portsmouth upon which Japan's own claim to Karafuto was legally based. Consequently, according to Article III of Protocol A, the Japanese undertook to evacuate northern Sakhalin before 15 May 1925. Moreover, they solemnly affirmed the Soviet Union's absolute sovereignty to that part of the island. This promise crushed wistful hopes among some Japanese that somehow, sometime, all of Sakhalin would fall like ripe fruit to the Empire.[32]

Although they lost all claims to northern Sakhalin, the Japanese managed by Article VI to retain rights to exploit minerals, forests, and other natural resources on U.S.S.R. territory. Protocol B outlined the conditions under which Japan could develop oil and coal on northern Sakhalin. The Japanese received concessions of forty-five years' duration for oil and coal. Their companies were allowed to drill in 50 per cent of certain designated oil areas and would pay a 5–15 per cent royalty depending upon the amount of oil produced (the rate for gushers was 45 per cent). Coal concessions granted at Dué and along the Agnevo River were also to be held up to forty-five years with royalties of 5–8 per cent on all coal extracted. The Japanese also maintained the right to send surveying missions to search for additional oil deposits. If such deposits were found, they would be shared on an equal basis. The details of these concessions were worked out and initialled on 14 December 1925. They constituted the legal basis for Japan's presence in northern Sakhalin from 1925 until 1944.

The twenty years from the Japanese invasion of Sakhalin in 1905 to the Soviet-Japanese Convention in 1925 witnessed more turbulent change than any comparable period of the island's history. Unlike the preceding years, the exercise of power in Sakhalin emanated principally from the south, from Japan. Excluded from Sakhalin in early 1905, Japan annexed the southern half of the island and for five years held the northern half as a hostage. External events gave Japan the opportunity to seize the north in 1920, and external events forced Japan to relinquish it in 1925.

Never before had the island of Sakhalin so occupied the thoughts of Russians and Japanese. For the Russians, it was the

[32] For relevant passages from the Soviet-Japanese Convention signed at Peking, see Appendix A.

last piece of Soviet territory occupied by the foreign interventionists. For the Japanese, it symbolized the dangerous proximity of Bolshevist Russia, the most northerly outpost of the Empire, a source of precious fuel, and a painful heritage from the past. For both countries, Sakhalin remained a divided, contested stretch of land that could only cause friction until one of the two powers gained total control over the entire island.

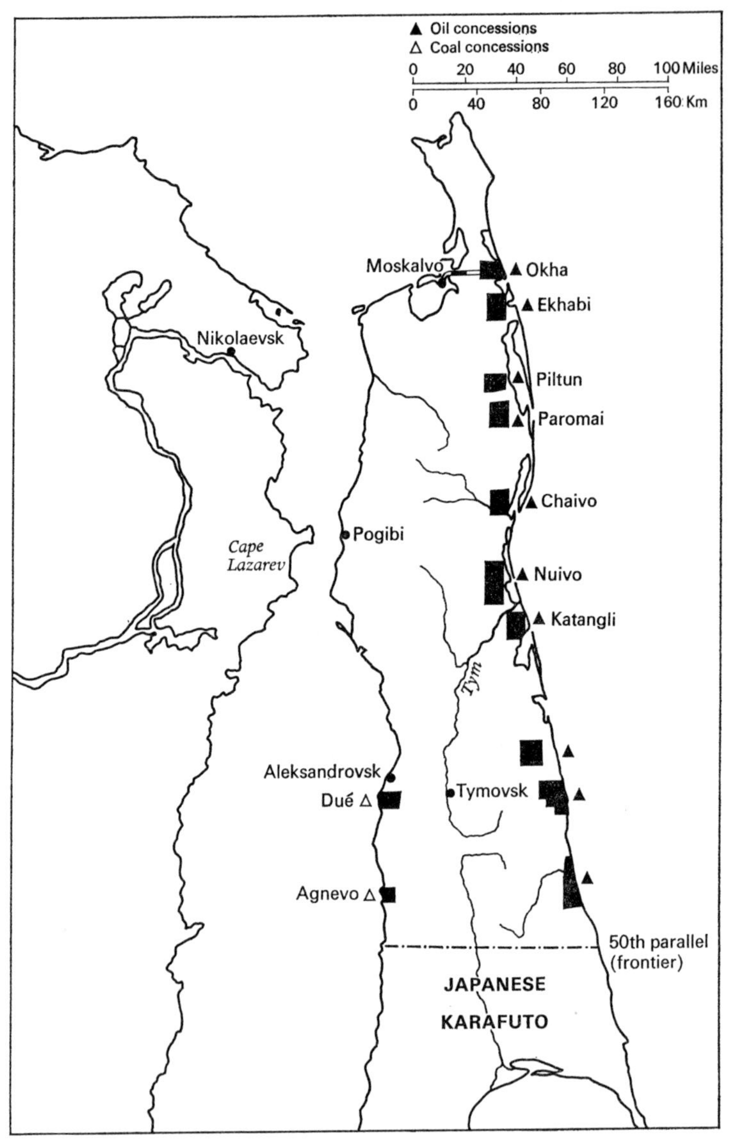

MAP V. Soviet Sakhalin and Japanese concessions (1925–44)

VII

KARAFUTO AND SOVIET SAKHALIN, 1925–1945

IN contrast with the preceding period, the twenty years from 1925 until the Soviet invasion in 1945 passed without a major crisis in Sakhalin. Both Japan and the Soviet Union devoted considerable efforts to developing their own section of the island. While Soviet-Japanese frontier incidents flared up with ominous intensity on the Soviet-Manchukuo and Mongolia-Manchukuo borders in the 1930s, the 50th parallel boundary line dividing Sakhalin preserved a relatively placid exterior until only six days before the end of the Second World War. Yet beneath this serene façade, mutual suspicion rarely abated. Each section of the island jealously preserved its identity. The frontier was sealed. Only the Japanese oil and coal concessions in the north offered occasions for direct contact. These 'two Sakhalins', one Japanese, one Soviet, followed different paths of economic and social development. The gap between them was buried only by the cataclysm of a short but destructive war. As Sakhalin's division was born in the embers of 1905, so its reunification was forged in the fires of a world holocaust.

Karafuto, 1925–1945

Karafuto underwent intensive colonization and development in the twenty years after 1925. Its 1925 population of 189,036 had jumped to 447,976 by 1944.[1] Close co-operation between government and large corporations struck the keynote for the exploitation of Karafuto's fisheries, forests, and coal. Agriculture remained primarily a small-scale enterprise of individual settlers, and its progress was less noteworthy.

During the inter-war years, Karafuto was not considered part of the home islands but was administered as a colony. As such,

[1] Hokkaido chō, Ryōdo Fukki Hoppō Gyogyō Taisaku Honbu, ed., *Karafuto shūsenshi nenpyō* (Sapporo, 1968), p. 24, for the 1944 figure. Karafuto chō, *Karafuto yōran*, 1942 (Toyohara, 1943), p. 20, for the 1925 figure.

it fell into a class with Korea and Formosa (Taiwan). Its governor was directly responsible to the Ministry of Colonization (*Takumushō*). Karafuto's governor enjoyed wide-ranging powers over taxation, police, defence, education, finance, communications, and the regulation of economic activity. He was assisted in these myriad duties by four department heads (Internal Affairs, Colonization, Communications, and Police). The Karafuto Office, including technical advisers, police, teachers, forestry and fisheries inspectors, and interpreters numbered about 2,000 personnel.[2]

The Karafuto Office's annual budget showed a remarkable growth from 1916 until the Second World War. Total expenditures rose from 1,851,843 yen (1916), to 17,734,099 yen (1926), to 27,462,435 yen (1936). In 1942, the Office's expenditures soared to 125,420,638 yen with increased funds being devoted to railroad construction and maintenance (35,000,000 yen), port construction (5,000,000 yen), extraordinary military expenditures (55,000,000 yen), and investment in coal (including oil distillation from shale) and forestry (for pulp, boats, and aviation fuel). Income came principally from taxes, railway revenues, the tobacco and salt monopolies, and public bonds. Subsidies from Tokyo reached a peak of 1,577,343 yen in 1926 and fell steadily until by 1936 the colony received no government subsidies. Subsidies resumed after 1941 and constituted almost 6,000,000 yen of the Office's income in 1942.[3]

Fishing was the oldest occupation of Japanese in Karafuto, and up to 1916 it led all other sectors in income and personnel. The island's coastal waters and rivers abounded in herring, trout, salmon, cod, scallops, and king crabs. *Konbu,* a long flat seaweed highly valued as a food by the Japanese, was collected in large amounts. Herring proved to be the mainstay of the fishing industry. Dried, it was sent to Japan as a fertilizer. Canned and smoked herring processed in Karafuto reached China and Manchukuo. Coastal towns such as Rūtaka, Sakaehama, Honto, Maoka, and Shikuka developed modern canning factories that exported produce worth 10,000,000 yen (about 5,000,000 U.S. dollars) in 1934. During the 1930s specialists

[2] *Karafuto yōran,* 1942, pp. 37–8. Takumushō, ed., *Takumu yōran,* 1936 (Tokyo, 1937), pp. 41–2.

[3] *Karafuto yōran,* 1942, pp. 129–47.

developed several fish breeding and spawning farms. The island of Kaihyōtō (now called Tiulenii Island) located in Taraika (Terpenie) Bay boasted thousands of seals that had attracted hunters from Europe and America since the 1840s. Protected by law since 1911, seals on Kaihyōtō were slaughtered by a quota system each autumn (generally 5,000 per annum) and their prized fur sent to Japan.[4]

Forestry and wood processing were Karafuto's largest industries after 1916. The pine, spruce, larch, and birch trees that covered most of the island were exploited with reckless abandon by lumber concerns until stringent controls were introduced in 1924. Indiscriminate cutting nevertheless resumed during the war years (1941–5), when the demand for wood became insatiable. Before wartime demand absorbed lumber for boats and even planes, Karafuto's wood was processed locally. Some of it became mine supports, railroad ties, or charcoal. The rest passed through more sophisticated processing and ended up as pulp, paper, wood alcohol, cardboard, turpentine, tar, rayon constituents, and even airplane fuel.

Karafuto's pulp industry grew up quickly after 1914 with the Mitsui and Fujii companies building factories at Ōtomari, Toyohara, and Ochiai to take advantage of the wartime boom. After a recession in the 1920s, the Ōji Paper Company emerged as the principal pulp producer in Karafuto with eight modern factories located throughout the island. The Ōji plants also produced a variety of wood derivatives such as alcohol and tar. During the Second World War, considerable research was devoted to distilling aeroplane fuel from pine tree roots and pine needles. While this particular experiment never proved economically feasible, Karafuto's pulp industry nevertheless supplied Japan with 70 per cent of its pulp and paper during the 1930s and early 1940s.[5]

Forest fires were Karafuto's *bête noire*. They broke out regularly and often raged out of control for weeks, causing awesome destruction. One holocaust in 1929 burned out 1,250

[4] Ibid., pp. 282–311. Herman R. Friis, 'Pioneer Economy of Sakhalin Island', *Economic Geography*, XV (Jan. 1939), 61–3. Karafuto chō, ed., *Karafuto sōsho*, VI (Toyohara, 1941), 350–4. Matsuda Genji, 'Glimpses of Saghalien', *Trans Pacific* XVIII (23 Oct. 1930), 5, 13.

[5] Karafuto Ringyō shi Hensan Kai, ed., *Karafuto ringyō shi* (Tokyo, 1960), pp. 306–7. *Karafuto yōran*, 1942, pp. 262–81.

square miles of forest. The government tried desperately to reduce the incidence of fires by sponsoring 'love the forests' campaigns among schoolchildren, covering locomotive stacks with high funnels, posting warning notices, and maintaining an army of fire fighters. Several Japanese universities established forestry research stations in Karafuto to study problems of conservation, fire prevention, and forestation.

According to a 1939 estimate, Karafuto had about 2,000,000,000 tons of coal reserves.[6] Two-thirds of this was soft bituminous coal, and the rest was black lignite. The richest deposits lay along the west coast at Esutoru, Naibuchi, and Kawakami. Coal production stagnated until the 1930s because of the lack of a good port and the government's policy of resource conservation. Consequently, until 1931, Karafuto actually imported coal to satisfy local demand. Later, the railroads and pulp factories generated such a strong local demand that the government slowly relaxed the restrictions on exploitation. By 1938, thirty-five mines were in full operation extracting 3,440,000 metric tons of coal of which about half was exported to Japan proper. After all restrictions were lifted on coal-mining in 1940, production exceeded 4,000,000 tons annually. To bolster the labour force in the mines, the government brought in Koreans. Karafuto's Korean population reached 20,000 in 1940 and doubled again before the end of the war.[7]

Karafuto disappointed Japanese hopes as a source of oil. While northern Sakhalin yielded significant quantities of petroleum, no comparable deposits were found south of the 50th parallel. During the 1920s and 1930s, several companies prospected assiduously but fruitlessly for the precious liquid. One foreign visitor heard in 1936 of an experimental station at Naihoro on the west coast where the Mitsubishi Mining Company was attempting to distil oil from shale coal. The progress of this operation was kept a tight secret, but the Karafuto Office issued a terse statement in 1943 that 'extremely good results' had been obtained. As Japan's fuel situation grew critical during the final stages of World War II, efforts to distil oil reached a

[6] Friis, 'Pioneer Economy of Sakhalin Island', p. 67.

[7] The Russians found 40,000 Koreans in Karafuto in 1945. K. I. Kniazev, ed., *Sakhalinskaia oblast* (Iuzhno-Sakhalinsk, 1960), p. 364. For coal production figure and government policy, *Karafuto yōran*, 1942, pp. 313–29.

feverish pitch. Some oil was actually produced in this fashion, but it never reached Japan for lack of transport.[8]

Agriculture grew steadily but less remarkably than the pulp and coal industries. Evidently, the cold climate and the psychological if not physical remoteness from the home islands discouraged the immigration of permanent settlers. After the first rush of immigrants in 1908–14, the number of incoming farmers remained low until a revival in 1928 which continued for ten years. The Karafuto Office made strenuous efforts to attract colonists. Twenty to twenty-five acres of land were distributed to each arriving family. Full ownership rights were granted after five years provided that 60 per cent of the area were under cultivation. In addition, the immigrant enjoyed regular cash subsidies, complete tax exemption for three years, free tools, and technical advice from the local agricultural research station. The settlers came mainly from Hokkaido and northern Honshū, having generally been attracted by a recruiting campaign sponsored by the Karafuto Office throughout rural Japan. Coming from the cold climate of northern Japan, these colonists were able to adapt to the harsh local climatic conditions. For crops, they grew barley, buckwheat, beans, and potatoes. Some engaged in dairy farming. It is interesting that many of the agricultural practices in Karafuto were borrowed from the American Midwest, in particular from Minnesota and Wisconsin.

As Karafuto never attained self-sufficiency in food, shortages had to be made up by imports from Japan and Manchukuo. During the Second World War, local officials staged strident campaigns to open new lands for potatoes and wheat in order to turn the colony into a 'logistic base'. Although 75,000 acres of new land were brought under cultivation between 1940 and 1944, dependence upon food imports remained the island's Achilles' heel.[9]

Life was extremely arduous for Karafuto's rural settlers. Yet it was also cosmopolitan. Several hundred Russians and some Polish farmers lived there, most of them descendants of exiles or

[8] William Henry Chamberlain, 'Japan's Northern Outpost', *Christian Science Monitor Weekly Magazine* (November 11, 1936), p. 10. *Karafuto shūsenshi nenpyō*, p. 19. *Karafuto yōran*, 1942, p. 330.

[9] *Asahi nenkan*, 1945 (Tokyo, 1945), pp. 242–3. Chamberlain, 'Japan's Northern Outpost', p. 10. Friis, 'Pioneer Economy of Sakhalin Island', p. 74.

free settlers who had decided to remain on the island after 1905. A few were refugees from the Russian Revolution and Civil War. These European families lived in harmony with the Japanese settlers. One product of this mixed society was the birth of a special Karafuto brand of *saké* called *rikyū* that was made from potatoes. *Rikyū*'s role in Karafuto paralleled that of vodka in Siberia—it helped make a harsh life bearable.

In addition to Japanese, Koreans, Russians, and Poles, there lived about 1,700 aborigines in Karafuto (1941 census). 1,300 of these were Ainu, some of whom had been repatriated from Hokkaido in 1905 after thirty years of self-imposed exile while Russia ruled the entire island. Those Ainu who had returned to Karafuto from Hokkaido were reputed to have been better educated than their cousins who had spent thirty years under Russian rule. The Karafuto Ainu lived in nine scattered rural settlements and engaged primarily in fishing.[10]

Some 300 Oroki natives (a Tungus tribe) resided along the upper reaches of the Poronai River. The Oroki raised reindeer for skins, milk, meat, and transport. The men led a semi-nomadic life, hunting deer and marten in the mountains during the winter, catching seals along the coasts from March to May, fishing for salmon and trout from June to August, and returning up the rivers in the autumn. Before border conditions grew tense in the 1930s, Oroki natives rarely heeded frontier regulations. They crossed and recrossed the 50th parallel dividing Karafuto and Soviet Sakhalin with innocent impunity.[11]

One of Japan's most far-reaching contributions to the development of Sakhalin was railways. Even today, about 80 per cent of the island's railway mileage is below the 50th parallel. The Japanese began building tracks only weeks after the Russian garrison surrendered in 1905. Notwithstanding the difficult terrain, the colony had 564 miles of tracks in 1945.[12]

Karafuto relied heavily on sea communications as very few airfields were constructed on the island before World War II. Ōtomari was originally the largest port, but its harbour froze from November to April. In winter vessels could only approach

[10] *Karafuto yōran*, 1942, pp. 22, 410–12.

[11] H. E. Krueger, 'Present Day Conditions in Karafuto, Japanese-owned Saghalin', *China Journal*, XVII (Nov. 1937), 240–1

[12] *Karafuto shūsenshi nenpyō*, p. 24.

to within one mile of the shore where they had to unload their cargo on to dog sleds. Honto and Maoka on the south-west coast were ice-free all year round. They developed into bustling ports. Regular steamship service to Hakodate, Otaru, and Wakkanai in Hokkaido provided the main transport links with Japan. Freighters loaded canned fish, lumber, pulp, and paper for shipment to Japan, Manchukuo, Korea, and occasionally to England, the United States, Germany, and the Dutch East Indies. Very little trade took place with the Soviet Union.[13]

Karafuto's economy underwent remarkable changes in magnitude and structure between 1907 and 1941. Total annual valued production increased forty times in this period, reaching the figure of 380,000,000 yen (U.S. $190,000,000) in 1941. While agriculture and fishing dominated the economy between 1907 and 1916, pulp manufacture outpaced all other sectors after 1916. The growth rate of coal-mining exceeded that of pulp manufacture from 1932 to 1941, but never matched it in valued output. The following chart illustrates the changing structure of the island's economy:[14]

Sector	*1915 Proportion per cent*	*1938 Proportion per cent*
Manufacturing (92 per cent pulp, paper)	23	60
Fishing	65	8
Coal mining	3	13·8
Forestry	1·8	14
Agriculture	5	4

As a frontier country, Karafuto could claim few cultural amenities. To fill the void, the Japanese went about building schools with characteristic alacrity. By 1942, there were 126 primary schools, 142 middle schools, 3 high schools, a trade school, and a teachers' college, comprising altogether 1,706 teachers and 73,328 pupils. Ainu and Oroki children were given a haphazard education by peripatetic instructors until 1933 when they were encouraged to enrol in Japanese schools. Integration came too shortly before the war for the results to be evaluated.

13 *Karafuto yōran*, 1942, pp. 342–3.

14 Based on figures in: Japan, Foreign Office, *Saghalien* (*Karafuto*) *Island* (Tokyo, 1949), pp. 14–23; Okuyama Ryō, *Aa Karafuto* (Sapporo, 1966), pp. 119–20.

The Karafuto Office built a large, well-equipped historical museum in Toyohara which published books regularly on local history, fauna, and flora. Anton Chekhov's monumental account of Sakhalin's penal system was translated and published in Karafuto on local paper—an event that would have evoked a wry smile from the author had he been alive.[15]

The Japanese left three 'cultural monuments' in Karafuto during their forty-year rule there. The majestic Toyohara Historical Museum (now the Iuzhno-Sakhalinsk Museum) with its imposing tile roof and guardian stone lions is one of them. The second was the Karafuto Jinja, a spacious Shinto shrine located in a virgin pine forest eight miles outside of Toyohara. This northernmost national shrine enjoyed its greatest moment of glory on 10 August 1925 when it was visited by the Crown Prince (now Emperor) Hirohito. The third such relic was the Higashi Honganji temple in Toyohara. Once a highly revered spot, it has been turned into a movie theatre by the Russians. Other memorable traces left by the Japanese include Fujiwara Ginjirō's Toyohara Park with its exquisitely sculptured landscapes, and the Swiss chalet proudly surveying the Asahigaoka ski resort. In the prewar days, Japanese skiers flocked to Asahigaoka for the national ski-jumping championships. It is now a Soviet vacation centre called 'Gornii Vozdukh' ('mountain air'). In 1964 one Japanese visitor was informed by a proud caretaker how the Russians had built it.[16]

The 50th Parallel

The Japanese image of Karafuto in the inter-war years was coloured by the consciousness that it formed a frontier with a Communist state. The 50th parallel which divided Soviet Sakhalin from Japanese Karafuto never received the publicity accorded to the Soviet-Manchukuo or Manchukuo-Outer Mongolia frontiers where Russo-Japanese clashes flared up sporadically in the 1930s. Although unpublicized, the frontier

[15] Anton Chehofu 'Sagaren shima', in *Karafuto sōsho*, VII (Toyohara, 1941), translated by Dazai Toshio.

[16] Miyatake Shōzō, *Shiberia* (Tokyo, 1965), pp. 207, 214–15. For Hirohito's visit to Karafuto: *Karafuto sōsho*, VI, 343–6. An agricultural research institute built by the Japanese in the 1930s was photographed in 1947 and depicted as the Russian-built Academy of Sciences Research Centre. S. N. Rakovskii, 'Na iuzhnom Sakhaline', *Geografiia v shkole*, III (May-June 1947), 11.

region nevertheless evoked an atmosphere of frigid inhospitality and ominous quietude. The infrequent sightseers who pushed their way up the narrow dirt road from Shikuka entered a vast silent expanse of swampy forest. Mile after mile, the traveller continued northwards, through depressing hamlets each more lonely and bleak than its predecessor—Kami Shikuka, Ōki, Hattoi, Aton, Keton, and Koton. This road was the only artery connecting Karafuto with Soviet Sakhalin. Traffic grew less and less visible as one approached the last Japanese settlement before the frontier itself—Handenzawa.[17]

Handenzawa qualified as one of the loneliest and most remote frontier stations imaginable. The ten to twenty Japanese frontier guards posted there left their families in Shikuka and spent an isolated, usually uneventful, but always raw winter inside the confined wooden hut that served as a guardhouse.

The Russo-Japanese frontier in Sakhalin was a product of the Portsmouth Treaty of 1905. It was not a natural frontier along a mountain range or a river or even a valley. The boundary ran brutally along the 50th parallel in a relentless straight line cutting through the forests of larch, pine, and birch from the east to the west coast of the island. When this line was demarcated in 1906–7, the surveyors cut a path ten metres wide through the forest and placed seventeen stone markers at equidistant intervals across the island. On the south side of the marker at Handenzawa, there was a chrysanthemum design with the inscription 'Dai Nippon Teikoku' ('Great Empire of Japan'). The obverse side read 'Rossiia Granitsa 1907' ('Russia Frontier 1907') with the double eagle emblem of the Romanov dynasty. The Soviet government did not bother to change the tsarist emblem on the marker. Someone, however, had tried to scratch out the eagle, leaving it a bit deformed.

During the 1930s, the Japanese entertained deep suspicions of any foreigner visiting Karafuto. The police viewed even the casual tourist as either an eccentric (why else would he come to this forsaken place?) or as a spy. The accusations ranged from ferrying communists to Soviet Sakhalin on an 'underground

[17] Frontier descriptions are based on eyewitness accounts: Maedakō Hiroichirō *Kokkyō Karafuto* (Tokyo, 1939), pp. 116–33; Abe Etsurō, *Karafuto no tabi* (Tokyo, 1936), pp. 105–6, 275–8; Miyazaki Raihachi, *Karafutoshi monogatari* (Tokyo, 1944), pp. 447–54; Kikuchi Kieji, *Kita Nihon no hanashi* (Tokyo, 1944), pp. 176–8.

railway' to outright espionage. When the Italian orientalist Fosco Maraini toured Karafuto in 1939, he was accompanied literally twenty-four hours by an endless succession of detectives who even shared his lodgings. A German geographer, Martin Schwind, was arrested in 1937 as a Russian spy and released only after the direct intervention of the governor of the colony.[18]

Relations with the Russians at Handenzawa rarely went beyond the bi-weekly exchange of mail that was instituted in 1927. There was no local telephone service. Messages were exchanged by raising signal flags or, if that failed, by tying written notes around rocks and hurling these missiles discreetly near the opposite guard post fifty yards away. Although neither side kept any appreciable military force permanently at the frontier, relations at this remote outpost grew increasingly tense after the Manchurian Incident in 1931. In May of that year a group of Japanese communists, accompanied by a Russian, escaped through the forests around Handenzawa across the frontier into the Soviet Union. Occasionally a Japanese hunter or woodcutter found himself an involuntary guest of the Aleksandrovsk detention centre after inadvertently or intentionally wandering into Soviet Sakhalin. By far the most sensational border crossing occurred on 3 January 1938 when the celebrated thirty-six-year-old actress Okada Yoshiko and her reputed lover Sugimoto Ryōkichi, a producer in the proletarian theatre, abandoned their horse-drawn sleigh, fled on foot through the snow near Handenzawa, and disappeared into the forests on the Soviet side.[19]

More serious were the shooting incidents that reached a climax in 1938–9 when Soviet-Japanese relations came close to a total rupture. In August 1938 two Japanese police escorts were shot while a member of the Imperial Diet was touring the frontier region. The Japanese press indignantly reported a

[18] Interviews with Fosco Maraini in Florence, Italy (12 May 1969) and with Martin Schwind in Bochum, German Federal Republic (16 May 1969). See also, William Teeling, 'Migration to Sakhalin', *Great Britain and the East*, XLVIII (14 Jan. 1937), 62. Edith Stone, 'North Pacific Outposts of Japan', *Travel*, LXXXIII (May 1944), 10–13, 32.

[19] Okada and Sugimoto successfully sought asylum in the U.S.S.R. and lived for many years in Moscow. Hokkaido shimbunsha, ed., *Hokkaido hyakunen*, III (Sapporo, 1968), 240. For other Karafuto frontier incidents: Japan, Gaimushō, *Nisso kōshō shi* (Tokyo, 1942), pp. 344–5, 389–90; Maedakō, *Kokkyō Karafuto*, pp. 122–8; *New York Times*, 13 August 1938.

series of kidnappings, shootings, and aircraft harassment. Although small in themselves, these incidents erupted in an atmosphere charged with hostility. In 1938–9, Japanese and Soviet army forces engaged in sporadic undeclared warfare at Changkufeng on the Korean-Manchukuo-Soviet frontier seventy miles south-west of Vladivostok (July–August 1938) and at Nomonhan on the Outer Mongolia-Manchukuo frontier (June–August 1939).

As Soviet-Japanese relations deteriorated during 1936–9, both sides took steps to strengthen their military posture in Sakhalin. While precise statistics on the Soviet armed forces in northern Sakhalin are not at present available, it is generally recognized that there was a considerable build-up of the Red Army's infantry, artillery, and air power in the Far East after 1936. Despite a costly involvement in China after July 1937, the Japanese did not neglect the 50th parallel frontier. Late in 1937 the Hokkaido-based Northern Region Army Command took the decision to bolster Karafuto's garrison and to fortify the frontier. On 12 March 1938, Supreme Command Headquarters in Tokyo approved a plan to deploy an entire division in Karafuto. Early in 1939 a special Karafuto Mixed Brigade was created and assigned to frontier defence. The brigade consisted of élite infantry, artillery, and engineer units. Meanwhile, the Navy began the construction of an airfield at Shikuka, and the Army followed suit in Toyohara. Needless to say, these activities constituted a contravention of Article IX of the Portsmouth Treaty which forbade the construction of fortifications on either side of the frontier.[20]

The Japanese stepped up military preparations in Karafuto during 1940. A fifteen-mile belt south of the 50th parallel was declared off limits to all without special military passes. The Karafuto Mixed Brigade deployed along the frontier and began the construction of concrete bunkers at Koton and Horomi Pass, located about eight miles south of Handenzawa on the single road leading from the frontier to Nairo and Toyohara. Units of the 7th Division (based in Asahikawa, Hokkaido)

[20] Material on Japanese Army operations in Karafuto (1937–43) is taken from: Japan, Bōei chō, Bōei Kenshūjo, Senshi Shitsu, ed. *Hokutō hōmen rikugun sakusen*, vol. XXI of *Tōa senshi sōsho* (Tokyo, 1968), 11–16, 31–44, 53–5, 74, 132–4, 224–8, 312–13, 517.

deployed around the towns further south such as Toyohara, Maoka, and Honto. A wireless communications network was set up to connect Koton with divisional headquarters in Kami Shikuka, Northern Region Command in Sapporo, and Supreme Command in Tokyo.

The surprise German invasion of the Soviet Union (22 June 1941) threw the Japanese forces in Karafuto into a state of tense preparedness. Although Japan's Foreign Minister, Matsuoka Yōsuke, had concluded a Neutrality Pact with the U.S.S.R. barely two months previously (13 April), there were voices in Tokyo and in the Manchukuo-based Kwantung Army that a providential opportunity had arrived to open a 'second front' against the Soviet Union and push northwards into Siberia. During July, officers of the Kwantung and Northern Region armies made preparations for an offensive against the U.S.S.R., using the code name 'Kan-toku-en' (special Kwantung manoeuvres). Sakhalin was to be an important field of operations. The 7th Division was assigned to seizing the Okha oil-fields in a combined air and sea assault. Other units were to carry out an amphibious landing at Aleksandrovsk, Soviet Sakhalin's administrative centre. The Karafuto Mixed Brigade was to attack northward across the 50th parallel following the road leading to Tymovsk.

These 'special manoeuvres' did not advance beyond the planning stage. After a survey of northern Sakhalin's oil reserves, the Navy concluded that even should Japan occupy the entire island, Sakhalin's fuel resources alone were insufficient to support wartime operations of the combined fleet. Much richer fuel deposits awaited exploitation in the Dutch East Indies. This and a complex variety of other forces brought about the triumph of proponents of the 'southern advance' (to Indo-china, the Philippines, and the Dutch East Indies) over those of the 'northern advance' (into Eastern Siberia) during July and August of 1941. On 9 August Supreme Command Headquarters in Tokyo ordered the Northern Region Army to cancel all plans for an attack on the U.S.S.R. On 18 August the Northern Region Command directed all units in Karafuto to exert strict caution along the frontier in order to avoid friction with the Russians.

From August 1941 to the end of the war, Karafuto's forces preserved a basically defensive posture. Combat readiness remained high until the summer of 1942 after which the Aleutian campaign against the Americans drew attention away from the 50th parallel. It is true that there were unsettling rumours that the Soviet Union was about to sell Kamchatka to the United States and allow the construction of American air bases in the Maritime Region. Not a few Japanese feared a Soviet-American offensive through Karafuto and Manchukuo. An occasional Soviet defector brought reports of American ships reaching Moskalvo (northern Sakhalin) and of the growing air traffic between Eastern Siberia and Alaska. While the Japanese may have been alarmed by these developments, they were in no position after early 1942 to open a new front in the north. From August 1942 to May 1943, Karafuto's Mixed Brigade occupied itself with the improvement of Koton's fixed defences and road construction. Other units engaged in the expansion of Shikuka's port and railway construction.[21]

The annihilation of the Japanese garrison on Attu Island in the Aleutians (29 May 1943) wrought a fundamental shift in the Northern Region Army's strategy. Human and material resources were diverted to prepare for the expected American advance against the Kurile Islands. Crack units such as the Karafuto Mixed Brigade and the 7th Division were withdrawn from Karafuto and redeployed in the northern Kuriles. The vacuum on the frontier created by the departure of the Karafuto Mixed Brigade was filled by the untried 125th Infantry Regiment from Sapporo. Consisting largely of reservists and students, it possessed neither the experience nor the equipment of its predecessor.[22]

After the summer of 1942 Japan's military leaders had their hands too full in the wide theatre of hostilities to worry particularly about Karafuto. Despite the disturbing rumours concerning Soviet-American collaboration, Tokyo reasoned that as long as the U.S.S.R. was heavily engaged with Germany in the west, the Russians would not jeopardize their eastern frontier by offering military installations to the Americans. These calculations proved sound only as long as Germany held the initiative in the war. After 1943 the Red Army grasped and maintained the initiative, driving the Nazi invader steadily westward

[21] *Hokutō hōmen rikugun sakusen*, pp. 42–4, 53–5, 132–4, 224. Oka Sakae, *Kita Karafuto* (Tokyo, 1942), pp. 279–80.

[22] *Hokutō hōmen rikugun sakusen*, pp. 312–13.

towards eventual destruction. Russia's crushing offensives in 1944 and 1945 should have warned the Japanese that it was only a matter of time before Soviet forces would be re-deployed in the Far East facing Manchukuo and Karafuto. Wishful thinking and blind faith in the validity of the 1941 Soviet-Japanese Neutrality Pact (which the Japanese were considering breaking in the summer of 1941) prevented the Japanese from fully realizing the implications of Soviet victory in the west. Consequently, when Karafuto faced a full-scale invasion in the summer of 1945, its inhabitants were woefully ill prepared.

Although Karafuto remained a backwater during nearly all of World War II, its relationship with the home islands underwent a significant administrative change in 1942 and 1943. On 11 September 1942, the Tōjō cabinet announced that Karafuto was to be incorporated into the *naichi* (home islands). This measure removed Karafuto from the class of colonies and trust territories (Korea, Taiwan, Micronesia) administered by the Ministry of Colonization and designated it an integral part of Japan. In November Karafuto's governor was made responsible to the Home Ministry. The former colony's integration with Japan proper progressed quickly during 1943. Karafuto's currency, postal system, taxation, railways, and police, hitherto the responsibility of the colony's governor, were transferred to the appropriate ministries in Tokyo.[23]

Karafuto's incorporation into Japan proper took place during a general reorganization of the nation's administration. An Imperial Decree of 20 June 1943 outlined a consolidation of Japan's administrative units (*ken*), or prefectures, into seven large districts. When this order went into effect on 31 January 1945, Karafuto became a part of District Number 1 which included the island of Hokkaido.

Two forces seemed to have motivated the unification of Karafuto with the home islands: an emotional conviction that it was not a colony but historically part of Japan; and secondly, an awareness that administrative consolidation would reduce total costs and redundant personnel in the strained wartime economy. Karafuto's settlers had little time to celebrate their new status. Only seven months after its début as part of the homeland, Karafuto was totally lost to Japan.

[23] *Asahi nenkan*, 1944, pp. 99, 424.

Soviet Sakhalin, 1925–1945

It was a proud moment for the Soviet Union when at noon on 15 May 1925 the Japanese flag was lowered at Aleksandrovsk and the hammer and sickle emblem raised in its place. Yet the representatives of the Far Eastern Revolutionary Committee (*Dalrevkom*) who came to northern Sakhalin to take over its administration faced tasks far more formidable and less pleasant than participating in a flag-raising ceremony. Less than 5,000 Russians lived there, or about one-third of the 1917 population. Some among these inhabitants had Tsarist sympathies and had collaborated with the Japanese. The Japanese left behind an economy in ruins. During the five-year occupation, Sakhalin's coal had been recklessly exploited, leaving the mines flooded and the equipment in shambles. The forests had been decimated and the fur-bearing animals hunted almost to extermination. Oil-fields in the north-east were occupied by Japanese concessionaires.[24]

The Soviet government confronted this challenge with stern determination. During the first three years of Soviet rule (1925–8), consolidation and reconstruction were priority objectives. The Dalrevkom assumed responsibility for administration and economic planning. It divided northern Sakhalin into four administrative (*raion*) districts—Aleksandrovsk, Rykovsk, Vostochnyi, and Rybnovsk—which together formed 'Sakhalin *oblast*'. Sakhalin *oblast* in turn constituted a territorial unit in Khabarovsk *krai* (region).

Parallel to this government structure was the Communist Party organization which provided comprehensive guidance and surveillance. The secretary of the Sakhalin party bureau was an *ex officio* member of the Central Committee of the Far Eastern Bureau at Khabarovsk. The bureau secretary held responsibility for all the island's party cells inside the regional *revkoms* (government administrative committees), the trade unions, the frontier guards units, and (after 1928) inside fishing and agricultural collectives.[25]

[24] V. Ia. Aboltin, 'Vosstanovlenie Sovetskoi vlasti na severnom Sakhaline', *Voprosy istorii*, XLI (Oct. 1966), 109–10.

[25] E. V. Mushkareva, 'Vosstanovlenie i uprochenie Sovetskoi vlasti na severnom Sakhaline: 1925–1928 gg.' K. I. Kniazev, ed., *Sakhalinskaia oblast* (Iuzhno-Sakhalinsk, 1960), pp. 159–66. For documents of party and state organs in Sakhalin

Soviet planners made sustained efforts to organize the efficient exploitation of the island's natural resources. A surveying expedition conducted in 1925 reported that Sakhalin had a rich potential if sufficient labour could be mobilized. As the 5,000 existing inhabitants hardly amounted to adequate manpower to propel an ambitious development programme, the Russians implemented massive immigration by central planning. The Dalrevkom brought in Komsomol (Communist Youth Organization) shock brigades from European Russia to build roads, clear forests, and construct much-needed housing. Coal-miners were brought from Suchan (near Vladivostok) to bolster the Chinese and Koreans working at Dué. Oil engineers and workers were recruited from Baku and Grozny by offers of relatively high wages. Peasants were transported from the Ukraine to settle the upper Tym Valley and fishermen from the Black Sea and Baltic regions to staff the co-operatives at Rybnovsk. To organize the workers, the Dalrevkom created trade unions among miners, lumbermen, fishermen, and among the Russian nationals working for the Japanese oil concessionaires.[26]

By 1928, on the eve of the First Five-Year Plan, the Dalrevkom could point with some satisfaction at the results of central planning. Coal production stood at 120,000 tons, equalling the 1916 output. Fishing and forestry showed promising signs of a revival. Settlers in the Tym Valley were raising crops of grain, vegetables, and fruit. Agricultural settlements for the island's aborigines (1,800 Gilyaks, 200 Evenki, 170 Oroki, and a handful of Yakuts and Ainu) were built at Moskalvo, Viskro, and Nogliki with rudimentary housing, educational, and medical facilities. The island's population had jumped five times to 25,000. Undeniably, these were hard times for all concerned. Acute housing shortages proved endemic. Discipline was uneven at best. However, Sakhalin's inhabitants enjoyed political stability for the first time in eight years. Soviet power brought one priceless quality to northern Sakhalin—optimism.

(1925–45), N. I. Kolesnikov, ed., *Sotsialisticheskoe stroitelstvo na Sakhaline 1925–1945 gg.* (Iuzhno-Sakhalinsk, 1967).

[26] Mushkareva lists 308 Russians working on the Japanese oil concessions in this period. 'Vosstanovlenie i uprochenie Sovetskoi vlasti na severnom Sakhaline', p. 170.

Under the First and Second Five-Year Plans (1928–37), northern Sakhalin's population and economy grew at a steady pace. The population mushroomed from 25,000 in 1928 to 106,000 in 1941. The 1941 total fell short of Karafuto's 417,000, but given the logistic problems, the increase represented no mean achievement. The most fundamental structural changes in Sakhalin's economy came about as a result of the collectivization of agriculture and the integration of the island's extractive fuel industries (oil and coal) with the new industrial complexes at Khabarovsk and Komsomolsk on the Amur River. Centrally planned immigration, both forced and induced, continued to play an important role in building up a labour force. The co-ordination of economic enterprises was administered after 1929 by the Sakhalin State Company.[27]

The collectivization of agriculture forced painful changes upon residents of the Tym Valley where most of the island's peasants lived. By 1932, collectivization had overtaken not only Russians but the aborigines, including the reindeer-raising Oroki. The Red Partisan Commune at Ada on the Tym River was one of the model collectivist experiments. About 400 Russian and Gilyak peasants and fishermen lived in several spacious communal houses cut out of the surrounding virgin forest. The community undertook a variety of tasks including road construction, fishing, and raising crops (oats, barley, vegetables) and livestock. A machine tractor station was attached to the commune with a staff of mechanics and drivers. For the children, the commune provided a kindergarten and primary school. This self-contained unit came to typify the emerging settlement patterns that Soviet power introduced in Sakhalin. Some of the older inhabitants regretted the demise of independent enterprise, yet few denied that collectivization stimulated agricultural production in northern Sakhalin. Indeed, the Russians seem to have made more progress than the Japanese in reducing their dependence upon food imports.[28]

In building up Sakhalin's fishing industry, the Russians failed to equal the scale of the Japanese in Karafuto. Neverthe-

[27] P. A. Lebedev, 'Ekonomika i kultura severnovo Sakhalina v gody dovoennykh piatiletok', Kniazev, ed., *Sakhalinskaia oblast*, pp. 186–7. *Atlas Sakhalinskoi oblasti*, p. 9. Vladimir Kantorovich, *Soviet Sakhalin* (Moscow, 1933), p. 21.

[28] P. V. Sliotov, *Na Sakhaline* (Moscow, 1933), pp. 114–29. Kantorovich, *Soviet Sakhalin*, pp. 62–6. Lebedev, 'Ekonomika i kultura', pp. 195–6.

less, between 1928 and 1941 central planning achieved a 64 per cent growth in total output of fish products. The Sakhalin State Fishing Trust, established in 1932, directed both fishing and processing operations. Nineteen new canning factories for salmon, dolphin, and crab sprang up in Aleksandrovsk, Rybnovsk, Shirokopadsk, and Vostochno-Sakhalinsk. The cleaning and canning machines in these factories came from the United States, and instruction in their use was given by American engineers. A substantial portion of the labour force consisted of Chinese who had come to the island as miners at the turn of the century.[29]

Lumbering fell mainly on the shoulders of young Communists who came to Sakhalin in large Komsomol shock brigades. Unlike the Japanese in Karafuto, the Russians did not develop a modern pulp industry. The processing of wood in northern Sakhalin rarely went beyond the sawmill stage. Nevertheless, the 337,500 cubic metres of wood cut in 1937 represented a threefold gain over 1928. The wood was used locally for housing, mine shaft supports, and railroad ties.

At the end of the Second Five-Year Plan (1937), northern Sakhalin's mines produced 320,000 tons of coal or almost three times the 1916 level. By 1943, coal output passed the 500,000-ton mark. This coal played an important role in fuelling the Chinese Eastern Railroad, the Ussuri section of the Trans-Siberian Railway, and the Pacific Fleet. Before 1928, coal for the railways in the Soviet Far East had to be shipped from Cheremkhovo on the west side of Irkutsk. In transporting Cheremkhovo coal to Vladivostok (a journey of over 2,000 miles), the supply trains burned up 40 per cent of their loads. Despite the breakthrough in fuel extraction, Soviet Sakhalin did not approach its coal export potential because of inadequate port facilities.

Of all the production indices, it was oil in which Soviet leadership generated the most impressive gains. Although the Japanese concessionaires in northern Sakhalin enjoyed more than a five-year head-start in drilling and pumping operations, the Russians overtook and surpassed them through a sustained investment in labour and capital.

Northern Sakhalin's oil deposits constituted the only known reserves in eastern Siberia and as such were considered doubly

[29] Lebedev, 'Ekonomika i kultura', p. 193. Kantorovich, *Soviet Sakhalin*, pp. 43–7. Sliotov, *Na Sakhaline*, pp. 24–30.

precious by Soviet planners during the inter-war years. Hardly had the ink dried on the Soviet-Japanese Convention of 1925 when geologists, engineers, and skilled workers began arriving in northern Sakhalin from Baku and Grozny. Some Russians were assigned to work in the Japanese concessions in order to acquire technical know-how. From the First Five-Year Plan onwards, crude oil production grew steadily under the management of the Sakhalin Oil Trust.[30]

	metric tons
1929	28,000
1932	210,000
1937	356,000
1939	473,000
1940	505,000
1942	550,000
1944	650,000

To expedite the transportation of crude oil from northern Sakhalin to refineries and industrial complexes on the Amur River, the Russians built a railway from the main oilfield at Okha across the island to Moskalvo on Baikal Bay. From there, the oil was loaded onto barges and taken up the Amur. In 1942, an oil pipeline passing beneath the Tatary Straits was built which connected Okha and Komsomolsk.

In contrast, the Japanese concessionaires suffered from unfavourable conditions of transport between northern Sakhalin and the home islands. No suitable harbour existed, forcing them to load their tankers offshore using lighters. This task proved hazardous, as the Okhotsk Sea sent breakers one yard high against the coast even in calm weather. Moreover, the sea froze over during six months of the year, leaving the Japanese only a brief interval in which to load their tankers. Lacking storage facilities in northern Sakhalin, the Japanese were forced to restrict production. Consequently, total annual crude oil output never surpassed the 195,000 ton mark set in 1933 although the Japanese boosted their total oil exports to the home islands by purchasing up to 134,000 tons (1932) from the Russian Sakhalin Oil Trust. The Soviet government halted these sales in 1937.[31]

[30] Lebedev, 'Ekonomika i kultura', pp. 188–90.
[31] Oka, *Kita Karafuto*, pp. 151–2.

Despite remarkable progress in agriculture, coal, fishing, and oil, transport remained largely undeveloped in Soviet Sakhalin. With the exception of the twenty-mile railroad from Okha to Moskalvo and an eight-mile narrow gauge railway from Aleksandrovsk to the edge of the mountains, no rail system existed. The unpaved road from Aleksandrovsk to Derbinskoe and its two branches to the Karafuto frontier and Ada-Tymovo were the only roads of any consequence in the Russian half of the island. Outside of these meagre routes, one travelled by river-raft, coastal steamer, or on foot along forest tracks. External communications improved with the completion during 1934–7 of an extension of the Trans-Siberian line to Sovetskaia Gavan, located about one hundred and fifty miles south-west of Aleksandrovsk across the Tatary Straits. This new link with the mainland obviated the old roundabout route that led through Nikolaevsk by steamer and along the sinuous lower reaches of the Amur River.

Several comparisons can be made between Japanese Karafuto and Soviet Sakhalin. First, notwithstanding compulsory immigration and shock brigades used by the Russians, the Japanese population in Karafuto grew at double the rate and by 1941 was four times that of Soviet Sakhalin. Geographical propinquity, high population pressures on the home islands, and the relatively mild climate of Karafuto help to explain this discrepancy.

Secondly, the economic structures of the two areas differed. In Soviet Sakhalin, centralized planning executed under Communist Party supervision and implemented by state trusts (oil, fishing, coal) introduced an element of stability into northern Sakhalin's economy. In Karafuto, private corporations exploited vast parcels of public lands, with only a supervisory role played by public authorities. In contrast to northern Sakhalin's steady growth, Karafuto's extractive and manufacturing industries oscillated in response to world market trends, visible in the pulp boom (1914–19), recession (1920s), and recovery (1930s).

Thirdly, the life styles of agricultural settlers varied. The Russian peasant of the Tym Valley worked in a regimented environment framed by communal dwellings and collectivized agriculture. His Japanese counterpart in the Poronai and Susui valleys generally owned his house and land and lived less closely integrated with the larger social community.

Fourthly, while Russian planners emphasized coal and oil production to supply the fuel for the Amur industrial complexes, the Japanese concentrated on forestry (pulp, paper, tar, alcohol), and fishing (food, fertilizer).

Fifthly, while the Japanese controlled the economy of Karafuto, the Russians did not exercise complete sovereignty in northern Sakhalin. The Japanese oil concessions in northern Sakhalin were the product of the Soviet-Japanese Convention of 1925 which had sanctioned them in exchange for the Japanese military withdrawal from the northern half of the island. The concessions had more than a purely economic significance. They symbolized both Russia's momentary weakness during the Revolution and Civil War, and Japan's abiding interest in asserting 'special rights' to northern Sakhalin. These concessions created a volatile situation in which Japanese and Russians competed face to face for the same precious resource in the same area in a charged political atmosphere.

Japanese Concessions in Soviet Sakhalin, 1925–1944

Competition for northern Sakhalin's oil and coal resources was a constant source of friction between Japan and the Soviet Union between 1925 and 1944. To meet the needs of the Five-Year plans, Russia needed increasing amounts of fuel. At the same time, Japan's growing involvement in Manchuria and China placed heavy demands upon all sources of fuel but especially oil. Combined with tensions generated by other issues (fisheries, frontier disputes on the continent, relations with China), Russo-Japanese rivalry over northern Sakhalin's resources nearly reached the stage of open hostilities in 1938–9. The explosion was temporarily averted by the outbreak of war in Europe, the Soviet-Japanese Neutrality Pact, the German invasion of Russia, and the Pacific War. Only after the U.S.S.R. had turned the tide against Germany in 1943 and after Japan's wartime position had deteriorated in 1944 did the northern Sakhalin concession problem end—in a Russian triumph.

When the Soviet Union and Japan established diplomatic relations by a Convention signed in Peking on 20 January 1925, the Russians agreed (according to Article VI of the Convention) to grant Japanese subjects 'concessions for the exploitation of mineral, timber and other natural resources in all parts of the territory of the Union of Soviet Socialist Republics'.[32] More specifically, Protocol B outlined the terms for Japanese oil and coal concessions in northern Sakhalin that would come into effect provided that all Japanese military forces had withdrawn from northern Sakhalin by 15 May 1925. After the Japanese had duly completed this withdrawal, negotiations began in Moscow over the details of the concessions. An agreement was reached and signed on 14 December 1925 for three concessions (two for coal, one for oil) which were to extend until 1970.

The terms for the oil concession accorded Japan the right to prospect (for eleven years) and exploit (for forty-five years) the oilfields at Okha, Nutovo, Piltun, Ekhabi, Chaivo, Niyvo, Ugleikuty, and Katangli. These areas were checkerboarded with every other square going to the Japanese. Payment for the oil extracted was determined at a *pro rata* share of annual production. It amounted to 5 per cent for production up to 30,000 metric tons and rose to 15 per cent for 620,000 metric tons. Royalties on gushers were set at 45 per cent. Gasoline from well gases was taxed at 15–30 per cent. A 4 per cent rental tax was levied on all equipment. The agreement fixed the ratio of Russian and Japanese workers at 50 per cent each for skilled labour and 75 per cent Russian to 25 per cent Japanese for unskilled labour. All labour disputes between the Japanese concessionaires and the Soviet trade unions were to be decided on the basis of Soviet law.[33]

The two coal concessions were located at Dué and along the Agnevo River. They represented about 15 per cent of the total proven coal deposits on Soviet Sakhalin. Here, the Japanese agreed to abide by the same rules governing labour relations in the oil concessions. Taxes were slightly lower, ranging from 5 per cent to 8 per cent of annual production depending on the

[32] For the relevant tests of the Soviet-Japanese Convention of 1925, see Appendix A.

[33] Material in this and following paragraphs concerning the northern Sakhalin concessions is taken from: Harriet L. Moore, *Soviet Far Eastern Policy*, 1931–1945 (Princeton, 1945), p. 73. George A. Lensen, *Japanese Recognition of the U.S.S.R.; Soviet-Japanese Relations*, 1921–1930 (Tokyo, 1970), pp. 194–6, 230–2. Japan, Gaimushō, ed., *Nisso kōshō shi* (Tokyo, 1942), pp. 113–24. Ōta, *Nichiro Karafuto gaikō sen*, pp. 311–12. A. K. Ilin, 'K likvidatsii Iaponskikh kontsessii na severnom Sakhalin i prolongatsii na piatlet rybolovnoi konventsii', *Bolshevik*, 9 (1944), 70.

output (5 per cent to 100,000 tons, adding 0.25 per cent for each additional 50,000 tons up to 8 per cent for anything over 650,000 tons). Furthermore, the Japanese undertook to obey not only all existing Soviet laws but any laws that might be passed in the future. Clearly, the Russians engineered these two agreements so as to retain a powerful legal lever in the event of any dispute.

The Japanese established two companies to exploit Sakhalin's coal and oil. Both were outgrowths of the Hokushinkai consortium (see Chapter VI) that had been active from 1919 to 1925. Unlike the Hokushinkai, the new companies had no direct government participation. To develop the oil concessions, the Hokushinkai shareholders created the Kita Karafuto Sekiyū Kabushiki Kaisha (Northern Sakhalin Oil Company, Ltd.) in June 1926. The company was capitalized at 10,000,000 yen. A retired admiral who had formerly been the chief of naval ordnance, Nakazato Jūji, was elected president. Nakazato defined the company's objective as developing northern Sakhalin's oil resources for profit. Investors flocked to buy the company's stock.

For the two coal concessions, the Mitsubishi Mining Company founded the Kita Karafuto Kōgyō Kabushiki Kaisha (North Sakhalin Mining Company, Ltd.) which was capitalized at 10,000,000 yen and directed by Kawakami Toshihiko, a former Foreign Office minister in Moscow, Harbin, and Vladivostok and currently a director of the South Manchurian Railroad Company. The public demonstrated little enthusiasm for buying shares in this concern and with good reason, for one of the two coal concessions remained inactive and the other operated at a loss.[34]

Although disagreements arose between the Soviet authorities and the Japanese concessionaires regarding the employment of Russian workers and the apportionment of new drilling sites, the northern Sakhalin concessions created no serious friction during the first six years of operation. In 1927 the Japanese obtained permission to enlarge the scope of prospecting activities. In 1928 the Sakhalin Oil Trust consented to sell oil from Russian wells to the Japanese concessionaires.

While oil purchases from the Russians enabled the Japanese

[34] Ōta, *Nichiro Karafuto gaikō sen*, pp. 312–16.

concessionaires to boost oil exports to the home islands, their own efforts to increase productivity in northern Sakhalin were frustrated by climatic and labour problems. Consequently, although the Japanese concessionaires enjoyed several years' head start over the Russians, the Soviet's Sakhalin Oil Trust succeeded in overtaking them in total production in 1932. The following chart illustrates the changing production patterns.[35]

Year	Kita Karafuto S.K.K. Output million tons	Sakhalin Oil Trust Sales to Japanese million tons	Sakhalin Oil Trust Output million tons
1926	34,000		
1927	77,000		
1928	122,000		
1929	184,000	28,000	28,000
1930	193,000	37,000	?
1931	189,000	113,000	?
1932	188,000	134,000	210,000
1933	195,000	125,000	?
1934	164,000	123,000	?
1935	168,000	40,000	?
1936	181,000	40,000	?
1937	151,000	100,000	356,000
1942	?	0	550,000
1943	16,000	0	590,000
1944	0	0	650,000

The above chart shows that (1) after a rapid growth in the late 1920s, oil production in the Japanese concessions stagnated after 1930 and fell sharply after 1937; (2) while the figures are incomplete, oil production in the Russian wells increased steadily after 1930, surpassing the Japanese in 1932; and (3) oil sales from the Soviet Sakhalin Oil Trust to the Japanese concessionaires terminated in 1937. During the early 1930s, the Russians became more and more reluctant to sell oil to the Japanese. The Second Five-Year Plan (1933–7) placed heavy demands on Sakhalin's oil as fuel for emerging industrial centres at Khabarovsk and Komsomolsk. Moreover, Japan's

[35] This chart is based on data compiled from Oka, *Kita Karafuto*, pp. 151–2; Lebedev, 'Ekonomika i kultura', pp. 188–90; and Moore, *Soviet Far Eastern Policy*, p. 141.

military ventures into Manchuria and Inner Mongolia forced the Russians to re-evaluate their accommodating posture in northern Sakhalin.

Japan's interest in northern Sakhalin's oil deepened perceptibly in the 1930s. Shortly after the Manchurian Incident (18 September 1931), the Japanese government began paying subsidies to the Kita Karafuto Oil Company. The Imperial Navy revived its active participation in company affairs. The newly elected company president, Admiral Sakonji, inaugurated his term in July 1935 by stressing the importance of northern Sakhalin's oil to national defence. Indeed, oil imports from northern Sakhalin amounted to nearly half Japan's total domestic production.

Starting in 1935, the Japanese government showed signs of reviving the question of northern Sakhalin's territorial sovereignty which had been a dormant issue since the Soviet-Japanese Convention of 1925. Foreign Minister Hirota Kōki heralded this new posture by publicly alluding to an alleged Soviet promise to sell northern Sakhalin to Japan. Moscow met this statement with a chilly silence. By injecting the territorial issue into the delicately poised oil-concession problem (already strained by sharpened competition for oil resources), the Japanese took the risk of transforming northern Sakhalin into a scene of serious hostilities.[36]

The Anti-Comintern Pact signed by Japan and Germany on 25 November 1936 quickened the deterioration of Soviet-Japanese relations in general and precipitated a change of Soviet policy in northern Sakhalin. Reacting sharply, the Russians began systematic efforts to dislodge the Japanese concessionaires from the island. The Sakhalin Oil Trust announced that all oil sales to the concessionaires would cease after 1937. Secondly, the Trust vetoed the pending Japanese requests to build additional storage tanks and underwater oil pipelines to facilitate the loading of tankers. Thirdly, the Soviet government inaugurated a campaign of protests over the mistreatment of Russian workers by the concessionaires.

[36] For Russo-Japanese disputes over Sakhalin oil (1932–7); 'Island of Bad Repute: Forthcoming Russo-Japanese Struggle Over Sakhalin Oil', *China Weekly Review*, LXX (6 Apr. 1935), 172–5; Baba Hideo, 'Japanese Oil Wells in North Sakhalin,' *Far Eastern Review*, XXXII (Feb. 1936), 79–80; Ōta, *Nichiro Karafuto gaikō sen*, pp. 324–8; Oka, *Kita Karafuto*, p. 81.

The Japanese retaliated with mass dismissals of Russian workers and brazenly began construction of the prohibited underwater pipeline. The Russians then arrested some Japanese workers on charges of spying. Waves of apprehension rippled through the Japanese community. Many among the 2,500 Japanese employees expressed the wish to return home. Oil production in the company's wells plummeted sharply. Then, in late 1937, the Russians turned their attention to the coal concessions.

Japan's two coal concessions at Dué and the Agnevo River were a disappointment to managers and investors alike. The Mitsubishi Mining Company activated only the Dué mines, as the lack of a suitable port and low home demand depressed production to between 100,000 and 130,000 metric tons annually. After 1935, however, a revival of domestic demand spurred output to 232,000 metric tons, and the company began to consider the activation of the Agnevo River pits. In September 1937 the Sakhalin Coal Trust suddenly ordered the liquidation of the Agnevo River concession. The Russians argued that the Mitsubishi Mining Company had broken the 1925 agreement by failing to mine coal, thereby creating unemployment among Soviet labourers and causing a loss of revenue to the Soviet government. In retaliation, the Mitsubishi Mining Company carried out drastic dismissals at Dué and cut output to 69,000 metric tons for 1937. The Coal Trust angrily demanded compensation. After months of rancorous exchanges, the Japanese conceded the loss of the Agnevo mines and virtually brought operations at the Dué mines to a shutdown. The Dué concession ceased operations altogether in 1939 but remained officially in Mitsubishi's hands until 1944.[37]

Soviet aid to China (with whom Japan was at war after July 1937) and frontier tension on the Amur River formed an ominous background to the acrimonious accusations that passed between Japan and the U.S.S.R. regarding Sakhalin during 1938. On January 22 Foreign Minister Hirota delivered a stern speech in the Diet warning the Russians that his government would not tolerate being 'pressured' out of northern Sakhalin. When Moscow demanded the closure of the Japanese consulate

[37] Oka, *Kita Karafuto*, pp. 261–5. Ōta, *Nichiro Karafuto gaikō sen*, pp. 333–4. Ilin, 'K likvidatsii Iaponskikh kontsessii', p. 70. *Nisso kōshō shi*, pp. 493–5.

in Okha, Hirota made a scathing attack (26 July) on the 'vicious oppression' of Japanese rights in northern Sakhalin. These exchanges took place against a background of a large-scale Soviet-Japanese military confrontation at Changkufeng on the Korean-Russian frontier during July and early August of 1938. The Changkufeng crisis had hardly passed before events in 1939 brought the two countries even closer to open hostilities.

Speeches in the Imperial Diet during early 1939 reflected a mounting militancy of Japanese views on the concession problem. In February several members of the Diet publicly urged the immediate military occupation of northern Sakhalin. Meanwhile, Russian restrictions had brought oil production almost to a standstill in the concessions.[38]

On 27 April Japan submitted a memorandum of grievances to the Soviet Foreign Ministry which remained unanswered until its rejection in July. During July Japan's ambassador in Moscow, Tōgō Shigenori, and the Vice-Commissar of Foreign Affairs, Lozovsky, engaged in a running exchange of recriminations. Tōgō protested Soviet obstructions, high-handed pressures, and accused the Russians of attempting to recruit Japanese employees in the northern Sakhalin oil concessions as spies. Lozovsky retorted with complaints of contraventions of the 1925 agreement such as violations of safety requirements, smuggling, failure to supply adequate housing to Russian workers, excessive employment of Japanese, the use of naval tankers, the non-payment of rent, and the import of rice for 'illicit distilleries'.[39]

Japan appeared to be contemplating the use of force when on 24 July Admiral Yonai Mitsumasa announced the departure of a naval squadron to northern Sakhalin 'in order to intimate clearly Japan's readiness to protect her vital oil and coal concessions'.[40] While the concession issue balanced on a fine edge between force and appeasement, a drama was being enacted at Nomonhan on the Outer Mongolia-Manchukuo frontier as

[38] Oka, *Kita Karafuto*, p. 265. Ōta, *Nichiro Karafuto gaikō sen*, pp. 337–8. *Nisso kōshō shi*, pp. 472–88.

[39] Moore, *Soviet Far Eastern Policy*, p. 114. *Soviet Documents on Foreign Policy*, III, 354–6. 'Russo-Japanese Oil Dispute', *Far Eastern Review*, XXXV (Aug. 1939), 308. *Nisso kōshō shi*, pp. 390–1.

[40] *China Weekly Review*, LXXXIX (29 July 1939), 271.

Soviet and Japanese forces savagely transformed a border incident into a dress rehearsal for World War II.

The Nazi-Soviet Non-Aggression Pact (23 August 1939) and the German attack on Poland (1 September 1939) launched Europe into World War II and simultaneously dampened the Soviet-Japanese confrontation in Manchukuo. The two countries nevertheless continued an abrasive rivalry in northern Sakhalin along the 50th parallel and in the oil concessions.

Starting in 1940, the Russians broadened the scope of their demands regarding Sakhalin. Hitherto, Soviet efforts had concentrated on the eviction of Japanese oil and coal concessions from the northern (Russian) half of the island. Gradually, there appeared signs that Moscow was seeking the expulsion of the Japanese from southern Sakhalin (Karafuto). From 11 to 15 March Soviet border guards directed sporadic gunfire at Japanese frontier posts at Anbetsu and Handenzawa. On 29 March the Commissar for Foreign Affairs, V. Molotov, suggested in a speech delivered at the Seventh Session of the Supreme Soviet that Russia would like to buy Karafuto. Later in 1940 Molotov articulated Russian attitudes more clearly by referring to Karafuto as a 'lost territory' of the U.S.S.R. (18 November). The following day, Molotov approached the Japanese ambassador in Moscow with the offer of a non-aggression pact in return for the Japanese abandonment of Karafuto. These irredentist expressions would have alarmed the Japanese more had it not been for the conclusion of the Soviet-Japanese Neutrality Pact on 13 April 1941.[41]

The Soviet-Japanese Neutrality Pact signed by the foreign ministers Matsuoka Yōsuke and Molotov was the occasion for an important agreement regarding northern Sakhalin's oil and coal concessions which was kept a secret until 1944. In effect Matsuoka gave the Soviet government a written pledge that the concessions would be liquidated before the end of the year.[42]

[41] For 1940 border incidents in Karafuto: *Nisso kōshō shi*, p. 560. For Molotov's speech of 29 March: Ōta, *Nichiro Karafuto gaikō sen*, p. 344. For Molotov's statement of 18 Nov.: Japan, Foreign Office, *Saghalien* (*Karafuto*) *Island* (Tokyo, 1949), p. 23. Molotov's proposal to the Japanese ambassador, Tatekawa Yoshitsugu, was related by Tatekawa to the American ambassador, Laurence Steinhardt, 'in strictest confidence', barely a week later: Steinhardt to Secretary of State, 28 Nov 1940, in U.S. Department of State, *Foreign Relations of the United States*, 1940, I (Washington, 1959), 676.

[42] Ilin, 'K likvidatsii Iaponskikh kontsessii', p. 70.

Matsuoka's dramatic abandonment of Japan's hitherto strongly maintained claims to northern Sakhalin's resources may have sprung from his assumption that Soviet neutrality in a Japanese move southwards against the oil-rich Dutch East Indies was worth the sacrifice. What Matsuoka failed to foresee in Moscow that April was the German attack on the Soviet Union on 22 June 1941.

The German invasion of the Soviet Union offered the Japanese an unexpected opportunity to exploit Russia's desperate involvement in the west. For a variety of reasons, of which only a few are known, Japan did not denounce the Neutrality Pact and join Hitler by starting a second front in the Soviet Far East. Some Japanese observers felt, however, that the time was ripe to 'solve' the Sakhalin problem by resorting to force.[43]

Although they stopped short of denouncing the Neutrality Pact, the Japanese took advantage of Russia's predicament by breaking Matsuoka's pledge regarding the liquidation of the concessions in northern Sakhalin. In October 1941 Tokyo pressed for an extension of drilling rights until 1943. The Russians had little choice but to accept, for in late 1941 the German invaders were literally at the gates of Moscow.

During 1943 and early 1944 a subtle shift altered the balance of power between Russia and Japan in north-east Asia. Soviet victories at Stalingrad, Kursk, and the headlong retreat of German forces from the Ukraine immensely strengthened Russia's posture in the Far East. Soviet triumphs in the west contrasted tellingly with Japanese reverses in New Guinea, Guadalcanal, and the Marshall Islands. The Japanese merchant marine suffered devastating losses from submarine warfare. In 1944 the country's need for oil reached a critical stage. Frantic efforts in Karafuto to distil gasoline from pine needles and oil from shale yielded meagre results. At this crucial moment in the war, Japan abandoned all the oil and coal concessions in northern Sakhalin.

Why did Japan give up these concessions when the country's war machine was faltering for lack of fuel? First, the extension of drilling rights extracted from the Russians in October of 1941 had expired in 1943. Secondly, in 1944 Japan could not afford

[43] Ōta, *Nichiro Karafuto gaikō sen*, p. 346. Oka, *Kita Karafuto*, pp. 268, 286, 288.

the loss of Soviet neutrality which might follow a refusal to give up the concessions. The Soviet Union was incapable of launching a successful offensive against Manchukuo in early 1944. However, far-sighted Japanese observers knew that Germany's capitulation, or even a stalemate on the western front, would allow the transfer of Russian forces to the Far East. Seeking to preserve Soviet neutrality, the Japanese elected to abandon a precious source of fuel.

The agreement to hand over the oil and coal concessions to the U.S.S.R. was signed in Moscow on 30 March 1944.[44] It provided for the annulment of all Japanese rights to exploit oil and coal resources in northern Sakhalin which were to have lasted until 1970. Furthermore, it stipulated the immediate transfer of all installations. In return the Russians paid the Japanese government five million rubles ($950,000) and promised to sell Japan 50,000 metric tons of crude oil from the Okha fields for five consecutive years 'from the time of the termination of the present war'.[45]

Most foreign commentators agreed that Japan's loss of the northern Sakhalin oil and coal concessions was a substantial gain for the Allied war effort.[46] In reality, the immediate loss may not have been as serious as contemporary observers estimated, for oil exports from northern Sakhalin to Japan remained at low levels after 1941. Nevertheless, as a potential source of fuel northern Sakhalin held considerable promise to Japan. In this sense, the demise of the concessions was a serious blow.

The Soviet-Japanese Protocol of March 1944 ended twenty-six years of Japanese involvement in northern Sakhalin. After two decades of compromises, the Russians could at last congratulate themselves on becoming absolute masters of northern Sakhalin's rich resources. Karafuto's turn followed in just over sixteen months.

May 1945 marked the twentieth anniversary of Soviet power in northern Sakhalin. May was also the month of Nazi Ger-

[44] Ilin, 'K likvidatsii Iaponskikh kontsessii', p. 73.

[45] For the relevant texts of the Soviet-Japanese Protocol signed on 30 Mar. 1944, see Appendix A.

[46] 'Sobering up in Sakhalin', *Time*, XLIII (10 Apr. 1944), 36. 'Last Concession', *Business Weekly* (8 Apr. 1944), 116–17. *New York Herald Tribune*, 2 Apr. 1944. *New York Times*, 9 Apr. 1944.

many's final defeat. The Allies turned their attention to the Far East where the last of the Axis powers continued a stubborn resistance. Karafuto's fate had been sealed even before the end of the war in Europe. At a meeting between Premier Josef Stalin, Prime Minister Winston Churchill, and President Franklin Delano Roosevelt at Yalta in February, the Soviet Union had promised to enter the war against Japan within two or three months after Germany's surrender. In return, the American and English heads of state promised the restoration of Russia's rights 'violated by the treacherous attack of Japan in 1904'. Among these rights was sovereignty over Karafuto (southern Sakhalin).

Unknown to the Japanese, massive forces were being deployed in the spring and early summer of 1945 for a blitzkrieg invasion of Manchukuo, Karafuto, and the Kurile Islands. In the last days of a world war, Karafuto, which had thus far escaped harm, stood unwittingly facing a cataclysm.

VIII

THE END OF KARAFUTO

THE first ten days of August 1945 witnessed historic events which signalled the end of World War II: America's unleashing of the atomic bomb on Hiroshima (6 August) and Nagasaki (9 August), and the Soviet declaration of war on Japan (8 August). By 11 August only three days remained until Japan's acceptance of the Potsdam Declaration and four days until Emperor Hirohito's broadcast announcing the end of hostilities. Up until 11 August Karafuto had avoided the scourges of war. It was an island of calm in a sea of chaos. Whereas the ordeal of the home islands had almost passed, Karafuto's was about to begin.

For sixteen days, Karafuto's inhabitants experienced a living hell of fire and death. The vast majority of the people there had not dreamed that such a remote island would become a battlefield. The American enemy was operating well to the south. True, the towns of Nemuro and Muroran on the island of Hokkaido had been bombed in July, and it was rumoured that American submarines were patrolling the La Pérouse Strait between Hokkaido and Karafuto. Yet very few, if any, realized that the source of imminent peril lay not to the south but to the north, from across the 50th parallel and the Tatary Strait.

On 11 August overwhelming Soviet forces smashed across the 50th parallel in one small part of a mammoth land, air, and sea offensive that engulfed Manchukuo, Inner Mongolia, North Korea, and the Kurile Islands. To Karafuto's 450,000 Japanese and Korean inhabitants this invasion came as a shock, progressed as a nightmare, and ended in detention, flight, or death. To the Russians, the invasion brought both important territorial gains and a sweet taste of revenge for the humiliating defeat of 1905.

The Soviet invasion of Karafuto in 1945 climaxed years of rivalry in Sakhalin in which force played a determining role. Force characterized the first Russo-Japanese confrontation in

Sakhalin in 1806. The overt or threatened use of force caused the Japanese to lose a foothold in Sakhalin in 1875 and in 1945. Two wars and a civil war impelled the Russians to recognize or countenance Japanese claims to Sakhalin in 1855, 1905, and 1925. Each country took advantage of the other's disabilities to extend its influence on the island.

The 1945 invasion had striking similarities with the Japanese attack on Sakhalin in 1905. Both were carried out during the final moments of the war when the enemy could offer little resistance. Both capitalized on the element of surprise. Both sought to nullify past treaties. The Japanese attack of 1905 was aimed at the Treaty of St. Petersburg (1875). The Russian attack of 1945 was directed against the Portsmouth Treaty (1905). Ironically, both campaigns had the approval of the President of the United States—Theodore Roosevelt in 1905 and Franklin Delano Roosevelt in 1945.

Both Russia and Japan have at one time possessed 'legal' claims to Sakhalin. The island first appeared in an international agreement in 1855 when the Treaty of Shimoda stipulated a state of 'joint occupation' by Russia and Japan.[1] Russia gained sovereignty over all Sakhalin in 1875 in exchange for the Kurile Islands which became Japanese territory (Treaty of St. Petersburg). The Portsmouth Treaty (1905) awarded southern Sakhalin (Karafuto) to Japan. In the Soviet-Japanese Convention of Peking (1925), the Soviet government implicitly recognized Japanese sovereignty in southern Sakhalin by re-affirming the validity of the Portsmouth Treaty. The Soviet Union again granted implicit recognition for Japan's sovereignty in Karafuto in Article I of the Soviet-Japanese Neutrality Pact (1941) which declared that both countries would respect each other's territorial integrity.[2]

Until 1945 both Japan and Russia used bilateral treaties between themselves to define Sakhalin's legal status. The Second World War introduced declarations of third powers and a secret treaty between the Soviet Union and third powers that legally decided Sakhalin's fate. The Cairo Declaration issued on 27 November 1943 by President Roosevelt, Generalissimo Chiang Kai-shek, and Prime Minister Churchill gave the first hint that

[1] For relevant texts of the Shimoda Treaty see Appendix A.
[2] See Appendix A.

third powers would preside over territorial transfers. The declaration stated that Japan was to be expelled from all areas 'which she has taken by violence and greed'.[3]

From 1942 until 1945 the prospect of the U.S.S.R. joining the war against Japan rarely ceased to intrigue the imagination of Allied planners. The first recorded expression of willingness came on the last night of the Foreign Ministers Conference in Moscow (30 October 1943) when Premier Stalin verbally affirmed to the American envoy Averell Harriman that he would consider entering the war against Japan after Germany's defeat. A few weeks later at the Teheran Conference, Stalin revealed that the price for Russia's participation in the Pacific War would be the retention of southern Sakhalin and the Kurile Islands. The Allies took no exception to these territorial demands. In October 1944 the U.S. Joint Chiefs of Staff actually recommended that the Russians occupy southern Sakhalin in order to safeguard sea communications between the Pacific Ocean and the Soviet Maritime Region.[4]

Russia transformed a verbal expression of intention into a secret written agreement by signing the Yalta Agreement on 11 February 1945. In return for a pledge to enter the war against Japan within two or three months after the termination of the European struggle, Russia was to be awarded (among other things) possession of southern Sakhalin. The justification for this territorial transfer was phrased in a manner which recalled the Cairo Declaration: '. . . former rights of Russia violated by the treacherous attack of Japan in 1904 shall be restored.'[5]

At Yalta, Russia negated the Portsmouth Treaty (1905), the Soviet-Japanese Convention of Peking (1925), and the Soviet-Japanese Neutrality Pact (1941), each of which had directly or indirectly confirmed Japan's sovereignty in southern Sakhalin. Neither Roosevelt nor Churchill seemed to have entertained doubts about Yalta's territorial transfers being a contravention of past Russo-Japanese treaties. Their approach was more pragmatic than legalistic, the overriding consideration being to win the war as quickly and with as little cost as possible. One

[3] U.S. Department of State, *Bulletin*, IX (4 Dec. 1943), 393.

[4] Herbert Feis, *Churchill, Roosevelt, Stalin* (Princeton, 1957), pp. 211, 255, 463, 511.

[5] See Appendix A for relevant texts of the Yalta Agreement.

American adviser did recommend that southern Sakhalin be placed under an international trusteeship with the U.S.S.R. as administrator. His words went unheeded, and probably unread. His recommendation was not included in the Yalta Briefing Book, and it is doubtful that it ever came to the attention of President Roosevelt or the Secretary of State, Edward R. Stettinius.[6]

In retrospect, the Yalta Agreement did not provide a conclusive legal justification for the Russian invasion of Karafuto. Nor can it be construed as a warrant for Soviet territorial sovereignty there. As the terms of the Yalta Agreement were secret, the Japanese had no knowledge that they included clauses regarding the transfer of Japanese territory. At the time of the agreement, Russia and Japan were bound by a Neutrality Pact which was not due to expire until 13 April 1946. Article II of this pact stated that if one of the contracting parties became involved in war with a third party or parties, 'the other contracting party will observe neutrality throughout the duration of the conflict'.[7]

That the Soviet Union denounced the Neutrality Pact on 9 April 1945 did not necessarily indicate that the validity of the pact ceased at that moment. Article III of the pact provided for denunciation only in relation to one party's rejection of the pact's *extension* for a further five years after 1946 which would have followed automatically in the absence of a denunciation. Moreover, Foreign Minister Molotov assured the Japanese that the denunciation of 9 April merely signified that the Neutrality Pact would expire naturally in 1946.[8]

Thus, when the Soviet Union denounced the pact in April 1945, the Japanese assumed that the Russians intended to maintain neutrality according to Article III until the pact's natural expiration in April 1946. No one imagined that the Yalta Agreement had already sealed Karafuto's fate. Nor did

[6] Hugh Borton, a noted scholar of Japanese history, prepared a memorandum for the Division of Territorial Studies in the Department of State. For the full text, see U.S. Department of State, *Foreign Relations of the United States, Diplomatic Papers, Publication 6199: the Conferences of Malta and Yalta, 1945* (Washington, 1955), pp. 385–8.

[7] For Article II of the Soviet-Japanese Neutrality Pact (13 Apr. 1941), see Appendix A.

[8] Yoshida Shien, *Hoppō ryōdo* (Tokyo, 1968, rev. ed.), p. 233.

the Japanese suspect that this territorial transfer would come about by a massive invasion heralded by only three days' notice. This lapse of acuity was uncharacteristic, for as past practitioners of surprise attacks in 1904 and 1941, the Japanese might have been expected to have foreseen a thrust from the north in the summer of 1945.

Soviet historians have explained the attack on Japan in 1945 as a response to Japanese 'aggression' and 'provocation' dating back to 1904.[9] Between 1941 and 1945, the Japanese allegedly committed serious acts of aggression against the U.S.S.R. They supplied 'vital strategic information' about Russia's defences to Nazi Germany. The Imperial Navy sank three Soviet merchant vessels and detained 178 others. The Kwantung Army held threatening manoeuvres in Manchukuo in late 1941 in preparation for an attack on the Soviet Far East. Large concentrations of Japanese troops in Manchukuo forced the Russians to deploy precious manpower in the Far East while a struggle in the west decided the nation's fate. Finally, the Japanese allegedly demonstrated warlike intentions in Karafuto by constructing 'offensive fortifications' along the 50th parallel using 'Chinese slave labour, American prisoners-of-war, and German technology'. These provocations aided the Nazi German enemy. As such, they were injurious to the Soviet Union. In view of these circumstances, the U.S.S.R. was justified in delivering the final blow which destroyed Japanese imperialism. Such is the Soviet view of the invasion.

The Invasion

Before August 1945 Karafuto was more of a forgotten backwater than a strategic outpost poised for attack. Admittedly, during 1939–41 the Japanese Army fortified the Handenzawa area and deployed crack forces along the 50th parallel. However, with the outbreak of the Pacific War in December 1941, Karafuto's best troops were gradually transferred to the Philippines, the South-West Pacific, and the Aleutians. After the annihilation of the Japanese garrison on the Aleutian island

[9] A. N. Ryzhkov, 'Sakhalinskaia oblast v gody velikoi otechestvennoi voiny Sovetskovo Soiuza: 1941–1945 gg.', *Sakhalinskaia oblast* (Iuzhno-Sakhalinsk, 1960), pp. 229–30. S. L. Lutskii, *Ostrov Sakhalin* (Moscow, 1946), p. 16. R. Ia. Malinovskii, *Kantōgun kaimetsu su* (Tokyo, 1968), p. 55. L. N. Kutakov, *Nisso gaikō kankei shi*, III (Tokyo, 1969), 614, 668.

of Attu (29 May 1943), first class troops were hastily withdrawn from the 50th parallel and were sent to the northern Kuriles. In 1944, frontier guards and military personnel posted along the 50th parallel were ordered to exert extreme caution not to arouse the Russians.[10]

At the beginning of 1945 the 88th Infantry Division, consisting of about 20,000 men, held responsibility for Karafuto's defence. The division fell under the command of the Northern Region Corps based in Sapporo, Hokkaido. The corps commander, Lieutenant General Higuchi Kiichirō, ordered the division deployed in a manner to meet the widely expected American amphibious landings along Karafuto's southern and eastern coasts. In April 1945, divisional headquarters were moved 200 miles southwards from Kami Shikuka to the Historical Museum in Toyohara so as to be better placed to direct the defensive preparations at Sakaehama and Jorei beaches for the anticipated American attack. To prepare for any contingency, the 125th Infantry Regiment (4,000 men) remained at Koton to guard the single road leading southwards from the Soviet frontier.[11]

The onset of summer brought disturbing indications that the Americans were approaching Karafuto. An American submarine shelled Kaihyōtō (Tiulenii Island) on 6 June. On 12 June a freighter was torpedoed in Aniwa Bay. Several ships exploded in Maoka harbour and in the La Pérouse Strait during the following few days. Fearing further loss of life, the authorities halted ferry service between Hokkaido and Karafuto on 7 July, thereby cutting off the island from the rest of Japan. On 17 July American commandos made a night landing from a submarine at Shirahama on the east coast of Karafuto and placed demolition charges on the main north-south rail line which later blew up a freight train.[12]

[10] *Nihon shūsen shi*, ed., Hayashi Shigeru, II (Tokyo, 1962), 212–14.

[11] Ibid., II, 212. Hokkaido chō, Ryōdo Fukki Hoppō Gyogyō Taisaku Honbu, *Karafuto shūsenshi nenpyō* (Sapporo, 1968), p. 27.

[12] *Karafuto shūsenshi nenpyō*, p. 28. Okuyama Ryō, *Aa Karafuto* (Sapporo, 1966), pp. 17–18. *New York Times*, 21 Aug. 1945, for the commando raid. Although the Americans did not invade Karafuto, some members of the U.S. Naval Reserve drew up a report in 1943 outlining the island's occupation and administration under American military authorities. U.S. Naval Reserve, Midshipman's School, 'Project Report, Karafuto (Japanese Sakhalin)', New York, 9 Sept. 1943. Typescript deposited in the East Asian Library, Columbia University, New York.

Meanwhile Karafuto's civilians were drafted into emergency defence work which consisted mainly of digging air raid shelters. Retired soldiers and young students formed a volunteer guard unit, but virtually no arms were available. August began with a dark premonition of impending disaster. Catastrophe came, but not from the expected source.

Although the civilian population in Karafuto were unaware of it, some officers in the 88th Division felt uneasy about unusual Russian movements along the border. Beginning in early June, all seven look-out stations along the 50th parallel reported considerable activity on the Soviet side of the frontier. Moreover, the Russians seemed to be going to considerable efforts to camouflage their operations. The chief of staff of the 88th Division, Suzuki Yasuo, sent repeated warnings during June and July to the Northern Corps headquarters at Sapporo (Hokkaido), but these urgent messages failed to elicit any response. Finally, on 3 August Suzuki notified Sapporo that a Soviet attack was imminent and at the same time put the 88th Division on full alert.[13]

On 8 August the Soviet Union informed the government of Japan that a state of war would exist between the two countries on the following day. This news was cabled to divisional headquarters at Toyohara at 7.00 a.m. on 9 August. Suzuki relayed the message to the commander of the 125th Infantry Regiment at Koton.

Koton was a derelict hamlet lying astride the single road connecting the Russo-Japanese frontier with population centres in southern Karafuto. It was also the northern railhead of the island's rail network. Surrounded by virgin forests, bracketed by mountain ranges to the west and the Poronai River to the east, Koton formed the axis of Karafuto's defence, through which the advancing Russian forces would have to pass. The commander of the 125th Regiment, Colonel Kobayashi, enjoyed only a few hours to digest and act upon the momentous message from divisional headquarters. He deployed the poorly armed 4,000 infantrymen across the road at Koton and at the Horomi Pass located slightly less than a mile to the north-west. The Japanese had not long to wait before a hail of artillery shells and a tidal wave of Soviet infantry bore down upon them.

[13] *Nihon shūsen shi*, II, 215.

After Germany's capitulation in May 1945, the Soviet Union began to transport massive forces across Siberia to deploy along the frontiers of Manchukuo and Karafuto for a final, overwhelming offensive against Japan. Altogether, three army groups or 'Fronts' and the Pacific Fleet, comprising over 1,600,000 men, 5,000 airplanes, 4,000 tanks, and hundreds of destroyers, submarines, and transports were massed in an awesome display of taut preparedness. Marshal of the Soviet Union A. M. Vasilevskii assumed over-all command of these Far Eastern armies from his headquarters at Khabarovsk. In the west, poised in Outer Mongolia, the Zabaikal Front commanded by Marshal R. Ia. Malinovskii waited to plunge into Manchukuo with motorized divisions. The First Far Eastern Front led by Marshal K. A. Meretskov was to cross the Ussuri River and push westward as the other jaw of this huge vice. The Second Far Eastern Front under General of the Army M. A. Purkaev was to attack southwards across the Amur River from Blagoveshchensk and Lazarevo while smaller detachments were assigned to occupy Karafuto and the Kurile Islands. Finally, the Soviet Pacific Fleet commanded by Admiral I. S. Iumashev had the task of mounting amphibious attacks against Karafuto (from Nikolaevsk and Sovetskaia Gavan), northern Korea (from Vladivostok), and the Kurile Islands (from Petropavlovsk in Kamchatka). The Soviet Far Eastern campaign required precise timing, perfect co-ordination, and remorseless speed to achieve its aim: the destruction of the Kwantung Army in Manchukuo, the occupation of Korea north of the 38th parallel, and the seizure of Karafuto and the Kurile Islands. The campaign was executed with admirable vigour, efficiency, and individual heroism. The much-vaunted Kwantung Army in Manchukuo crumbled under the three-sided blow. Japanese resistance in Karafuto, however, proved unexpectedly stubborn.[14]

The Soviet attack on Karafuto began on the morning of 9 August with an artillery bombardment of the Handenzawa frontier post. The frontier guards defended themselves in bunkers for three days until they were surrounded and wiped out by two battalions of Russian infantry.

[14] 'Kampaniia Sovetskikh vooruzhennykh sil na Dalnem Vostoke v 1945 g.: fakty i tsifry', *Voenno-istoricheskii zhurnal*, VIII (Aug. 1965), 64–73, is an excellent factual and statistical survey of the Far Eastern campaign of August 1945.

Having annihilated the first line of defence, the main 35,000-man assault force (an infantry division and several infantry, artillery, and tank brigades) under the command of General Baturov divided into three groups. The largest group (including motorized units) followed the road southwards. Two smaller forces advanced tortuously through the forests and swamps on either side of the road. The Soviet objective was to destroy Koton where the Japanese had grouped to block any advance to the south. To reach the Japanese rear behind Koton, the 179th Regiment overcame the natural obstacles of the Poronai swamps. Taking advantage of the mist and tall grasses, the right wing of the Russian advance (165th Regiment) made a wide arc around Koton's western flank thus completing the encirclement of the Japanese defences.[15]

On 13 August the encircling Soviet forces launched an assault on the Japanese positions at Koton. The entrenched defenders fought desperately and repulsed the Russians, inflicting heavy losses. Overcast skies and the swampy terrain prevented the attackers from making maximum use of their airpower and armour. Frontal infantry assaults on Koton continued during 14 August, forcing the Japanese to withdraw to a last redoubt—the Horomi Pass. The skies cleared on 15 August, permitting aerial bombardment.

On 17 August the Russians fought their way into the Horomi redoubt. Soviet sources report that one heroic Russian soldier, Sergeant A. Buiukly, threw himself into the embrasure of an enemy bunker, using his own body to absorb machine-gun bullets that would have decimated his comrades. There was fierce hand to hand fighting and the air was pierced by screams and curses. The Soviet commander personally leading the first assault wave, Colonel Smirnykh, fell riddled with enemy fire.[16]

Soviet sources stress that the 17 August attack smashed Japanese resistance, leaving only isolated pockets in the adjacent hills and swamps. The Japanese allegedly made several false

[15] A. Diakonov, 'V boiakh na iuzhnom Sakhaline', *Voenno-istoricheskii zhurnal*, VIII (Aug. 1965), 61. V. N. Bagrov, *Iuzhno-Sakhalinskaia i Kurilskaia operatsii, avgust 1945 goda* (Moscow, 1959), pp. 60–9. S. E. Zakharov, et. al., *Tikhookeansky flot* (Moscow, 1966), pp. 210–20. Malinovskii, *Kantō gun*, p. 224.

[16] Koton was renamed Pobedino after the war, in honour of the Soviet victory. Two settlements further south, Keton and Hoe, were renamed Smirnykh and Buiukly respectively, after the two heroes.

surrenders, raising a white flag until the Russians ceased firing and then resuming their own volleys. After a third such attempt, the Japanese tried to break out of their encircled positions but were again repulsed and forced to surrender, yielding some 3,300 prisoners.[17]

Japanese accounts of these events differ remarkably. Suzuki Yasuo, chief of staff of the 88th Division, recalled that the defences held firm at Horomi Pass notwithstanding repeated frontal charges. Moreover, the 125th Regiment's surrender on 18 August came only after a cable from Imperial Headquarters ordered an immediate ceasefire (the Emperor had announced the end of the war by radio on 15 August). Finally, Suzuki insisted that the Russians were actually in a more disadvantageous position than the Japanese, for the attackers had only occupied low-lying swamps while the defenders fought from entrenched positions on high ground.[18]

The Japanese version of the Koton-Horomi Pass episode seems to have a certain validity. It would have been uncharacteristic of them to surrender an intact regiment without some extraordinary circumstance such as a direct order from the Emperor. Witness the record of Attu, Saipan, Iwo Jima, and Okinawa, where whole units resisted until they were annihilated (the Japanese honoured this practice with the expression *gyokusai* or 'crushed jewel'). Even Marshal Malinovskii referred to the Japanese soldier as a *smertnik* (*smert* meaning death) to whom war was a form of suicide. Suzuki's account errs on the side of optimism, however, when it declares that the Japanese surrendered in a more advantageous position than their Russian encirclers. By 18 August the Soviet attackers had extricated themselves from the swamps and were pushing southwards.

The fall of Koton and the Horomi Pass left southern Karafuto nearly defenceless before the attacking Russians. Confusion beset other units of the 88th Division as reports of Japan's surrender reached them over the radio. Most of the remaining Japanese forces retreated towards Toyohara. A few diehards rejected the surrender reports as a hoax and disappeared into

[17] Diakonov, 'V boiakh na iuzhnom Sakhaline', p. 63. Bagrov, *Iuzhno-Sakhalinskaia i Kurilskaia operatisii*, p. 69. Ryzhkov, 'Sakhalinskaia oblast', pp. 234–6. Malinovskii, *Kantō gun*, pp. 226–7.

[18] *Nihon shūsen shi*, II, 216. *Karafuto shūsenshi nenpyō*, p. 31.

the central mountain range declaring their determination to resist at all costs.

The bitter struggle for Horomi Pass was only one aspect of Karafuto's collapse and death. Soviet frontier guards, backed up by artillery, stormed into the undefended fishing settlements of Anbetsu and Ennai that perched just below the 50th parallel on the west and east coasts respectively. Both villages went up in flames, deserted by terrified inhabitants seized by an irrepressible desire to flee southwards. During 11–13 August Soviet bombers hit the towns of Kami Shikuka, Nairo, Esutoru, and Tōrō, turning them into infernoes. Streams of refugees abandoned houses and property and besieged rail stations in a desperate attempt to escape Karafuto before it was too late.

Although ranking officers in the 88th Division and bureaucrats in the Karafuto Office had advance warning of the Russian attack, the ordinary citizen remained blissfully ignorant until his ordeal began. Incomprehensibly, no preparations for evacuation of the civilian population had been made before 9 August. On the contrary, harried refugees from bombed-out urban centres on the home islands were actually *arriving* in Karafuto in late 1944 and early 1945. When the island's 450,000 inhabitants learned of the Soviet invasion, a great many of the more astute knew that most of them were trapped.[19]

One day after the Soviet declaration of war (10 August), officials in the Karafuto Office, shipping companies, railroads, and some army officers met in Toyohara and decided to evacuate immediately women, children, the aged, and the disabled. Already the scramble for boats in Maoka, Honto, and Ōtomari was turning into a stampede. A ship, a rowboat, a raft, a canoe—nearly anything that would float commanded instant interest. In drawing up lists for those to be given preference to board available steamers, favouritism was shown to the dependants of officials and military officers. Some men did not hesitate to disguise themselves as women to claim a ticket to safety. Despite the confusion, evacuation proceeded rapidly. Nearly 30,000 managed to leave Karafuto during August, and a further 87,000 escaped the island before New Years Day 1946.

After 15 August the Japanese military position deteriorated

[19] Izumi Tomosaburō, *Soren Minami Karafuto* (Tokyo, 1952), p. 22. Okuyama, *Aa Karafuto*, pp. 18–21. *Nihon shūsen shi*, II, 210.

rapidly. Northern Region Corps headquarters in Sapporo cancelled a plan to send reinforcements to Karafuto on 15 August. On the following day, Soviet amphibious forces landed at Tōrō on the west coast just north of Esutoru, an important rail centre. During the next two days, the Russians fought their way into Esutoru. The Japanese resisted fiercely, and casualties were heavy on both sides. The bitterness of feeling was attested to by the execution of Esutoru's mayor and police chief and the suicide of over 170 civilians who preferred death to captivity.

On 18 August, Supreme Command Headquarters in Tokyo ordered all Japanese forces to cease fire and lay down their arms. Several groups in Karafuto either failed to receive the message, disbelieved it, or fought on in self-defence as the Russians kept up a remorseless bombardment from the air, the sea, and the land. Then, two tragedies struck the Japanese population: the destruction of Maoka (20 August) and the sinkings at Rūmoi (22 August).

Maoka was Karafuto's principal port. As such, it constituted a top priority objective both for Japanese attempting to escape the island and for Soviet forces seeking to isolate and destroy the enemy. On 20 August Soviet landing craft of the 113th Mixed Brigade approaching Maoka harbour met small arms fire from unidentified assailants entrenched along the shore. The Russians interpreted this incident as organized resistance and came in shooting, while offshore warships bombarded the town. Two Japanese peace envoys tried to approach the attackers but were cut down. Two more followed. They too were shot. Thus began Maoka's ordeal.[20]

Aerial bombardments ignited fires. Soldiers on both sides committed atrocities. Caught in between were the civilians who absorbed the highest casualties. More than one family, trapped by approaching Soviet soldiers, sought escape through suicide. Seven out of eight girl telephone operators at the Post Office killed themselves as the invaders forced their way into the building. In general, the Russians behaved as men will under chaotic circumstances. The hostilities that erupted over a

[20] Soviet versions of the Maoka espisode: Bagrov, *Iuzhno-Sakhalinskaia i Kuril-skaia operatsii*, pp. 75–109. Ryzhkov, 'Sakhalinskaia oblast', p. 237. Malinovskii, *Kantō gun*, pp. 227–9. Japanese versions: *Nihon shūsen shi*, II. 209–10. *Karafuto shūsen shi nenpyō*, p. 32. Okuyama, *Aa Karafuto*, pp. 21–3.

misunderstanding claimed over 1,000 dead. Three thousand refugees streamed overland towards Toyohara. Their mecca proved to be illusory. Those who survived the trek found the city occupied by Soviet troops who ordered them to return to Maoka.

The second major tragedy occurred on 22 August when two refugee ships from Karafuto were torpedoed by a submarine of unknown origin outside Rūmoi harbour in Hokkaido. In one stroke, over 1,700 lives were lost.

Maoka's example was repeated to a lesser extent in Esutoru, Shikuka, and Toyohara. Civilians who had heard the Emperor's broadcast on 15 August announcing the end of the war were terrified and confused by the relentless Soviet air and artillery bombardments that continued without pause during the following week. The few diehards who resisted the attackers only made it more difficult for the Russians to distinguish between dangerous and harmless Japanese. Roads, harbours, and railroad stations teemed with refugees seeking escape. Unless the Japanese officials in Karafuto could organize an orderly ceasefire, the killing would continue.

Finally, on 22 August Karafuto's civil and military leaders managed to contact General Baturov. The commander of the 88th Division, the governor of the island, and the chief of police met with a delegation of Soviet officers at Shirutoru to arrange a ceasefire. Governor Ōtsu Toshio was able to reach remnants of the Maoka garrison and succeeded in bringing about an end to resistance there. Meanwhile, perhaps unaware that a ceasefire had been reached, Soviet planes continued to bomb the Toyohara Railroad Station, inflicting heavy casualties among the crowds of refugees awaiting trains that never came.

By 23 August virtually all the fighting had come to a standstill. Japanese forces throughout the island laid down their arms. Soviet warships sealed the La Pérouse Strait in an attempt to prevent further flight to the home islands.

The Russians conducted a peaceful landing at Ōtomari on 24 August. The scene that day on the long pier must have been imprinted upon the memories of all the participants. Over 20,000 Japanese refugees swelled the port, turning the harbour area into a seething mass of humanity. Every available school, temple, and public hall was packed with teeming throngs of all ages. On the waterfront, crowds pushed and jostled to board freighters, packets, and fishing boats that could not hold a fraction of the supplicating applicants.

As the first Soviet landing craft appeared, a shudder of apprehension rippled through the crowd. To an observer on the approaching Russian vessels, this scene might have been interpreted as a vast welcoming reception. The bulging crowds ringing the harbour area could well be the vanguard of Karafuto's downtrodden masses craning their necks to greet the liberator. Indeed, the Soviet press reported such incidents.[21] But this was not a full-throated ovation or even a polite applause. It was a sigh of anguish mixed with resignation as the crowd expressed its realization that further evacuation was hopeless.

The commander of the Soviet forces participating in the invasion announced that units under his command had taken 18,320 prisoners in Karafuto. This was an understatement. If those who could not return to Japan were included, there were over 300,000 prisoners.

The Occupation

The Russians announced the official inauguration of Karafuto's occupation on 23 August. On 27 August a military government was established under General I. Alimov (Alimov was replaced in October by the commander of the 2nd Far Eastern Front, General of the Army M. A. Purkaev). Alimov promptly ordered the confiscation of all radio sets, arms, and automobiles, and the return of all citizens to their homes. He placed Governor Ōtsu under house arrest and assigned two guards to survey his activities.[22] He allowed Japanese to continue freely their economic activities but warned against disorders.

On 28 August the Russians banned publication of the local newspaper (*Karafuto nichinichi shimbun*). Rules were posted ordering red flags to be flown from the windows of all houses and red identification badges to be worn by all inhabitants. A 6.00 p.m. curfew was imposed. Inevitably the occupying troops indulged in a certain amount of pillage during the confusion of

[21] Ryzhkov, 'Sakhalinskaia oblast', p. 243. 'Russians Report Sakhalin Amity', *New York Times*, 1 Sept. 1945.

[22] The Russians so feared that Governor Ōtsu would commit suicide that the two guards accompanied him even to the toilet. Izumi, *Soren Minami Karafuto*, p. 45.

the first week, but by 1 September Karafuto had regained a modicum of stability.[23]

At first, it was not clear what the Russians intended to do with Karafuto. Rumours circulated among the populace that Moscow would create an 'autonomous Japanese region' similar to the Finnish Karelian district in European Russia. Eventually, however, Soviet leaders decided to repatriate Karafuto's Japanese, re-settle the area with immigrants from other parts of the U.S.S.R., and assimilate the former Japanese colony into an enlarged Soviet Sakhalin.

Between surrender and repatriation, Karafuto's Japanese either worked in Soviet Sakhalin (the name 'Karafuto' was abolished on 31 December 1945) or were sent to detention camps in Siberia. The vast majority of the civilian population remained in Sakhalin until repatriation. After being disarmed, the 88th Division was reorganized into labour battalions (minus the officers). Half of these were transported to labour camps in the Russian interior. The rest were marched to northern Sakhalin where they worked in the coal and forestry industries. Ranking bureaucrats, company managers, army and police officers, publishers, judges, and other community leaders were eventually incarcerated in camps on the continent, but not before serving as advisers to incoming Soviet administrative personnel.

After re-establishing order, the military regime addressed itself to the resurrection of Karafuto's civil administration and the reconstruction of the economy. To achieve these aims, the Soviet authorities needed the active co-operation of former Japanese officials. Hence, there were few arrests or trials during the first few months of the occupation. The Russians urged community leaders to continue their work as usual. The transition from capitalist Japanese Karafuto to communist Soviet Sakhalin took place gradually.

The Soviet military authorities made skilful use of former officials of the Karafuto Office. During the remainder of 1945 the Russians relied heavily on their expertise and their familiarty with the area. On 7 September a 'Soviet Southern Sakhalin People's Department' was created under the direction of Colonel Kriukov to handle civil affairs. Kriukov set up eleven regional

[23] *New York Times*, 14 Sept., 23 Sept. 1945. *Karafuto shūsenshi nenpyō*, p. 35.

offices throughout Karafuto, staffed by former Japanese officials and supervised by a Russian adviser. Former bureaucrats found themselves taking a census, administrating food rationing, issuing identification papers, or just sitting around their old offices wondering what would happen next. Kriukov shrewdly retained the *tonarigumi* (neighbourhood associations) as an instrument to control the population. Such Japanese that were drafted into service for the Soviet state often received salaries higher than Russian clerks working in the same office. During October, ex-governor Ōtsu discovered himself fulfilling the implausible role of guide to Colonel Kriukov on a familiarization tour of the island.[24]

The Russians also retained Japanese businessmen and technical experts to resuscitate Karafuto's paralysed economy. In late August occupation authorities angrily announced that 'militarists' had committed industrial sabotage by flooding mines, blowing up factories, blocking tunnels, and severing underwater cables. Executives from Ōji Paper, Hokkaido Colonial Bank, Karafuto Electric, and other companies were accordingly drafted into a 'production committee' which held responsibility for economic reconstruction. Responsibility, however, did not entail the retention of ownership. In October, Japanese corporate assets were confiscated and declared to be the property of the Soviet Union.[25]

Radical changes transformed Karafuto's educational institutions during the first three months of Soviet rule. In late September, primary and secondary schools were ordered to reopen with a new curriculum that omitted instruction in morals (*shūshin*), history, and geography. Teachers were told to introduce the fundamentals of Marxist-Leninist doctrine into the classroom. Soviet advisers attached to each school verified the implementation of these educational directives. Some of the Japanese instructors made the transition from Yamato nationalism to Soviet-style communism with surprisingly little difficulty. Wages for competent and accommodating teachers proved

[24] For a first-hand account of a former Karafuto Office official who served in the Soviet administration in Sakhalin during 1945–9, see Izumi, *Soren Minami Karafuto*, pp. 45–145.

[25] *Karafuto shūsenshi nenpyō*, p. 38. *Nihon shūsen shi*, II, 219. Ryzhkov, 'Sakhalinskaia oblast', p. 244.

munificent, and the Russian authorities accorded them flattering social respect.[26]

Soviet propaganda activity blossomed only days after the guns fell silent. Karafuto's Japanese were presented in the Soviet press as extending an ardent welcome to the 'liberating' Red Army. Even the island's 1,200 Ainu reportedly revelled in their successful escape from the 'yoke of Japanese imperialism'.[27] When Anastas Mikoyan, Vice-Chairman of the Council of Ministers of the U.S.S.R., arrived in southern Sakhalin on 30 September he was regaled with brassy pageantry. In October the Red Army inaugurated publication of a Japanese language newspaper called the *Shin seimei* or 'New Life'.[28] Edited by two former staff members of the defunct Japanese newspaper *Karafuto nichinichi shimbun* (Mutō Tatsuhiko and Yamauchi Manshirō), it carried Tass dispatches and *Pravda* editorials on the front page, and stories of local production wonders on the inside columns.

On 7 November Karafuto's Japanese enjoyed their first public celebrations of the November Revolution. They beheld the incongruous spectacle of ex-governor Ōtsu and other leading Japanese officials attending a Soviet military parade at the banner-bedecked grounds of the Toyohara Middle School.

For all the encouragement to assume Marxist trappings, Karafuto's Japanese clung to their cherished ways. A craze for baseball (always popular in the home islands) helped the younger inhabitants to forget their predicament. The traditional festival dances were held with undiminished enthusiasm and must have bemused not a few Russian spectators. Characteristically Japanese was the Russian language 'boom' occasioned by the reports (partially true) that Russian-speaking Japanese could acquire a comfortable supplementary income as interpreters.

Inevitably, there were arrests. At first, the Russians rounded up only police and army officers. The commander of the 88th Division and all officers of the rank of colonel or above were flown to unknown destinations in Siberia on 29 September.

[26] For the experiences of a Japanese middle-school teacher in occupied Karafuto, see Okuyama, *Aa Karafuto*, pp. 41–3.

[27] N. Yakovlev, 'A Visit to the Ainu in Southern Sakhalin', *The Asiatic Review*, New Series, XLIII (July 1947), 278.

[28] The East-West Center Library, University of Hawaii, contains an incomplete set of the *Shin seimei* on microfilm (1 Aug. 1946–2 Sept. 1948).

Karafuto Office bureaucrats, company executives, publishers, and judges continued to function in an advisory capacity to the Soviet authorities during the autumn. Suddenly on 6 December General Alimov made a flying inspection of former Japanese government officcs and held interrogations of ex-officials. Meanwhile, Soviet MVD (Ministry of Internal Affairs) squads conducted investigations of selected community leaders. The first series of civilian arrests came on 10 December. Detained were the department heads of the Karafuto Office, the chief editor of the former local newspaper, and executives of the Ōji Paper Company, the Karafuto Coal Company, the Karafuto Electric Company, the Karafuto Development Company, and the Hokkaido Colonial Bank. Ex-governor Ōtsu's turn came on 30 December. Arrested with him were the president of the Chamber of Commerce and the mayors of Toyohara and Honto.

This élite crowd numbering around forty found themselves categorized as 'war criminals' guilty of 'anti-Soviet activities'. On 12 January 1946, they boarded special planes which flew them to Khabarovsk, where they were transported to the Krasnaia Rechka Prison in the city's suburbs. While some of this group remained at Krasnaia Rechka for the next few years, others were shifted to camps ranging from Birakan in the former Jewish Autonomous Province (between Khabarovsk and Blagoveshchensk) to Erabuka near Kazan (450 miles east of Moscow). Those who survived detention returned to Japan during 1950 on repatriation ships which carried them from Nakhodka (near Vladivostok)to Maizuru, a port on Honshū's Japan Sea coast.[29]

During 1946 the Russification of southern Sakhalin made rapid strides. Yen currency lapsed on 1 March. Towns and villages assumed Russian names on 1 June. Toyohara became Iuzhno-Sakhalinsk, Maoka became Kholmsk, Honto became Nevelsk (after the Russian explorer Nevelskoi), Esutoru became Uglegorsk ('coal town'), and Shikuka became Poronaisk. Toyohara's main thoroughfare, Jinja dōri, was predictably renamed Karl Marx Street.[30]

[29] *Karafuto shūsenshi nenpyō*, p. 40–3, 75. For an account of life in the Krasnaia Rechka Prison by the former head of Karafuto's Imperial Rule Assistance Association (*Taisei yokusankai*): Sugawara Michitarō, *Akai rōgoku* (Sapporo, 1949).

[30] For a detailed list of place name changes, see Appendix B.

Karafuto's absorption into the U.S.S.R. took place in several stages. On 2 February 1946 the Preasidium of the Supreme Soviet ordered the creation of 'south Sakhalin *oblast*' and designated it a component of the Khabarovsk region. On 2 January 1947, the Soviet government created a 'Sakhalin *oblast*' which was administratively independent of Khabarovsk. The newly formed *oblast* consisted of northern Sakhalin, southern Sakhalin (formerly Japanese Karafuto), and the Kurile Islands. The final step of Karafuto's incorporation into the Soviet Union came on 25 February 1947 when the Soviet Constitution was amended to include southern Sakhalin as an integral territory of the Russian Soviet Federated Socialist Republic.

These territorial transfers interested the 300,000 Japanese in Karafuto far less than the prospect of repatriation. The hope of repatriation had possessed the thoughts of every man and woman since August 1945. Organizations sprang up in Hakodate and Tokyo to receive refugees and to petition the occupation authorities in Japan to intervene on their behalf in Moscow. Large rallies convened in Tokyo's Hibiya Park to urge the repatriation of all Japanese held in Russian-occupied territories.[31]

Over a year passed after the invasion before the Russians indicated that they would consent to repatriation. On 15 October 1946 Soviet authorities in southern Sakhalin gave notice that 30,000 Japanese would be allowed to return to their homeland after November. From December 1946 until December 1948 nearly 250,000 Japanese were ferried from Maoka to Hakodate. During the busy summer months, up to 3,000 left Maoka daily on two dilapidated steamers overflowing with a grey mass of material and human baggage.

The Japanese settlers left southern Sakhalin with a mixture of relief, regret, and anticipation. Many had spent years creating a home in the wilderness only to lose all in a few terrible weeks. Stunned, they stood on the decks of refugee ships, looking weary and aged. Sometimes, the steamers carried a load con-

[31] 2,726,353 Japanese military and civilian personnel were captured by Russian forces in Manchukuo, northern Korea, the Kwantung Territory, Karafuto, and the Kurile Islands. U.S. Army, Military History Section, Headquarters, Armed Forces, Far East, *Japanese Monograph No. 155* (n.p., 1952), p. 18.

sisting almost entirely of corpses. The *Hakuryū maru* entered Hakodate on 23 July 1949 with 1,625 passengers of whom 1,554 were dead, killed during the fighting in 1945 or dead from natural causes.

By 1950 most of the enlisted soldiers had been repatriated from Siberia or Central Asia. A repatriation office in Hakodate announced on 23 September 1949 that only 1,900 Japanese still remained on what had been Karafuto. From December 1946 until New Years Day 1950, 218 ships brought back 312,452 former Karafuto residents.[32]

The Soviet news agency Tass declared on 22 April 1950 that the repatriation of Japanese from occupied areas had been completed, but the announcement failed to satisfy the Japanese government, refugee organizations, or friends and relatives of the missing. Japan's Foreign Office claimed in March 1951 that over 320,000 Japanese remained unaccounted for in Russian hands. The issue dogged Soviet-Japanese relations throughout the 1950s.

In August 1957 a trickle of former residents of Karafuto began reaching Japan. Repatriation ships arrived intermittently during 1957–9, carrying mainly Koreans with Japanese wives who had opted to leave Soviet Sakhalin. Some 200 Chinese also left the island. They had lived there under Japanese rule working mainly as merchants, craftsmen, and small retailers. After application to the Russian authorities, some of them succeeded in gaining permission to re-settle in Japan.[33]

Koreans constituted the largest single minority group in Japanese Karafuto. During the 1930s, the Japanese had brought in Korean labourers to work in the coal-mines, pulp factories, and fisheries. By 1941, Karafuto's Korean population had reached 150,000. About 100,000 of these were transferred to mainland Japan during the Pacific War to fill critical manpower shortages in the mining industry. At the end of the war, some 43,000 remained on the island. From 1910 to 1945, when Korea was a Japanese colony, its inhabitants suffered not only from a callous colonial rule but from humiliating discrimination by Japanese in general. Karafuto was no exception. Living and

[32] *Karafuto shūsenshi nenpyō*, p. 74.

[33] Yoshida Shien, *Hoppō ryōdo* (Tokyo, 1968 rev. ed.), pp. 284–6. *Karafuto shūsenshi nenpyō*, pp. 76–80. *New York Times*, 20 Feb. 1946; 18 Jan. 1948.

working conditions for Koreans fell far below those for Japanese. As victims of Japanese mistreatment, Karafuto's Koreans understandably expected favoured treatment from the Russian 'liberator'.[34]

The disposition of the Korean minority challenged Russian ingenuity. Unfortunately, the Russian method of dealing with the problem, while well intentioned, aroused considerable bitterness. Like the Japanese, Karafuto's Koreans hoped fervently for immediate repatriation. Local and international circumstances prevented their hope from being realized. A majority of Karafuto's Koreans came from southern Korea which was under American military occupation. Furthermore, Korean labour played a vital role in the coal, pulp, and fishing industries which the Soviet authorities wanted continued at all costs. Finally, the lack of available ships made repatriation even to northern Korea unthinkable in 1945.

After a brief 'honeymoon', Russo-Korean relations in southern Sakhalin began to show signs of strain. The critical food and clothing shortages prevented the Russians from improving Korean living standards. Ordered to continue the arduous work under degrading conditions, many Koreans had a feeling of disillusion. Strikes provoked repression. Cadres of Russian-born Koreans arrived from the mainland to conduct propaganda activities. Political surveillance tightened. As the 1940s drew to a close, factions formed around those sympathetic to the rival northern and southern regimes on each side of the 38th parallel on the Korean peninsula.

The repatriation of Japanese residents in 1947–8 aggravated Russo-Korean and Korean-Japanese relations in southern Sakhalin. Many Koreans interpreted the repatriation of Japanese as a Russian betrayal. The good luck of their former oppressors deepened Korean antagonism towards the Japanese. The Japanese were responsible for the Koreans being in Sakhalin; therefore, it was natural for the Koreans to resent both their early repatriation and their apparent indifference to the Korean predicament.

[34] Material on Sakhalin's Korean minority in this and following paragraphs is taken from: Chō Zai Jutsu, *Gokumontō* (Tokyo, 1966), pp. 3, 18–20, 24. Robert Trumbull, 'Sakhalin: a Scene of Korean Strife', *New York Times*, 21 Oct. 1957. V. Ia. Kantorovich, *Sakhalinskie tetradi* (Moscow, 1965), p. 251.

The outbreak of the Korean War (25 June 1950) intensified the rivalry between 'northern' and 'southern' factions inside Sakhalin. Those accepting North Korean citizenship received favoured treatment in education, housing, and wages. Those who refused North Korean or Soviet citizenship were classified as 'stateless' and became the objects of derision and intimidation. Tension between the two factions occasionally erupted into open clashes such as the disturbances at the Makarov pulp factory in September 1954 and the violent strikes in Iuzhno-Sakhalinsk in October 1957. Although Soviet censorship prevents detailed information from reaching the outside world, there is no doubt but that the disposition of Sakhalin's Korean minority persists as a serious social problem.

How many Japanese are there in Sakhalin at present? None are mentioned in the 1967 Soviet census of the *oblast*, but the Zenkoku Karafuto Renmei (National Karafuto League) estimated in 1969 that the figure stood at about 200.[35] A Japanese journalist visiting Iuzhno-Sakhalinsk in 1964 met some compatriots who had married Russian nationals and declined repatriation.[36] Lacking precise evidence and access to the island, one can only conjecture that scattered around Sakhalin are a few hundred middle-aged Japanese who for various reasons made the choice to remain as Soviet citizens.

With the passing of time, Japanese memories of Karafuto have undoubtedly dimmed. While Sakhalin is geographically close, access to it hardly exists because of political barriers. For their part, the Russians have played down the role of Japan in Sakhalin's past and are content to allow any physical vestiges to decay. A few structures have survived the years of change: some schools, a ski resort, a museum, several pulp factories, a rail network, some stolid bank architecture, an overgrown public garden, and a run-down temple converted into a movie theatre.

Perhaps the most lasting heritage left by the Japanese in Sakhalin has been their language. It is reported that Japanese is frequently heard in Iuzhno-Sakhalinsk, spoken not only by Koreans but by Russians. One Russian official told a visiting journalist that thirty-five per cent of the population of the

[35] Zenkoku Karafuto Renmei, ed., *Minami Karafuto o wasureru na* (Tokyo, 1969), p. 14.

[36] Miyatake Shōzō, *Shiberia* (Tokyo, 1965), pp. 203–4.

island could use the Japanese tongue. Furthermore, many listened to radio broadcasts from Hokkaido for entertainment.[37]

Before the Second World War, the town of Wakkanai in northern Hokkaido served as a bustling port and railhead for travellers to and from Karafuto, barely visible on clear days across the La Pérouse Strait. Today, Wakkanai is but a shell of its former self. Above the decaying wharf there is a large wooden arch surmounted by a placard with faded characters which read: 'Welcome'. Before 1945, ferries departed from this wharf for Karafuto, but service has not resumed since the end of the war. Only this melancholy message testifies to what once existed across the straits—a home for nearly 500,000 Japanese.

[37] Miyatake Shōzō, *Shiberia,* (Tokyo 1965), p. 206.

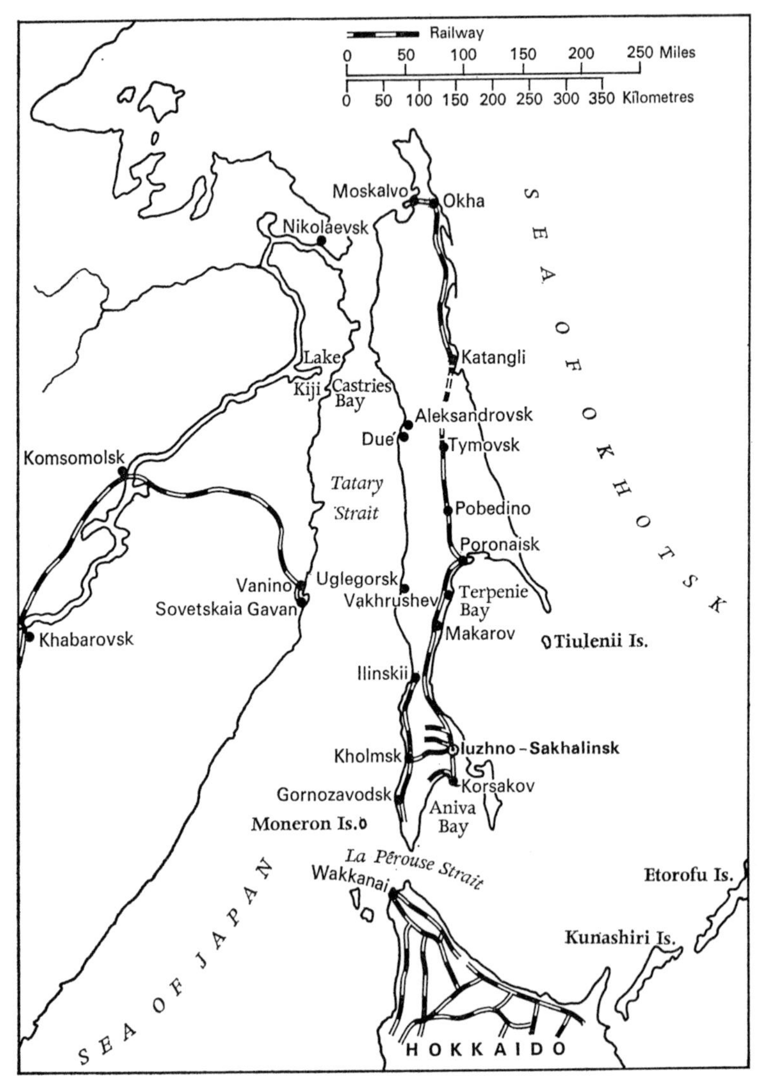

MAP VI. Soviet Sakhalin (1970)

IX

SAKHALIN SINCE 1945

'Don't fear Sakhalin, Svetlana.'

L. M. DEMIN (1965)

Sakhalin in International Relations

SINCE February 1947 the island of Sakhalin has been an integral part of the Soviet Union; 640,000 Russians, Ukrainians, Tatars, Mordvinians, Belorussians, Koreans, and Kazakhs populate the island. Under the guidance of the Communist Party, Sakhalin has been economically and administratively integrated with the Soviet Far East. It has developed into a strong, productive bastion of Soviet power in Northeast Asia. Nevertheless, the Russian claim to sovereignty in Sakhalin has not gone uncontested.

At present, the Japanese government makes no direct territorial claims to southern Sakhalin but maintains that its status has yet to be determined by international law.[1] By refusing to recognize Soviet sovereignty in southern Sakhalin, the Japanese appear to be trying to improve their bargaining position in relation to other territorial issues, namely the Japanese claims to Russian-occupied Kunashiri and Etorofu, the two southernmost Kurile Islands.

To cast doubt upon Russia's claim to sovereignty in Sakhalin, the Japanese cite their own prior exploration, the Portsmouth Treaty (1905) which gave them title to Karafuto, the Convention of Peking (1925) in which the Soviet government confirmed the validity of Portsmouth, and the Soviet-Japanese Neutrality Pact (1941) which contained a pledge to respect each other's territorial integrity. Furthermore, the Japanese dismiss the secret clauses of the Yalta Agreement (1945) awarding southern Sakhalin to Russia, insisting that Japan was not a party to the agreement nor was she even informed of its contents. In answer

[1] Japan, Ministry of Foreign Affairs, Public Information Bureau, *The Northern Territorial Issue* (Tokyo, 1968), p. 5.

to the argument that Japan abandoned Karafuto at the San Francisco Peace Treaty (1951), Tokyo asserts that the said treaty contained no provision as to whom Japan had abandoned her rights. Moreover, the Japanese hold that the Russian refusal to sign the San Francisco Treaty nullifies any Soviet prerogative to benefit by it.

The above legalistic reservations concerning Soviet sovereignty in southern Sakhalin appear to be bargaining points to be used in negotiations over other issues. However nostalgic Japanese might be about the loss of Karafuto, few entertain serious hopes of regaining it.[2] Irredentism is dangerously outdated in a nuclear age.

While realistic Japanese have privately renounced all hope of recovering southern Sakhalin, the island's strategic location has made it a scene of cold war tension. As early as 16 August 1945, when Soviet forces were moving into Karafuto, hints of Soviet-American friction appeared when Premier Stalin cabled President Truman that he hoped to occupy northern Hokkaido.[3] Perceiving the Russian intent to gain control of the La Pérouse Strait and acquire a foothold on Japan itself, Truman deftly declined the proposal. With Soviet power blocked from further expansion, southern Sakhalin and the Kurile Islands became Russia's closest outposts to Japan. Its strategic location dictated that Sakhalin be turned into an armed base. The La Pérouse Strait marked a sensitive contact point between not only the Russians and the Japanese but between the Russians and the Americans.

The official American attitude towards the Soviet acquisition of southern Sakhalin has been inconsistent and even oppor-

[2] With the return of Okinawa scheduled for 1972, there has been a revival of public interest in the northern territories occupied by the U.S.S.R. in 1945. While the position of the Japanese government remains unchanged, private individuals and organizations have begun to raise claims to southern Sakhalin. See Hanami Tatsuji, 'Hoppō zen ryōdo ga Nihon ryō da', *Seikai ōrai*, XXXVI (Jan. 1970), 36, 38. Zenkoku Karafuto Renmei, ed., *Minami Karafuto o wasureru na* (Tokyo, 1969), pp. 20–21. Minami Karafuto Henkan Kisei Dōmei, 'Zenshin no shuisho', (Tokyo, 1 Apr. 1969), a proclamation calling for national support in pressing for the return of southern Sakhalin.

[3] Personal and Secret from Premier J. V. Stalin to the President, H. Truman, 16 Aug. 1945. Document no. 363 in U.S.S.R., Ministry of Foreign Affairs, *Correspondence of the Council of Ministers of the U.S.S.R. and the Presidents of the U.S.A. and the Prime Ministers of Great Britain During the Great Patriotic War of* 1941–45, II (Moscow, 1957), 266.

tunist. President Franklin D. Roosevelt sanctioned the Soviet territorial gains at Yalta in 1945, yet ten years later the Secretary of State John Foster Dulles virtually denied their validity. Cold war rivalry brought about this reversal from support of Russian claims to qualified championship of the Japanese position.

Hardly had the Second World War ended when doubts arose regarding the relationship of the Yalta Agreement and recent Soviet territorial gains in the Far East. Russia's proclamation of sovereignty in southern Sakhalin and the Kurile Islands evoked reactions of surprise in Great Britain and the United States. Although there was no outright opposition, many observers felt that territorial transfers should be settled by peace conferences or by the United Nations. American officials limited themselves to cryptic statements. On 4 September 1945, Secretary of State James Byrnes announced that his government 'tacitly agreed' with the Russian occupation of southern Sakhalin and the Kurile Islands and that a transfer of territory had been 'discussed' at Yalta. He declined to clarify or amplify the relationship of Yalta to the Soviet Union's new Far Eastern acquisitions.[4]

Rumours about Yalta's secret clauses grew rife during the end of 1945, and Byrnes finally confirmed in February 1946 what many had suspected—that the United States had sanctioned Russian territorial gains in return for her participation in the war against Japan within two or three months after Germany's defeat. Angry reactions erupted ranging from accusations that President Roosevelt had violated the Atlantic Charter to a proposal that the United States should annex Okinawa in retaliation.[5]

The Japanese government voiced its first objections to the Yalta Agreement late in 1949. The Foreign Affairs Committee in the Diet's House of Representatives asserted that Yalta was not binding on Japan.[6] Japan's claim to southern Sakhalin, the committee concluded, could not be extinguished by third party agreements. A significant section of Japan's political leaders

[4] *New York Times*, 3 Sept. 1945, on world reactions to Russian territorial gains. For the Byrnes announcement, *New York Times*, 5 Sept. 1945.

[5] The proposal regarding an American annexation of Okinawa was made by Virginia's Senator Harry F. Byrd. *Time*, 11 Feb. 1946, p. 8. *New York Times*, 12 Feb. 1946.

[6] *New York Times*, 23 Dec. 1949.

continued to advance such arguments in the early 1950s. Since 1956, the Japanese have paid less attention to southern Sakhalin in favour of focusing on their territorial claims to some small islands off the east coast of Hokkaido (Shikotan and the Habomai Islands) and the two southern Kurile Islands, Kunashiri and Etorofu.

A change in the official American attitude towards the Soviet acquisition of southern Sakhalin first became apparent in 1951 during preparations for the Peace Treaty which was to be signed at San Francisco, ending the state of war between Japan and the former Allied Powers. Engaged in a global cold war rivalry, the United States and the Soviet Union differed over the contents of this treaty. When the Soviet representative intimated that his government would not sign a treaty that sanctioned American military bases in Japan, John Foster Dulles (then a high-ranking adviser in the State Department) declared that Moscow's non-participation in the treaty would invalidate the Russian claim to sovereignty in southern Sakhalin.[7]

At the San Francisco Conference in September the Russian Foreign Minister Andrei Gromyko presented an amended draft of the peace treaty in which the territorial clause read that Japan renounced all her rights in southern Sakhalin in favour of the Soviet Union. The Russian draft was rejected on 7 September. In its place, the Peace Treaty signed on 8 September by all members of the conference except Russia, India, and Burma simply stipulated that Japan renounced her claim to southern Sakhalin. Who should inherit these rights was left unsaid. When asked about the Peace Treaty's relationship to the Yalta Agreement with respect to southern Sakhalin and the Kuriles, Dulles answered that the Peace Treaty did not confirm Yalta but reversed it, leaving Russian ownership of the islands open to future settlement.[8]

Since 1952 American policy on the status of southern Sakhalin has remained static. The Eisenhower administration was not prepared to denounce Yalta's secret clauses, although some sections of the Republican Party reportedly advocated this

[7] Ibid., 1 Mar. 1951.

[8] For the Gromyko amendment: Nanpō Dōho Engo Kai, *Hoppō ryōdo no chi'i* (Tokyo, 1962), p. 597. For the Dulles statement: *New York Times*, 22 Jan. 1952.

measure.[9] On the other hand, the government viewed with displeasure any hints that the Japanese might abandon their territorial claims against Russia.

In August 1956, when Sovict-Japanese negotiations regarding the normalization of relations brought forth some optimistic Japanese talk of 'compromise' on the territorial issues, Dulles warned at a news conference that if Japan sacrificed her claims to southern Sakhalin and the Kuriles to the U.S.S.R., the United States might revise its attitude towards Okinawa and the Ogasawara (Bonin) Islands.[10] Concerned about the unfavourable repercussions of this remark in Japan, the State Department issued an *aide memoire* on 7 September 1956 in which the Yalta Agreement was defined as '. . . simply a statement of common purposes by the then heads of the participating powers, and not as a final determination by those powers or of any legal effect in transferring territories'. While supporting Japan's territorial claims in the Kurile Islands (but not in southern Sakhalin), the Americans cautioned Japan against transferring sovereignty of any of the northern territories to the Soviet Union. After 1956 the American government continued to follow the vague formula first enunciated at San Francisco in 1951: that the question of Japan's former territories must be determined by 'international solvents' in the future.[11]

Between 1949, when the Japanese first officially denounced the Yalta Agreement, and 1956, when the Soviet-Japanese Peace Declaration was signed, there occurred a subtle shift in the scope of Japan's territorial claims. As late as 1955 successive government spokesmen included southern Sakhalin in the category of territories that Japan sought to regain from the U.S.S.R. In May and June of 1955 Prime Minister Hatoyama Ichirō optimistically envisaged the recovery of southern Sakhalin in return for a promise of Japanese neutrality and the withdrawal of American military bases from Japan.[12] In a publication issued by the Foreign Ministry's Public Information Bureau in August, southern Sakhalin's historical links and

[9] William S. White, 'Republican Split on Yalta', *New York Times*, 17 Feb. 1953.

[10] James W. Morley, 'Soviet-Japanese Peace Declaration', *Political Science Quarterly*, LXXII (Sept. 1957), 378.

[11] *Hoppō ryōdo no chi'i*, p. 599.

[12] *New York Times*, 27 May, 7 June 1955.

economic importance to Japan received considerable attention.[13]

These hopes were crushed by the adamant attitude of the Soviet Union at the London and Moscow talks which stretched from June 1955 to October 1956. The Russians flatly refused to discuss the question of southern Sakhalin and stated that only the offshore islands of Habomai and Shikotan might be handed over at the conclusion of a peace treaty between the two countries.

After the conclusion of the Soviet-Japanese Peace Declaration (19 October 1956), which deferred the territorial issue to later negotiation, southern Sakhalin suddenly ceased to be mentioned in Japanese arguments as a territorial claim. Henceforth, the government concentrated its attention on the return of Kunashiri and Etorofu (the two southernmost Kurile Islands). A 1968 Japanese government publication concerning the 'northern territories' problem advanced no claim to southern Sakhalin. Instead, it characterized southern Sakhalin's status as 'yet to be determined by international law'.[14]

What had led Tokyo to play down the claims to southern Sakhalin? Dominant figures in the ruling Liberal Democratic Party may have seen a more realistic chance of success by advancing a limited, well-documented claim, encompassing only the two southernmost Kurile Islands. Japan's historical rights in the southern Kuriles are stronger than those in southern Sakhalin. Kunashiri and Etorofu have been part of Japan since 1798. Unlike southern Sakhalin, they have never been ruled by Russia (until 1945). While Japan seized southern Sakhalin in war (1905), Kunashiri and Etorofu hardly fit the Cairo Declaration's definition of 'territories seized by violence and greed' or Yalta's 'former rights of Russia violated by the treacherous attack of Japan in 1904'. Russia recognized Japan's sovereignty to Kunashiri and Etorofu in the Treaty of Shimoda (1855). Finally, the Japanese have used the legalistic argument that Kunashiri and Etorofu, as defined in the Treaty of Shimoda and in the Treaty of St. Petersburg (1875), are *not* part of the

[13] Japan, Ministry of Foreign Affairs, Public Information Bureau, *The Northern Islands* (Tokyo, 1955).

[14] *The Northern Territorial Issue*, p. 5. Yoshida Shien, *Hoppō ryōdo* (Tokyo, 1968 rev. ed.), p. 136.

Kurile Islands. It follows that Japan's abandonment of all rights in the 'Kurile Islands' at San Francisco (1951) does not apply to Kunashiri and Etorofu.[15]

Although the Japanese government makes no outright territorial claim to southern Sakhalin, various private individuals and organizations in Japan continue to call for the reversion of Karafuto. Perhaps the most strident spokesman for Sakhalin irredentism is the right-wing extremist Akao Bin. While Akao commands no great following, his inflammatory posters seem to decorate every other telegraph pole in Tokyo.

Another agency which keeps the issue of southern Sakhalin alive is the Zenkoku Karafuto Renmei (National Karafuto League). Established in 1949 to extend economic assistance to former Karafuto residents, the league is now actively promoting Japanese claims to southern Sakhalin. The league co-operates closely with the Hokkaido prefectural government in collecting documents on Karafuto's past; moreover, it issues pamphlets and manifestoes under its own name or under the name of a subsidiary organization called the Minami Karafuto Henkan Kisei Dōmei (Alliance for the Realization of the Return of southern Sakhalin).[16] The league's current director, Ogata Masakuni (formerly Karafuto's chief of police), asserts that Japan will not rest until southern Sakhalin has been regained, even if it takes 500 years.[17]

Assorted individuals also consider southern Sakhalin to be Japanese territory. Former residents naturally phrase their arguments like men who have been driven from their homes. A professor in the former Karafuto Normal School (Toyohara), Nishizuru Sadayoshi, has appealed for an international conference to decide southern Sakhalin's status.[18] His words are echoed by thousands of other ex-residents now living in Hokkaido. A number of conservative intellectuals emphasize strategic and economic factors in urging a more forceful government policy on the still unsolved problem of southern Sakhalin.[19]

[15] *The Northern Territorial Issue*, p. 7. [16] See note no. 2.

[17] Ogata Masakuni, personal interview, Tokyo, 13 Jan. 1970, with the author.

[18] Nishizuru Sadayoshi, 'Shijitsu ni motozuku hoppō ryōdo mondai ni tsuite', Unpublished MS (n.d.), p. 9.

[19] Hanami, 'Hoppō zen ryōdo ga Nihon ryō da', pp. 36–41. Morizawa Masateru, 'Chishima minami Karafuto mondai no shōten', *Chūō Kōron* (Aug. 1955), 158–68.

By acquiring southern Sakhalin and the Kurile Islands, the Soviet Union strengthened immensely its posture on the Pacific Ocean. Before 1945, the naval bases at Vladivostok and Sovetskaia Gavan were 'trapped' in the Sea of Japan by virtue of Japanese control of all the exits to the Pacific: the Tsushima, Tsugaru, La Pérouse, and Kurile straits. Possession of southern Sakhalin has opened the Tatary and La Pérouse straits to Soviet naval vessels. The island's proximity to Hokkaido makes it ideal not only as an observation point but also as a potential staging area for the occupation of northern Japan. Korsakov (formerly Ōtomari) in Aniwa Bay has become an important naval supply base with a squadron of modern destroyers stationed there. Southern Sakhalin is dotted with jet fighter and seaplane bases.[20]

Unvisited by foreigners until the mid-1960s, Sakhalin has eluded outside scrutiny and has even assumed a touch of the mystery associated with it in the end of the nineteenth century. Reports of varying reliability have occasionally reached the non-communist world. In early 1946, the Nationalist Chinese government in Chungking claimed that Russia was forming military units from Japanese prisoners of war in Sakhalin.[21] Chinese refugees from Sakhalin reaching Japan in 1948 brought reports (probably exaggerated) of the construction of a huge submarine base in Korsakov and of the deployment of 400,000 Soviet ground troops on the island.[22] In October, 1952, after an American B-29 had been shot down over Habomai Island (off Hokkaido's east coast), there were speculations of a military build-up on Sakhalin and rumours that an underwater tunnel had been dug to join the island with the continent.[23]

Just before the Soviet-Japanese Peace Declaration was signed in October 1956, the journalist Robert Trumbull wrote a series of articles on Sakhalin in which he declared that the Russians had 'converted the island into a vast military complex'.[24] He

20 Andrew J. Grajdanzev, 'Soviet Position in the Far East', *Far Eastern Survey*, XIV (21 Nov. 1945), 334–7. Ohmae Toshikazu, 'The Kuriles and Sakhalin', in M. G. Saunders, ed., *The Soviet Navy* (New York, 1958), pp. 277, 282–3.

21 *New York Times*, 20 Feb. 1946

22 Ibid., 18 Jan. 1948.

23 Ibid., 28 Oct. 1952.

24 Robert Trumbull, '2 Tips of Sakhalin Threat to Japan', *New York Times*, 18 Sept. 1956. Other Trumbull articles on Sakhalin: *New York Times*, 11, 13, 19, 23 Sept. 1956.

reported that there were thirty airfields on the island which accommodated enough fighters to give the Russians a fifteen to one superiority in tactical air strength over American and Japanese forces stationed on Hokkaido. To counter this, the Americans have built a radar station at Wakkanai (on the northern tip of Hokkaido facing Sakhalin) which monitors Russian air movements and relays information to air bases in Hokkaido and northern Honshu. Both sides conduct reconnaissance flights over the La Pérouse Strait. Mutual observation and harassment has been a common characteristic of this frontier.

Japan's Self-Defence Force leaders are acutely aware of Sakhalin's strategic and tactical implications. A large proportion of Japanese ground and air forces are stationed in Hokkaido in the event of a sudden thrust from the north. In the summer of 1969, the Maritime Self-Defence Force established a small but significant naval base at Yōichi on the Japan Sea coast of Hokkaido, just 200 miles south of the La Pérouse Strait. Yōichi is Japan's northernmost naval base since the end of World War II. These movements suggest that after a lapse of twenty-four years, the Japanese are re-establishing themselves as a military force along the northern frontier.[25]

In the early 1960s, there appeared signs that Sakhalin was shedding its tight insularity and becoming more accessible, at least to Japanese citizens. On 3 October 1964, Soviet Premier Nikita Khrushchev met the prominent politician Fujiyama Aiichirō at the Black Sea resort of Sochi and responded favourably to the latter's appeal to allow family visits to the graves of former settlers on the island.[26] Although Khrushchev fell from power only eleven days later, the Soviet government honoured the ex-leader's promise. From 27 to 31 July 1965, the first 'grave-visiting' group reached Sakhalin and toured Kholmsk (formerly Maoka), Iuzhno-Sakhalinsk (Toyohara), and Nevelsk (Honto). In July 1965 a group of Hokkaido Trade Union leaders led by Hoshino Kenzō were entertained by their Russian counterparts in Sakhalin.[27] A television team from

[25] *New York Times*, 24 Sept. 1969. For details of the Japanese military forces in Hokkaido, see *Bōei nenkan* 1970 (Tokyo, 1970).

[26] *New York Times*, 5 Oct. 1964. Yoshida, *Hoppō ryōdo*, p. 295.

[27] M. Shepelenko, 'Prolivom druzhbi', *Sovetskie profsoiuzy* XXII (May 1966), 41–3.

Japan Broadcasting System toured Iuzhno-Sakhalinsk in October 1964 and made a film that was shown throughout Japan, giving most people their first glimpse of the island since the war.[28]

Soviet-Japanese negotiations regarding Japan's assistance in Siberia's development have been conducted since 1966. Sakhalin would play an important role in such a project. Many Japanese business leaders have recognized Sakhalin's potential as a source of oil and natural gas and as a market for consumer goods and industrial equipment. In September 1967 the first Japanese economic survey team visited Sakhalin and returned with an optimistic forecast of the island's trade potential.

At present, the most ambitious joint project concerning Sakhalin is the contemplated construction of a 925-mile pipeline designed to transport natural gas from the Okha fields of northern Sakhalin to the steel and pulp factories of Muroran in Hokkaido. If constructed, the pipeline will pass through the Tym and Poronai valleys to Cape Krilon, under the La Pérouse Strait to Wakkanai, and southwards to Muroran. The plan envisages the pipeline's completion in late 1971, after which Japan would receive 2,400,000,000 cubic metres of natural gas annually for twenty years. The Teikoku Oil Company, Marubeni Iida Company, Hokkaido Tōhoku Development Finance Corporation, and the Hokkaido Prefectural Office have decided to form a joint firm to handle the gas imports. However, several outstanding problems prevented the plan from being finalized at consultations of the Japan-Soviet Joint Economic Committee which took place in Moscow during 11–17 February 1970. Among these were: (1) disagreement over the quantity and price of the gas, (2) Japanese reluctance to build a pipeline from Yakutsk to Magadan, and (3) disagreement regarding the extension of credits to the U.S.S.R.[29]

Unfortunately, the trend towards relaxation of restrictions on travel to Sakhalin apparent in 1964–7 has been slowed by a renewal of Russo-Japanese friction over the territorial issue. In August 1969 *Izvestiia* carried a scathing editorial condemning an 'anti-Soviet movement' behind the growing Japanese demands for the return of Habomai, Shikotan, Kunashiri, and

[28] Miyatake Shōzō, *Shiberia* (Tokyo, 1965), pp. 200–20.
[29] *Yomiuri shimbun*, 21 Dec. 1969; 12–18 Feb. 1970.

Etorofu. The annual invitation for 'grave visiting', which had been extended in 1965, 1966, and 1967, ceased in 1968. Indeed, with the return of U.S.-occupied Okinawa set for 1972, the Japanese have turned their attention towards the 'northern islands' occupied by the U.S.S.R. in the final days of World War II. The construction of a Japanese naval base at Yōichi in Hokkaido, the strengthening of Japan's Self-Defence Forces, and the conservative party election victory in 1969 all contributed to the Soviet reimposition of travel restrictions to Sakhalin. Moreover, Sino-Soviet frontier tensions have heightened security consciousness throughout the Soviet Far East.[30]

On the other hand, should tension decrease as a result of any number of factors (an end to the Vietnam War, a Sino-Soviet border treaty, the withdrawal of U.S. bases from Japan and Okinawa), there is every reason to expect that Sakhalin will have an economic impact upon Japan and vice versa. Sakhalin's isolation since the first decade of this century has been a result primarily of political, not geographical, barriers. A relaxation of cold war tensions might give the island an opportunity to assume its older historical role of being a bridge, not a barrier, between Japan and the continent.

Soviet Sakhalin: Economic Growth

Sakhalin *oblast* formally came into being on 2 January 1947 with the amalgamation of northern Sakhalin, Japanese Karafuto, and the Kurile Islands. The *oblast*'s area occupies only 1.4 per cent of the Soviet Far East (including Yakutia), but Sakhalin's population comprises 11.6 per cent of the Soviet Far East's inhabitants.[31]

Sakhalin's population grew from 200,000 in 1945 (excluding Japanese and Koreans) to 660,000 in 1957. In 1966 it stood at 640,000. Russians make up 78 per cent of the inhabitants. Other nationalities include: Ukrainians (7.4 per cent), Koreans (6.5 per cent), Belorussians (2.1 per cent), Tatars (1.8 per cent), and Mordvinians (1.7 per cent). In 1959 there were 2,531 aborigines

[30] *Izvestiia*, 1 Aug. 1969, for the editorial on 'anti-Soviet' movements in Japan. *Asahi nenkan* 1969 (Tokyo, 1969), p. 307, for the termination of 'grave visiting'.

[31] For current population data: Akademiia nauk S.S.S.R., Sakhalinskii kompleksnyi nauchno-issledovatelskii institut, *Atlas Sakhalinskoi oblasti* (Moscow, 1967), p. 9. U.S.S.R., Sakhalinskaia oblast, *Sakhalinskaia oblast v tsifrakh za* 1946–1966 *gody: statisticheskii sbornik* (Iuzhno-Sakhalinsk, 1967), p. 9.

on Sakhalin, of whom about 1,800 were Gilyak (Nivkhi) followed by small groups of Ainu and Oroki. Although precise data is not available, there are probably several hundred Japanese and Chinese living on the island.

Sakhalin has a semi-urban society. Over 80 per cent of its inhabitants live in towns exceeding 3,000 in population. The populated areas are concentrated in the south around Iuzhno-Sakhalinsk (100,000 in 1968), Korsakov (40,000), Kholmsk (40,000), Dolinsk (30,000), and Nevelsk (30,000). The central regions are dominated by the towns of Poronaisk-Shaktersk-Uglegorsk (together around 90,000) and Aleksandrovsk-Tymovsk (together approximately 60,000). The Okha area in the extreme north has around 90,000 inhabitants.

Iuzhno-Sakhalinsk is the *oblast*'s administrative centre. Formerly called Toyohara, the town was also the capital of Japanese Karafuto. Today it serves as headquarters not only for government agencies but for the Communist Party, trade unions, and the Komsomol (Communist Youth Organization). The town boasts a teachers' college, a publishing house, and a historical museum among its education and cultural facilities.

Since the island's unification under Soviet power, Sakhalin has undergone remarkable economic development. Although small in land area compared to the adjacent continental mass, Sakhalin's peculiar concentration of natural resources and its proximity to industrial complexes on the Amur River have attracted heavy investment in capital and labour. The total output value of Sakhalin's products (oil, coal, fish, timber, paper, construction materials) increased more than five times between 1946 and 1965. During this period the island's economic structure underwent notable alterations. An increasing proportion of the total labour force entered the manufacturing and processing industries at the expense of the extractive industries. For example, from 1946 to 1965 the proportion of fishermen in Sakhalin's working population fell from 32 per cent to 21 per cent while coal-miners declined from 27.4 per cent to 15 per cent. In the same period, the number of workers employed in the metal-working and construction materials (brick, cement) industries rose by thirty times.[32]

Fishing has been the traditional mainstay of Sakhalin's

[32] *Atlas Sakhalinskoi oblasti*, p. 12.

economy and still comprises 40 per cent of the *oblast*'s valued output (1965) and 20 per cent of the total valued output for the Soviet Far East. The fishing fleet has recently been enlarged and modernized and operates not only in coastal waters but in the Sea of Okhotsk and the North Pacific. Hauls more than doubled between 1958 and 1965 and are expected to continue to grow rapidly in the 1970s. Sakhalin produced 7 per cent of the U.S.S.R.'s fish in 1965.

Fish canning is carried on both in Sakhalin and on floating canneries that accompany the fleet. Large, automated canneries process herring, crab, salmon, trout, whale, and dolphin at Kholmsk, Nevelsk, Korsakov, and Poronaisk. A number of marine breeding farms produce about 500 million young fish annually. Learning from the example of the Japanese, the Russians have begun to harvest seaweed. Whether or not seaweed will become part of the Soviet citizen's diet is not made clear.[33]

A remarkable sight in Sakhalin is a rocky islet called Tiulenii (or Kaihyōtō by the Japanese) which lies off the central east coast. Tiulenii's abundant seal population attracted American hunters in the 1840s and 1850s. Since 1911, seal-hunting has been strictly controlled by the Japanese, and more recently by the Soviet, governments. It has been reported that Russian scientists are carrying on intensive research on the living habits of Tiulenii's seals by 'bugging' them with tiny microphones which eavesdrop on the unsuspecting colony.[34]

Sakhalin's oil is perhaps the island's unique natural asset. It is the only oil currently found in the Soviet Far East, and since 1950 has been one of the fastest growing industries there. The eight principal oilfields are located on the north-east coast facing the Sea of Okhotsk. From north to south they are: Kolendo, Okha, Ekhabi, Vostochnyi, Tungor, Sabo, Paromai, and Katangli. Natural gas deposits have been found and exploited on the Schmidt Peninsula, at Moskalvo, and around Baikal Bay. Intensive prospecting for oil and natural gas has also

[33] *Atlas Sakhalinskoi oblasti*, p. 12. *Sakhalinskaia oblast v tsifrakh*, p. 14. E. G. Meerson, 'Sakhalinskaia oblast', in Institut geographii, AN, SSSR, *Dalnii Vostok, ekonomiko-geographicheskaia karakteristika* (Moscow, 1966), p. 374. D. N. Trubachev et. al., 'Ekonomika i kultura oblasti v poslevoennye period', in K. I. Kniazev, ed., *Sakhalinskaia oblast* (Iuzhno-Sakhalinsk, 1960), pp. 274–87.

[34] *The Times* [London], 31 July 1969.

been conducted in southern Sakhalin (particularly at Krasnogorsk, Chekhov, and Gornozavodsk) with promising results. Sakhalin's crude oil is transported to refineries in Komsomolsk by a 350-mile pipeline built in 1942 that runs from Okha southwestward, crosses the Tatary Straits at Pogibi to Lazarev, and cuts overland to the Amur River. A gas pipeline and a second oil pipeline are at present under construction. Oil refineries may be built in Sakhalin in the near future that will supply the fuel needs of Kamchatka and Magadan.[35]

Crude oil output in Sakhalin has grown from 750,000 metric tons in 1945 to 2,608,000 metric tons in 1966. Assuming that output reached 3,000,000 metric tons in 1969, the island's oil would still amount to only 1 per cent of total U.S.S.R. production (309,000,000 metric tons in 1968, 350,000,000 metric tons projected for 1970). Nevertheless, its strategic location makes Sakhalin oil considerably more valuable than the volume of its output alone suggests. Without the Sakhalin reserves, the Russians would have to transport oil on the Trans-Siberian railroad from distant fields in the Urals, the Caucasus, and the Caspian regions in order to supply the Amur industrial complexes. For the strategically located steel and aircraft factories in Komsomolsk and Khabarovsk, Sakhalin oil is of vital importance. Improved drilling and refining technology should bring steady increases in the exploitation of Sakhalin's estimated 400,000,000 metric tons of oil reserves in the 1970s.[36]

Sakhalin's coal deposits rank among the foremost in quality and quantity in the Soviet Far East. Total deposits are currently estimated at 19,400,000,000 metric tons of which 10,000,000,000 metric tons are at a depth not lower than 300 metres. About half is brown coal, while the rest is lignite. The coal lies mainly along the west coast and is mined in seven areas: Mgachi, Arkovo, Dué, Boshniakovo, Ternovskii, Shaktersk-Uglegorsk, and Gornozavodsk. On the east coast, Vakhrushev and Makarov are important mines. Mines also operate just north of Iuzhno-Sakhalinsk at Sinegorsk and Bykov.

Coal output stood at nearly 5,000,000 metric tons in 1966 and

[35] Trubachev, 'Ekonomika etc.', pp. 266–74. Meerson, 'Sakhalinskaia oblast', p. 371. *Neftianik*, XI (June 1966), 18–20; XIII (Dec. 1968), 21. I. M. Siryk, *Neftegazonosnost vostochnykh sklonov zapadno-sakhalinskikh gor* (Moscow, 1968), *passim*.

[36] *Atlas Sakhalinskoi oblasti*, pp. 12, 36, *Sakhalinskaia oblast v tsifrakh*, p. 18.

should rise rapidly in the 1970s after extensive modernization of the mines has been completed. Coal represents 60 per cent of the island's locally consumed fuel. Large quantities are exported to the Komsomolsk area. Since 1953 the Russians have been offering to sell Sakhalin coal to Japan on a barter basis, but such shipments have yet to exceed 200,000 metric tons anually.[37]

As 60 per cent of Sakhalin is covered with trees, forestry had naturally become one of the island's major enterprises. The rudimentary efforts of Komsomol shock brigades in the 1930s have been superseded by a network of modern sawmills, mechanized transport, and a sophisticated group of wood-processing factories which produce paper, cardboard, turpentine, and cellulose. These factories are almost entirely in the southern half of the island and were inherited from the Japanese in 1945. Since then they have been modernized and re-equipped. In 1965, 3,600,000 cubic metres of wood (mostly pine) were cut, and with the completion of four new sawmills the 1970 output should exceed 5,000,000 cubic metres. In contrast to the reckless exploitation of Karafuto's forests by the Japanese, the Russians have undertaken considerable reafforestation work. Sakhalin is the only paper-producing area in Eastern Siberia. In 1965, the *oblast* produced 158,000 metric tons of paper and 83,000 metric tons of cardboard. This constitutes about 7 per cent for total U.S.S.R. paper output.[38]

With the rapidly growing mechanization of Sakhalin's extractive industries, machine maintenance stations have sprung up in profuse numbers. Some like the shipyards at Kholmsk and Nevelsk are impressive complexes. Maintenance shops for railroad stock, canning machinery, logging equipment, coal and oil extraction machines, and pulp processing works have appeared in nearly all of the major towns.

The production of construction materials is Sakhalin's newest and fastest growing industry. An insatiable demand for housing has led to a mushrooming of factories manufacturing

[37] *Atlas Sakhalinskoi oblasti*, pp. 12, 36. Trubachev, 'Ekonomika', pp. 257–66. Meerson, 'Sakhalinskaia oblast', p. 368 *Sakhalinskaia oblast v tsifrakh*, p. 18.

[38] V. F. Baliaevskii, Ia. L. Markovich, 'Bumazhnaia promyshlennost Sakhalina v poslevoennyi period', *Bumazhnaia promyshlennost*, XXXII (Dec. 1957), 15–18. Meerson, 'Sakhalinskaia oblast', pp. 372–3. Trubachev, 'Ekonomika', pp. 287–93. *Atlas Sakhalinskoi oblasti*, p. 12.

prefabricated reinforced concrete sections. The *oblast*'s sand and clay deposits provide ready-made raw material for cement and bricks. In the 1960s an annual production of 100,000 cubic metres of prefabricated concrete and 20,000,000 bricks has propelled the 170,000 square metres of living space constructed every year. Row after row of cream-coloured, five-storey apartment blocks now transform the vistas of Iuzhno-Sakhalinsk and Kholmsk.[39]

There are a variety of light industries located in Iuzhno-Sakhalinsk, Aleksandrovsk, and Kholmsk, including breweries, vodka distilleries, food processing plants, and clothing and footwear factories. These enterprises do not satisfy local demand. Most consumer commodities must be imported from the mainland.

Notwithstanding the rosy expectations of the First and Second Five-Year Plans, Sakhalin has still not achieved self-sufficiency in food production. This is due less to the shortcomings of collectivization than to the six-fold increase in population since the beginning of World War II. The postwar growth of the island's agriculture does not match that of the extractive and processing industries, but there has been a steady improvement in harvests and livestock production.

Sakhalin possesses 480,000 acres of arable land of which about 250,000 acres are under cultivation or are used for grazing. In 1965, the island's crops by value were potatoes (23.7 per cent), dairying (18.6 per cent), poultry (14.9 per cent), fur-bearing animals (12.1 per cent), pigs (11.2 per cent), vegetables (7.1 per cent), and reindeer (0.9 per cent).[40]

Potatoes (34,000 acres) are grown principally in the Uglegorsk area and to a lesser extent along the Poronai and upper Tym rivers. Vegetables (6,000 acres) are also grown around Uglegorsk, the Poronai River, and in the suburbs of Iuzhno-Sakhalinsk. Cabbages comprise about 65 per cent of the vegetable crops with carrots, beets, and radishes harvested on a smaller scale. Attempts have recently been made to introduce warm climate plants such as pears, grapes, tomatoes, cucumbers, and even grapefruit and ginseng, but these are still strictly

[39] Trubachev, 'Ekonomika', pp. 300–9. *Atlas Sakhalinskoi oblasti*, pp. 12–13.

[40] *Atlas Sakhalinskoi oblasti*, p. 17. *Sakhalinskaia oblast v tsifrakh*, pp. 27–72, for statistics on agricultural production.

luxury items for local consumers. Few plant crops have been cultivated successfully in the northern third of the island.[41]

About thirty per cent of Sakhalin's arable land is used for pasturage. Recently, some success has awarded efforts to raise livestock, especially dairy cows, pigs, and poultry. Most of Sakhalin's dairy farms are in the upper Tym valley or along the west coast between Uglegorsk and Kholmsk. The island is said to have the dairying potential of Denmark.[42] Fur-bearing animals (mostly foxes and martens) are also raised and their pelts exported to the mainland. The Gilyak and Oroki have been organized into reindeer co-operatives, but such exotic pursuits have remained economically marginal.

The most remarkable structural transformation in Sakhalin's agriculture since 1950 has been the growth of *sovkhozes* or 'state farms' which numbered ninety in 1967. Organized in every branch of agriculture, their share of total valued output has jumped from 7.4 per cent in 1950 to 56.2 per cent in 1965. The *sovkhoz* has been particularly successful in livestock enterprises, especially dairy and meat concerns where output has more than doubled since 1950. Nor does the *sovkhoz* ignore the smaller animals. Sakhalin boasts some of the finest collectivized beehives in the Soviet Union. [43]

Electric power in the *oblast* was supplied up to 1966 by over 900 small thermo-electric stations scattered throughout the island. A large electric generator station is scheduled for completion at Vakhrushev in 1970. The Vakhrushev 'elektroblok' will supply electricity to every town on Sakhalin through an integrated grid system.

The fact that Sakhalin is an island makes communications a vital factor in the *oblast*'s economic life. Bad communications led the Tsarist regime to select the island as an 'escape proof' penal colony. Inadequate communications plagued Soviet development plans during the inter-war years. Since 1945, the Russians have made progress in overcoming Sakhalin's isolation. The

[41] *Priroda*, LV (Aug. 1966), 92. N. E. Tikhomirov, 'Greipfrut na severe Sakhalina', *Priroda*, XLII (Mar. 1953), 119, T. N. Kriukova, T. A. Zimina, 'Opyt introduktsii zhenshenia na Sakhaline', Sakhalinskii kompleksnyi nauchno-issledovatelskii institut, *Trudy*, 17 (1966), 180.

[42] *Atlas Sakhalinskoi oblasti*, p. 17.

[43] 'Bolshe vnimaniia pchelovodstvu na Sakhaline', *Pchelovodstvo*, XXIX (May 1952), 58–9.

completion of an extension of the Baikal-Amur railway from Komsomolsk to Vanino and Sovetskaia Gavan (ports on the Tatary Strait) has greatly improved transport between Sakhalin and the mainland. Regular steamer service is now in operation between Vanino and the Sakhalin ports of Aleksandrovsk, Uglegorsk, Kholmsk, and Korsakov. Since 1942 more and more of Sakhalin's oil has been transported by pipeline from the Okha fields to refineries and consumption centres in Komsomolsk, replacing the cumbersome process of barge transport up the Amur River.

The Tass Agency announced late in 1969 that Soviet planners had decided to build a sixty-mile canal from the Amur River to the Sea of Japan.[44] Although its route was not specified, the canal will most likely originate in the neighbourhood of Mariinsk and pass through Lake Kiji and the northern tip of the Sikhote Alin Range to debouch at the Tatary Strait just north of Castries Bay. When completed, the canal will shorten the water route from Khabarovsk to ports in southern Sakhalin by nearly 400 miles, bypassing the sinuous lower courses of the Amur River.

Modern airports have been constructed at Okha, Nogliki, Zonalnoe (near Tymovskoe), and Shakhtersk. All offer direct flights to Khabarovsk. From Sakhalin's main airport at Iuzhno-Sakhalinsk, flights of Ilyushin 18s and Antonov 10s depart regularly for Vladivostok, Khabarovsk, Burevestnik (Etorofu Island in the southern Kuriles), and Moscow. The 4,800-mile flight to Moscow takes about eleven hours with a stopover at Khabarovsk.

Internal communications centre around a rail network which the Russians inherited from the Japanese. The north-south line from Korsakov, which the Japanese extended as far as Pobedino (Koton) in 1944, has been further extended since the war across the 50th parallel to Tymovsk. A 130-mile line has been constructed along the east coast from Okha and Moskalvo down to Katangli through the oilfields. When the Tymovsk-Katangli section is completed, it will be possible to travel the whole length of the island by rail. It is not clear whether the Russians have replaced the narrow gauge Japanese lines with the broad gauge used in the rest of the U.S.S.R. The completion of a rail ferry

[44] *Yomiuri shimbun*, 30 Nov. 1969.

between Vanino and Kholmsk (170 miles) will provide a direct link between mainland and Sakhalin rail networks.

Sakhalin's roads are scarce and rugged. Only one route connects the northern and southern halves of the island, via Pobedino and Onor. The east coast from Poronaisk to Katangli still remains largely inaccessible.

To summarize, Sakhalin plays a role in the U.S.S.R. economy out of proportion to its population and area. While its inhabitants comprise only 0.3 per cent of the Soviet Union's population, the *oblast* supplies 7 per cent of the country's fish, pulp, and paper. Sakhalin paper is shipped not only to the Amur region (28 per cent) but to Western Siberia (8 per cent), Soviet Central Asia (24 per cent), Moldavia and the Ukraine (together 7 per cent), and Moscow (13 per cent). It supplies essential oil to the industries of Khabarovsk and Komsomolsk. Coal shipments provide an important source of fuel for Magadan and Kamchatka.

About 8 per cent of Sakhalin's valued output is exported outside of the Soviet Union. Japan buys coal, oil, and lumber. India takes most of the paper and pulp exports. Paper is also sent to Cuba, Indonesia, Hong Kong, Thailand, and the German Democratic Republic.

Sakhalin's economic future looks promising. Growing industrial demands in the Soviet Far East will continue to propel increases in coal, oil, and pulp production. Fishing, food processing, and construction industries should also expand to meet strong local demands. If the negotiations that began in 1966 with the Japanese are successful, the *oblast* will be exporting natural gas in considerable quantities to Hokkaido. The Russians are even considering the construction of a four-mile wide dam to bridge the straits between Sakhalin and the mainland.[45] By allowing the warm currents from the Sea of Japan to flow through the straits and by blocking the seasonal return of this warm water, climatic changes are envisaged.

Cultural Life

Located on the fringe of the Soviet Union's Far Eastern possessions, Sakhalin might at first appear to be a cultural Sahara. The island's remoteness and loneliness attracted poets

[45] G. Paderin, *Rediscovered Country* (Moscow, n.d.), pp. 186–7.

and writers from both Russia (Anton Chekhov) and Japan (Kikuchi Kan, Kitahara Hakushū) who commiserated with its inhabitants and wondered at its silent, fog-enshrouded forests. The Soviet authorities, however, have not relied on the island's 'natural lure' to define the content of cultural life. Since 1945 strenuous efforts have been made through schools, libraries, workers' clubs, and the mass media to instil Sakhalinites with pride in their island's past and confidence in its future.

Each town in Sakhalin has its own schools, public libraries, and clubs. To foster 'local patriotism' among children, teachers arrange local history exhibits, show films, and assign books by local authors. Soviet achievements on the island are naturally given top priority. The predatory American whalers come off only a bit worse than the Japanese plunderers who 'seized' parts of the island after 1805.[46]

Local libraries encourage members of Sakhalin's trade unions to read books on local history as well as on purely technical matters.[47] In 1968 a library in Aleksandrovsk organized a meeting where former exiles from the penal colony reminisced about Sakhalin under the Tsarist regime, and veterans from the 1945 campaign recounted stories about the liberation of the south from the Japanese.[48]

The Russians have gone to great lengths to give Sakhalin a new 'positive' image. Starting in 1945, Moscow published a series of books and pamphlets extolling the island's rich natural resources. In 1959 a publishing house was established in Iuzhno-Sakhalinsk that has since issued popular local histories for national consumption. Epithets such as 'treasure island', 'gem', 'Soviet forepost on the Pacific', 'order-bearing island', and 'beloved island' have been promoted in the hope of ridding Sakhalin of its unfavourable connotations.

A school of 'Sakhalin writers' has grown up to carry on, discreetly, the work pioneered by Anton Chekhov in 1890. Whereas Chekhov evoked the degradation and inhumanity of an island penal colony, Sakhalin's younger writers concentrate on

[46] F. Uryvskii, 'Kraevedenie v shkolakh Sakhalina', *Narodne obrazovanie* (Aug. 1966), pp. 54–8.

[47] A. Zasukha, 'Na Sakhalin', *Sovetskaia knizhnaia torgovlia*, I (1955), 16–17. A. Zasukha, 'Sredi vekovoi taigi', *Bibliotekar*, II (Feb. 1958), 30–1. L. Kucherov, 'Dla tekh, kto v more', *Bibliotekar*, XII (May 1968), 23–5.

[48] L. Tikhonina, 'Ordenonosnii ostrov', *Bibliotekar*, XII (Sept. 1968), 32.

eulogizing socialist progress. Nowhere is this metamorphosis more apparent than with the case of Sergei Chekhov, Anton's grand-nephew, who toured Sakhalin in 1959 and produced a dutiful homily on Soviet achievements.[49]

Sakhalin has figured in Soviet literature since the early days of the regime. Hardly had the Japanese evacuated the north in 1925 when Boris Ellinskii wrote his memoirs about his ordeal as a political exile in Tsarist Sakhalin. Max Polianovskii and Vladimir Kantorovich captured the rough, makeshift life of the First Five-Year Plan (1928–32). Shortly before his death in 1936, Maxim Gorki, who had for many years felt an especial attachment to 'the isle of misery', wrote a letter to some Sakhalin schoolchildren encouraging them to love their island. 'Writer brigades' roamed around the island in the 1930s, but even their prolific output could not match the spate of publications that appeared in 1945–6 celebrating the liberation of the south. While the reporter's notes of I. Osipov realistically evoked the Russian exhilaration at Japan's eviction from Karafuto, the quota-fulfilling novels of Semion Buitovoi and A. Chakovskii of the late 1940s rank among the jewels of soporific literature. Patriotic fatuity reached a climax with Sergei Feoktistov's 'Sakhalin morning' in which Stalin's rising sun banishes 'forty years of dark night' (1905–45) during which southern Sakhalin was ruled by 'Japanese samurai brigands'.[50]

Such unpromising material may have been in a Russian commentator's mind when he remarked that not a single professional writer lived in Sakhalin before 1955.[51] In the summer of 1955, however, a group of young local aspiring writers met and decided to devote themselves to evoking faithfully the manifold aspects of life on the island. Since then, an uninterrupted succession of novels, short stories, poems, and drama have flowed from the pens of these writers on to the pages of local (and occasionally national) publications.

[49] S. Chekhov, 'Poiezdka na ostrov Sakhalin: iz dnevnika khudozhnika', *Moskva*, IV (1960), 188–94.

[50] Sergei Feoktistov, 'Sakhalinskoe utro', *Oktiabr*, VI (June 1950), 122. I. Osipov, *Sakhalinskie zapisi, osen* 1945 *goda* (Moscow, 1945). Semion Buitovoi, *Sadi i okeana* (Leningrad, 1957 rev. ed.). Vladimir Kantorovich, *Soviet Sakhalin* (Moscow, 1933). B. Ellinskii, *Pod zvon tsepei* (Leningrad, 1927). For a survey of other writers (1917–50), see M. V. Teplinskii, *Sakhalinskie puteshestviia* (Iuzhno-Sakhalinsk, 1962), pp. 46–9.

[51] Viacheslav Kuznetsov, 'Sakhalin literaturnyi', *Oktiabr*, XLI (Dec. 1964), 211.

Nikolai Maksimov, Anatolii Tkachenko, and Nikolai Petrochenkov have emerged as prominent practitioners of the unfortunate genre exemplified by Chakovskii in the 1940s. Aleksandr Mandrik, a participant in the 1945 campaign against Japan, has received wide acclaim for his impassioned verse, 'My Kuriles'. Boris Dediukhin has gained a reputation as a sympathetic observer of oil-workers in action. K. Rendel wrote a little vignette of his experiences in Japan. The sailor-poet Aleksandr Kiselev and the worker-poet Olga Prishchep have joined Sakhalin's bard laureate Ivan Belousov in chanting paeans to socialist man mastering rugged nature. Finally, the Gilyak poet Vladimir Sangi who passed through studies at the Leningrad Pedagogical Institute has won applause for his articulate descriptions of his tribe's emergence into the modern world of socialist construction. Even Sangi, however, could not resist the temptation to consign Sakhalin's past misfortunes to 'American whalers, Japanese militarists, Russian merchants, gendarmes, and shamans'.[52]

Concurrent with the development of an indigenous literature, a group of artists closely associated with the island began exhibiting in the early 1950s. A Studio of Fine Arts was organized in 1950 with twenty members all duly accredited by the Khabarovsk branch of the Union of Artists of the Russian Soviet Federated Socialist Republic. The artists adhere to three axiomatic themes: nature, people, and socialist realism. This genre is best exemplified by I. Minusov's 'Portrait of Tractoress' which as one of the 'toilers' series has been blessed with official approbation. G. Montkava specializes in the historical aspects of socialist realism (e.g. 'Bolshevik exiles'). The younger painters and sculptors, V. Buraka, G. Mazanko, M. Fediaeva, and A. Ni show no signs of deviating from well-trodden paths. If practitioners of abstract expressionism, pop, op, or other forms of non-representational art exist in Sakhalin, they are not being exhibited.[53]

While art and literature in Sakhalin have been hampered by the preoccupation with stereotyped forms, there has been

[52] D. A. Rachkov, *Pisateli Sakhalina* (Iuzhno-Sakhalinsk, 1962), p. 10. For a discussion of contemporary writers, see Teplinskii, *Sakhalinskie puteshestviia*, pp. 50–63; Kuznetsov, 'Sakhalin literaturnyi', pp. 211–13; *Literaturnyi Sakhalin, literaturno-khudozhestvennyi sbornik* (Iuzhno-Sakhalinsk, 1959).

[53] B. Shakhnazarov, 'Khudozhniki Sakhalina', *Khudozhnik*, V (1959), 16–19.

an impressive record of scientific research on the island, especially in geology, hydrology, botany, and zoology. These activities are co-ordinated and publicized largely through an institution called the Sakhalin Joint Scientific Research Institute, a branch of the Siberian Department of the U.S.S.R. Academy of Sciences. The institute publishes a journal carrying the latest results of scientific research concerning the island.[54]

The aspect of scientific research in Sakhalin with the widest international ramifications may well be the earthquake-measuring centre of the Sakhalin Research Institute located at Novo-Aleksandrovsk just outside of Iuzhno-Sakhalinsk. As part of the earthquake-prone Pacific rim (Indonesia, Japan, the Kurile and Aleutian islands, Alaska, and the Pacific seaboard of North and South America), Sakhalin frequently experiences earth tremors. Measuring and reporting tremors that can cause tidal waves is the institute's speciality. After identifying the source and magnitude of the tremor, warnings are dispatched through an international wire service to such widely separated points as Japan, Chile, Alaska, and Hawaii. Sakhalin's monitoring service has been a genuine contribution to disaster prevention.[55]

What does the word 'Sakhalin' mean to the inhabitant of Moscow, Kiev, Omsk, or Tiflis? Judging from the popular press, the expression might evoke images of a distant island, vaguely exotic for its proximity to Japan, rich in natural resources, and endowed with stunning scenery. Although hardly a tourist mecca, the island has attracted more and more Russian visitors. No longer does one publicly hear epithets of fear and revulsion that made Sakhalin an object of universal dread. Now, pundits extol the invigorating mineral springs, the medicinal muds, and the ski resorts. Over one hundred hostels greet thousands of hikers and skiers every year from all over the U.S.S.R. Even Premier Nikita Khrushchev toured the island in 1954 in a state visit equalled only by that of Crown Prince (later Emperor) Hirohito to Japanese Karafuto in 1925. If the English language pamphlets on display at Khabarovsk Airport are any indication

[54] For a discussion of the Sakhalin Research Institute, see Akademiia nauk, SSSR, *Vestnik*, XXXIV (June 1964), 106. The institute's journal: Akademiia nauk, SSSR, Sakhalinskii kompleksnyi nauchno-issledovatelskii institut, *Soobshcheniia* (nos. 1–196), renamed *Trudy* for issues after no. 196.

[55] G. Vladimirovka, 'Sluzhba tsunami', *Ogoniok*, XXXV (Feb. 1957), 24.

of future policy, Sakhalin may soon offer hospitality to foreign tourists.[56]

Should the visitor come to Sakhalin by air, his point of arrival is likely to be Iuzhno-Sakhalinsk. Iuzhno-Sakhalinsk is the island's administrative and cultural centre. A modern city of 100,000 population, it was formerly called Toyohara during the period of Japanese rule (1905–45). Iuzhno-Sakhalinsk today boasts the usual amenities found in a provincial Soviet city: some light industries (breweries, leather and furniture shops, a chocolate factory), thirteen movie houses, the Chekhov Drama Theatre, a suburban ski resort, a teachers' college, twelve local libraries, government and party offices, trade union headquarters, and a sprinkling of sports clubs. What makes Iuzhno-Sakhalinsk fascinating, however, are the vestiges of Japanese influence.[57]

Since 1945 the Russians in Sakhalin have worked assiduously to expunge all evidence of any constructive role that the Japanese may have played in Sakhalin's past. Japanese buildings, monuments, and parks in Iuzhno-Sakhalinsk have consequently been demolished, disguised, or claimed as Russian-built.

The observant traveller in Iuzhno-Sakhalinsk can discover several fascinating examples of Japanese enterprise from the prewar period. The solid neo-classical building in the downtown area with the neon sign 'Sakhalin' (a department store) was once the Karafuto branch of the Hokkaido Colonial Bank. The imposing tile-roofed Museum of Regional Studies with its stone lion guardians formerly housed the exhibits of the Karafuto Historical Museum. The exhibits have changed, but the building has remained with surprisingly few alterations. A run-down wooden movie house called the 'Vostok' was at one time the Higashi

[56] For popular views of Sakhalin: Tamara Ilatovskaia, 'Kogda za plechami riukzak', *Smena*, XL (Feb. 1963), 16–17. I. Osipov, 'Na Sakhaline', *Ogonoik*, XXXI (Dec. 1953), 4–5. A. Baiukanskii, 'U vostochnykh granits', *Ogoniok*, XXXI (June 1953), 2. Galina Shergova, 'Na dalnem ostrove', *Ogoniok*, XXXIII (Sept. 1955), 7–9. A. Starkov, 'Na Tikhom Okean', *Ogoniok*, XXXVI (Sept. 1958), 14–19. Mykola Sheremet, 'Na Sakhalini', *Vitchyzna*, XXVI (Dec. 1958), 115–24. B. T. Komissarenko, *Mineralnyi istochniki i lechebnye griazi Sakhalina i Kuril* (Iuzhno-Sakhalinsk, 1964).

[57] This and succeeding paragraphs on Iuzhno-Sakhalinsk are based on: I. Belousov, ed., *Yuzhno-Sakhalinsk* (Moscow, 1968); K. P. Obzhigalin, ed., *Sakhalin, chudesnyi krai: fotoalbom* (Iuzhno-Sakhalinsk, 1965); Miyatake, *Shiberia*, pp. 205–10.

Honganji temple. The graceful public gardens, laced with artificial lakes built by the paper-magnate, Fujiwara Ginjirō, have now become the 'People's Park'. Other Japanese schools, shrines, government offices, research institutes, and factories remain, but nearly all of the small fragile wooden houses of private citizens have been swept away by rows of cream-coloured prefabricated apartment blocks.

Economic growth and cultural efflorescence have raised problems of their own. Inefficiency, the housing shortage, and 'hooliganism' plague Sakhalin no less than other parts of the U.S.S.R. Since the mid-1950s, there have been complaints about the over-centralization of the decision-making process on local economic matters.[58] Communist Party officials have been accused of spending too much time travelling and not enough time familiarizing themselves with local conditions. Projects have fallen behind from lack of local supervision. More serious than the peccadilloes of party officials has been the friction between seasoned workers and young high-handed managers, especially in the coal-mines.[59]

Housing shortages persist despite the construction of thousands of apartments in the principal towns. The first influx of Russians after the war could not be accommodated in the available living space. Many Russian immigrants were assigned to Japanese houses. Russian and Japanese families not infrequently shared the same house until the completion of repatriation. The new arrivals recoiled from the thin walls and *tatami* (straw mat) floors. They had no choice but to resign themselves to a cold, cramped, and austere winter. As new apartments became available, competition for early access grew intense. Favouritism in the assignment of these new flats inevitably caused bitter resentment among the less fortunate, erupting in a minor scandal in 1964 that involved some local party officials and the chairman of a trade union committee.[60]

[58] V. Obukhov, 'Nepravnie metodi', *Partiinaia zhizn* (Nov. 1956), pp.57–9; (Feb. 1957), p. 78. 'Ucheba na polozhitelnom primere', *Partiinaia zhizn* (Nov. 1966), pp. 59–60.

[59] K. Rendel, 'Uvolit po sobstvennomu zhelaniiu', *Sovetskie profsoiuzy*, XXII (May 1966), 36.

[60] V. Barskaia, 'Moia sovest ne pozvoliaet molchat', *Partiinaia zhizn* (Mar. 1965), pp. 59–61. V. Ia. Kantorovich, *Sakhalinskie tetradi* (Moscow, 1965), pp. 248–9.

In the words of the First Secretary of Sakhalin's Communist Party, P. Leonov, some of the island's most serious social problems are lack of discipline, drunkenness, truancy, theft, hooliganism, and 'political philistinism'. Despite heightened vigilance against bourgeois propaganda, iniquitous influences have apparently penetrated even the party hierarchy. In 1967, Comrade F. Uryvskii, chairman of People's Instruction in Sakhalin, was dismissed after his son had been branded a 'systematic hooligan' for theft and drunkenness. A brigade leader in the coal-mines lost his position for 'vicious drunkenness' and 'rampant hooliganism'.[61]

Such colourful incidents form the veneer under which the party is attempting to eradicate ideological indifference and indiscipline. Sakhalin probably differs little from other areas in the Soviet Union in respect to petty crime and juvenile delinquency, but it is instructive to note the role of local history as a tool in re-establishing single-minded patriotism and working-class allegiance. In 1967 the party organized mass youth pilgrimages to the 1945 battlefields and strengthened ideological instruction at all levels through books, television, newspapers, magazines, and seminars. A Writers' Union was formed that year to channel clerical talents into the extolment of unity, orthodoxy, vigilance, and patriotism.[62]

How have Sakhalin's 2,500 aborigines fared under Soviet rule? It has been a cardinal tenet of Soviet historiography that the Ainu, Gilyak, and Oroki peoples welcomed the coming of the Russians in the eighteenth and nineteenth centuries. The novelist Nikolai Zadornov induced one of his Ainu characters to exclaim: 'We have been waiting for them [Russians] for many years'. The historian Iuri Zhukov wrote that the Ainu proudly considered themselves as Russians from the beginning of the nineteenth century. A. N. Ryzhkov characterized the Ainu as grateful to the Russians for 'liberating them from inevitable enslavement and extermination which threatened them from Japanese, Americans, and other plunderers'.[63]

[61] P. Leonov, 'Vospityvat ubezhdennykh stroitelei kommunizma', *Kommunist*, XLV (May 1968), 52–7.

[62] Ibid., pp. 58–61.

[63] Nikolai Zadornov, *Daliokii krai* (Leningrad, 1950), pp. 374–5. Iuri Zhukov, *Russkie i Iaponiia* (Moscow, 1945), p. 73. A. N. Ryzhkov, 'Iz istorii otkrytiia, issledovaniia, i osvoeniia Sakhalina', *Sakhalinskaia oblast*, p. 59.

Soviet nationality policy in Sakhalin eludes judgement, because the available literature often reads more like a sales prospectus than a critical evaluation. It is known that the approximately 1,800 Gilyak (or Nivkhi) in northern Sakhalin were organized into thirteen collectives in 1932 and resettled in designated areas throughout the island. Some Gilyak, such as the poet Vladimir Sangi, have received a higher education in European Russia and have returned to teach among their own people. Another Gilyak, Chuner Taksami, is enjoying a successful career as an ethnographer studying his own people. Today the Gilyak live in settlements along the east coast, facing the Sea of Okhotsk at Piltun, Chaivo, and Veni. Few (5.4 per cent) have entered into mixed marriages with the Russian majority. Nevertheless, they speak the Russian language freely, and the younger men and women are seeking improved employment opportunities in the larger towns.[64]

Little is known about the state of the Sakhalin Ainu at present except that they have declined in numbers from 1,200 in 1945 to about 600 in 1967.[65] This sharp fall is explained by the fact that many Ainu left southern Sakhalin with the Japanese during 1947–8. These are now settled in Hokkaido in small hamlets such as that of Tokoro on the outskirts of Abashiri.[66] Those Ainu who remained in Sakhalin under Soviet rule have been organized into fishing co-operatives around eight settlements in the southern part of the island.[67]

There is no evidence of racial discrimination against any of the aborigines. While traditional cultural forms have been preserved as 'folk art', further assimilation into the Russian majority is only a matter of time. The Soviet nationalities policy appears to be successful in terms of providing vocational

[64] A. V. Smoliak, 'O sovremennom etnicheskom razvitii narodov nizhnevo Amura i Sakhalina', *Sovetskaia etnografiia* (May–June 1967), pp. 95–102. Chuner M. Taksami, *Nivkhi* (Leningrad, 1967), pp. 267–9.

[65] N. Yakovlev, 'A Visit to the Ainu in Southern Sakhalin', *The Asiatic Review*, New Series, XLIII (July 1947), 278 for the 1945 figure. *Atlas Sakhalinskoi oblasti*, p. 9, for the 1967 figure.

[66] For a study of the Sakhalin Ainu in Hokkaido, see E. Ohnuki Tierney, 'A Northwest Coast Sakhalin Ainu World View', unpublished Ph.D. dissertation, University of Wisconsin, 1968.

[67] These are Ochikho, Tomihama, Shirahama, Niitoi, Tarantomari, Torutsu, and Chirai. S. N. Rakovskii, 'Na iuzhnom Sakhaline', *Geografiia v shkole*, III (May-June 1947), 16.

education and guaranteeing a modest but acceptable standard of living to the 'small peoples' of this area.

Sakhalin's 43,000 Koreans (1966) comprise the island's largest single alien minority group. Brought there largely by the Japanese as labourers in the 1930s, only very few have been repatriated to their homeland since 1945. The emergence of two mutually hostile Korean states (the communist north and the anti-communist south), the Korean War (1950–3), and the global cold war have split Sakhalin's Koreans into two warring factions. A majority have taken North Korean (65 per cent) or Soviet (25 per cent) citizenship and receive favourable treatment from the authorities. However, about 10 per cent or 4,300 of Sakhalin's Koreans have refused both Soviet and North Korean citizenship and demand repatriation to Japan or South Korea. Until Stalin's death (1953) this latter group suffered discrimination, arrest, and imprisonment. Political surveillance has relaxed since 1954, but violence occasionally erupts between the two factions. In October 1957 1,000 Koreans gathered at Iuzhno-Sakhalinsk for a three-day sit-down strike demanding repatriation to Japan. The outcome of this incident was eclipsed by a Soviet communications black-out. In 1967 the South Korean government made representations to the International Red Cross in Geneva for the repatriation of those desiring to leave Sakhalin. As of 1970 this problem remains unsolved.[68]

Some refugee reports seem to give an overly pessimistic impression of the Korean problem in Sakhalin. The Russians have made genuine efforts to attune local institutions to the needs of the Korean minority. In 1960 there were forty-nine schools where Korean children were taught in their own language. Korean teachers in these schools received training at a special department in the Iuzhno-Sakhalinsk Pedagogical Institute designed to prepare them for teaching children in their own cultural group. A glance at the names of research workers at the Sakhalin Joint Scientific Institute reveals that Koreans are serving in respected occupations. The *oblast* has a Korean language newspaper, a local Korean radio station, a publisher of Korean books, and Korean libraries. There is no reason to assume that the Korean minority

[68] *The Japan Times*, 17 Dec. 1967 for the South Korean government's appeal. Robert Trumbull, 'Sakhalin a Scene of Korean Strife', *New York Times*, 21 Oct. 1957. Chō Zai Jutsu, *Gokumontō* (Tokyo, 1966), pp. 3–20.

in Sakhalin is significantly worse off than their compatriots in Japan. Both groups are divided by factions supporting either the North or the South Korean governments. Both have suffered from the tragic succession of events that has seen their homeland undergo Japanese colonialism followed by partition.[69]

In 1970 Sakhalin celebrated its twenty-fifth anniversary since the unification of the island under Soviet rule. The Russians have achieved remarkable economic progress in that period, especially in the fishing, coal-mining, oil, paper, and construction materials industries. Agriculture has failed to keep pace with the extractive and processing industries. Transport and housing still leave much to be desired. Nevertheless, the island has come a long way since 1945.

The Soviet economic forecasts for Sakhalin are optimistic. In 1970 the island's estimated oil production (4,000,000 metric tons) surpasses all the oil produced in Sakhalin between 1927 and 1940 by both the Japanese and the Russians. Coal production is estimated to be 6,000,000 metric tons in 1970, and the total fish catch for 1970 will more than double the 1958 figure.[70]

As important as the economic forecast is Sakhalin's political future. At present, the perennial territorial rivalry between Russia and Japan over Sakhalin seems buried. Barring some radical transformation in leadership or the climate of opinion, Japan is not likely to continue the vicious circle of 1905 and 1945 by embracing irredentism. More likely, mutual economic self-interest may make Sakhalin a scene of unprecedented Soviet-Japanese co-operation.

As a foreigner who has yet to visit Sakhalin, I can only hope that in the coming decade the Soviet Union will relax the restrictive policies regarding non-Russian visitors to the island. Only when the island has opened its doors to all will it cast off the last vestige of its nineteenth-century reputation. Only then can L. M. Demin's advice to a young immigrant ('Don't fear Sakhalin, Svetlana') embrace an international audience.[71]

[69] For Soviet views on Sakhalin's Koreans, see Trubachev, 'Ekonomika', pp. 364–5; V. Ia. Kantorovich, *Sakhalinskie tetradi* (Moscow, 1965), p. 251; L. M. Demin, *Za Tatarskim prolivom: Sakhalinskie ocherki* (Moscow, 1965), p. 57.

[70] V. S. Tiurin, ed., *Sakhalin, Kurily: rodnye ostrova: sbornik ocherkov* (Iuzhno-Sakhalinsk, 1967), pp. 289–92.

[71] Demin, *Za Tatarskim prolivom*, p. 99.

APPENDIX A

TREATIES AND AGREEMENTS

THIS Appendix contains extracts of treaties and agreements that are relevant to Sakhalin Island. For the complete text of each treaty or agreement, please consult the sources cited below each extract.

I. *Treaty of Peace and Friendship (7 February 1855): Treaty of Shimoda*

ARTICLE II

Henceforth the boundaries between Russia and Japan will pass between the islands Etorofu and Uruppu. The whole island of Etorofu belongs to Japan and the whole island of Uruppu and the other Kuril Islands to the north constitute possessions of Russia. As regards the island Karafuto (Sakhalin), it remains unpartitioned between Russia and Japan, as has been the case up to this time.

Japan, Foreign Office. *Treaties and Conventions between the Empire of Japan and other Powers together with Universal Conventions, Regulations and Communications since March 1854* (Tokyo, 1884 rev. ed.), p. 585.

II. *Sakhalin-Kurile Islands Exchange: the Treaty of St. Petersburg (7 May 1875)*

ARTICLE I

His Majesty the Emperor of Japan, for Himself and His descendants, cedes to His Majesty the Emperor of all the Russias, the part of territory of the island of Sakhalin (Karafuto) which he possesses at present together with all the rights of sovereignty appertaining to this possession, so that henceforth the said island of Sakhalin (Karafuto) in its entirety shall form an integral part of the Russian Empire, and that the boundary between the Empires of Russia and Japan in these areas shall pass through the La Pérouse Strait.

ARTICLE V

The residents of the territories ceded from one and the other, the Russian and Japanese subjects, may retain their nationality and return to their respective countries; but if they prefer to remain in the ceded territories, they shall be allowed to stay and shall receive protection in the full exercise of their industry, their right of property and religion, on the same footing as the nationals, provided that they submit to the laws and jurisdiction of the country to which the possession of the respective territories passes.

ARTICLE VI

In consideration of the benefits accruing from the cession of the island of Sakhalin, His Majesty the Emperor of all the Russias accords:

(1) to Japanese vessels the right to frequent Korsakov harbour (Kushunkotan), exempted from all harbour dues and customs duties for the period of ten years from the date of the exchange of ratifications. Upon the expiration of that term it will depend on His Majesty the Emperor of all the Russias whether to continue this exemption or to suspend it. His Majesty the Emperor of all the Russias furthermore grants to the Japanese Government the right to station a Consul or Consular Agent in the port of Korsakov.

(2) to Japanese vessels and merchants the same rights and privileges as those enjoyed in the Empire of Russia by the vessels and merchants of the most favoured nations in regards to navigation and commerce in the ports of the Sea of Okhotsk and of Kamchatka, as well as fishery in those waters and along the shores.

Japan, Foreign Office, *Dai Nihon gaikō bunsho*, VIII (Tokyo, 1940), 216–26. For a complete English text of the St. Petersburg Treaty and the Supplementary Article, see the Appendix of George A. Lensen, *The Russian Push toward Japan* (Princeton, 1959).

III. *Supplementary Article to the Sakhalin-Kurile Islands Exchange: the Treaty of Tokyo (22 Aug. 1875)*

a. The inhabitants of the ceded territories, the Russian and Japanese subjects, who wish to remain domiciled in the localities which they presently occupy, shall be maintained in the full exercise of their industries. They shall retain the right to fish and to hunt within the limits belonging to them and shall be exempted from any tax on their respective industries for the rest of their life.

d. The aborigines of Sakhalin and of the Kurile Islands shall not enjoy the right to remain domiciled in the localities which they now occupy and at the same time retain their present subjection. If they desire to remain subject to their present government, they must leave their present domicile and go to the territory which belongs to their Sovereign; if they desire to remain domiciled in the localities which they occupy at present, they must change their subjection. However, they will be allowed a period of three years from the date of their notification of this supplementary treaty for making a decision on this matter.

Japan, Foreign Office, *Dai Nihon gaikō bunsho,* VIII (Tokyo, 1940), 259–62.

IV. *The Transfer of Southern Sakhalin from Russia to Japan: the Treaty of Portsmouth (5 Sept. 1905)*

ARTICLE IX

The Imperial Russian Government cede to the Imperial Government of Japan in perpetuity and full sovereignty, the southern part of the island of Saghalin and all islands adjacent thereto, as well as all public works and properties there situated. The fiftieth parallel of north latitude is adopted as the northern boundary of the ceded territory. The exact boundary line of the territory shall be determined in accordance with the provision of additional Article II, annexed to this treaty.

Japan and Russia mutually agree not to construct in their respective possessions on the island of Saghalin or the adjacent islands any fortifications or other similar military work. They likewise mutually agree not to take any military measures which might hinder the free navigation of the Straits of La Pérouse and Tartary.

Japan, Foreign Office, *Nihon gaikō bunsho,* XXXVII–XXXVIII, *bessatsu, Nichiro sensō,* V (Tokyo, 1960), 528–34; or United States, Department of State, *Foreign Relations of the United States, 1905* (Washington, 1906), p. 826.

V. *Japanese Concessions in Northern Sakhalin: the Soviet-Japanese Convention of Peking (20 Jan. 1925)*

ARTICLE II

The Union of Soviet Socialist Republics agrees that the Treaty concluded in Portsmouth in 5 Sept. 1905, remains in full force.

ARTICLE VI

In the interests of the development of economic relations between the two countries, and taking into consideration the needs of Japan with respect to natural resources, the Government of the Union of Soviet Socialist Republics is ready to grant to Japanese subjects, companies and associations concessions for the exploitation of mineral, timber and other natural resources in all parts of the territory of the Union of Soviet Socialist Republics.

PROTOCOL A

ARTICLE III

In view of the fact that the climatic conditions in northern Sakhalin prevent immediate transportation home of the Japanese troops now stationed there, these troops will be completely evacuated from the said region by 15 May 1925.

This evacuation must commence just as soon as climatic conditions permit, and in each and all of the districts in northern Sakhalin thus evacuated by Japanese troops will immediately afterwards be restored full sovereignty of corresponding authorities of the Union of Soviet Socialist Republics.

Details regarding the transfer of administration and of the termination of the occupation will be arranged in Aleksandrovsk between the commander of the Japanese army of occupation and representatives of the Union of Soviet Socialist Republics.

PROTOCOL B

1. The government of the Union of Soviet Socialist Republics agrees to give to Japanese concerns recommended by the Japanese government concessions for the exploitation of 50 per cent of the area of every oilfield in northern Sakhalin, mentioned in the memorandum presented to the representative of the Union of Soviet Socialist Republics on 29 Aug. 1924. In order to ascertain the area which is to be leased to Japanese concerns for such exploitation, each of the mentioned oilfields is to be divided into checkerboard squares, from 15 to 40 dessiatins each, the Japanese being given such a number of these squares as will represent 50 per cent of the entire area; it being understood that the squares thus to be leased to the Japanese should not as a rule be adjacent, but should include all wells which are now being drilled or worked by the Japanese. As regards the remaining unleased oil lands mentioned in the same memorandum, it is agreed that should the government of the Union of Soviet Socialist Republics decide to offer these lands, in full or in part, on concessions to foreigners, Japanese concerns will enjoy equal chances in regard to such concessions.

2. The government of the Union of Soviet Socialist Republics will grant to Japanese concerns recommended by the Japanese government the right, for a period from five to ten years, of carrying on exploration work on the oilfields along the eastern shore of northern

Sakhalin over an area of one thousand square versts, which must be allotted within a year from the date of the conclusion of concession agreements, and if, as a result of such exploration work by the Japanese, oil should be located, a concession for the exploitation of 50 per cent of the oilfield area thus established will be granted to the Japanese.

3. The government of the Union of Soviet Socialist Republics agrees to grant to Japanese concerns recommended by the Japanese government concessions for the exploitation of coal deposits on the western shore of northern Sakhalin over a definite area, which is to be established by concession contracts. The government of the Union of Soviet Socialist Republics further agrees to grant to such Japanese concerns concessions for coal-mining in the Dué district over an area to be established in the concession contracts. As regards coalfields situated outside the definite area mentioned in the previous two sentences, it is also agreed that should the government of the Union of Soviet Socialist Republics decide to offer them on concession to foreigners, Japanese concerns will be given equal rights in regard to such concessions.

4. The period of the concessions for the exploitation of oil and coalfields, as set forth in the previous paragraphs, is to be established for 40 to 50 years.

5. As payment for the above-mentioned concessions, Japanese concessionaires will turn over annually to the government of the Union of Soviet Socialist Republics—in the coalfields, from 5 to 8 per cent of the gross output; in the oilfields, from 5 to 15 per cent of the gross output. It is proposed that in the event of striking oil gushers, the payment may be increased to 45 per cent of the gross production.

The percentage of production thus to revert as payment will be finally determined in the concession contracts, it being subject to change in accordance with the scale of annual production by a method to be established in the above mentioned contracts.

6. The said Japanese concerns shall have the right to cut timber necessary for the needs of the enterprise, and to erect various structures to facilitate communication and transportation of materials and products. The details in connection therewith will be stipulated in the concession contracts.

7. In view of the above-mentioned rental and taking into consideration the unfavourable conditions in which the enterprises will be placed owing to the geographical position and other general conditions in the said regions, it is agreed that there will be a duty-

free import and export of all articles, materials and products necessary for such enterprises or produced in the latter, and that the enterprises will not be subject to such taxation or limitations as would actually make profitable exploitation impossible.

8. The government of the Union of Soviet Socialist Republics will provide for the said enterprises all reasonable protection and facilities.

Japan, Foreign Office, *Nihon gaikō nenpyō narabi shuyō bunsho*, II (Tokyo, 1965), 67–72. U.S.S.R., Ministerstvo inostrannykh del S.S.S.R., *Dokumenty vneshnei politiki S.S.S.R.*, VIII (Moscow, 1963), 70–7. For an English text, see Harriet L. Moore, *Soviet Far Eastern Policy, 1931–1945* (Princeton, 1945), pp. 175–81.

VI. *Soviet-Japanese Neutrality Pact (13 Apr. 1941)*

ARTICLE I

Both contracting parties undertake to maintain peaceful and friendly relations between themselves and mutually to respect the territorial integrity and inviolability of the other contracting party.

ARTICLE II

Should one of the contracting parties become the object of hostilities on the part of one or several third Powers, the other contracting party will observe neutrality throughout the entire duration of the conflict.

ARTICLE III

The present pact comes into force from the day of its ratification by both contracting parties and shall remain valid for five years. Should neither of the contracting parties denounce the pact one year before expiration of the term, it will be considered automatically prolonged for the following five years.

Japan, Foreign Office, *Nihon gaikō nenpyō narabi shuyō bunsho*, II (Tokyo, 1965), 491–2. For an English text, see Jane Degras, ed., *Soviet Documents on Foreign Policy*, III (London, 1953), 486–7.

VII. *Protocol on the Transfer of Japanese Oil and Coal Concessions in Northern Sakhalin (30 Mar. 1944)*

ARTICLE I

The Government of Japan transfers to the Union of Soviet Socialist Republics all rights to the Japanese oil and coal concessions in northern Sakhalin in accordance with the provisions of the present Protocol and the terms of application of the Protocol appended hereto.

The concession contracts concluded between the Government of the Union of Soviet Socialist Republics on the one hand, and Japanese concessionaires on the other hand, concluded on 14 Dec. 1925, as well as the supplementary contracts and agreements concluded subsequently, are annulled by the present Protocol.

ARTICLE II

All the property (structures, equipment, materials, spare parts, provisions, etc.) in the possession of the Japanese concessionaires in northern Sakhalin is to be turned over to the Government of the Union of Soviet Socialist Republics in its present condition insofar as nothing different is provided for by the present Protocol and the terms of application of the Protocol appended hereto.

ARTICLE III

In connection with the provisions of the two preceding articles the Government of the Union of Soviet Socialist Republics agrees to pay to the Government of Japan the sum of five million roubles in accordance with the provisions of the terms of application of the present Protocol appended hereto.

The Government of the Union of Soviet Socialist Republics also agrees to supply annually to the Government of Japan on the usual commercial terms 50,000 metric tons of oil extracted at the Okha oilfields in the course of five consecutive years as from the time of the termination of the present war.

ARTICLE IV

The Government of the Union of Soviet Socialist Republics guarantees to the Government of Japan unobstructed and free of duty removal from the concession territories of oil and coal stocked in stores and belonging to Japanese concessionaires, in conformity with the provisions of the terms of application of the present Protocol appended hereto.

Moscow News, 1 Apr. 1944, p. 2, as quoted by Harriet L. Moore, *Soviet Far Eastern Policy, 1931–1945* (Princeton, 1945), pp. 202–4.

VIII. *Agreement Regarding Entry of the Soviet Union into the War Against Japan: Yalta Agreement (11 Feb. 1945)*

The leaders of three Great Powers—the Soviet Union, United States of America and Great Britain—have agreed that in two or three months after Germany has surrendered and the war in Europe has terminated the Soviet Union shall enter into the war against Japan on the side of the Allies on condition that:

2. The former rights of Russia violated by the treacherous attack of Japan in 1904 shall be restored, viz:

A. The southern part of Sakhalin as well as all islands adjacent to it shall be returned to the Soviet Union.

B. The commercial port by Dairen shall be internationalized, the pre-eminent interests of the Soviet Union in this port being safeguarded and the lease of Port Arthur as a naval base of the U.S.S.R. restored.

C. The Chinese-Eastern Railroad and the Southern Manchurian Railroad, which provides an outlet to Dairen, shall be jointly operated by the establishment of a joint Soviet-Chinese company, it being understood that the pre-eminent interest of the Soviet Union shall be safeguarded and that China shall retain full sovereignty in Manchuria.

3. The Kurile Islands shall be handed over to the Soviet Union.

The Heads of the three Great Powers have agreed that these claims of the Soviet Union shall be unquestionably fulfilled after Japan has been defeated.

United States, Department of State, *Foreign Relations of the United States, Diplomatic Papers, Publication 6199, the Conferences of Malta and Yalta, 1945* (Washington, 1955), p. 984.

IX. *The Potsdam Declaration: Signed by China, Great Britain, the United States (26 July 1945), and by the Soviet Union (9 Aug. 1945)*

8. The terms of the Cairo Declaration shall be carried out and Japanese sovereignty shall be limited to the islands of Honshu, Hokkaido, Kyushu, Shikoku and such minor islands as we determine.

United States, Department of State, *Foreign Relations of the United States, 1945, Conference of Berlin (Potsdam)*, II (Washington, 1960), 1281.

X. *Treaty of Peace with Japan: the San Francisco Treaty (8 Sept. 1951)*

ARTICLE II

c. Japan renounces all right, title and claim to the Kurile Islands, and to that portion of Sakhalin and the islands adjacent to it over which Japan acquired sovereignty as a consequence of the Treaty of Portsmouth of 5 Sept. 1905.

Raymond Dennet and Katherine D. Durant, ed., *Documents on American Foreign Relations, XIII (1951)* (Princeton, 1953), 471.

APPENDIX B

RUSSIAN AND JAPANESE PLACE NAMES IN SAKHALIN

Although Sakhalin is at present a part of the Soviet Union, the island has a long historical association with Japan. Japan ruled the southern half of the island (Karafuto) from 1905 to 1945. It is therefore important to be aware of both the Russian and the Japanese place names for towns, bays, mountains, capes, and other geographical features. To facilitate reference, this appendix gives both the Russian-Japanese and the Japanese-Russian name conversion tables.

For a complete gazetteer of Sakhalin's Russian and Japanese place names, see: U.S. Air Force, 6004th Air Intelligence Service Squadron, Evasion and Escape Section, *Gazetteer of Sakhalin* (n.p., 1956); U.S. Army, Headquarters, Far East, 8th U.S. Army, Office of the Assistant Chief of Staff, G–2, Intelligence A.P.O. 343, *Gazetteer of Russian Place Names in Sakhalin and the Kurile Islands* (3rd ed., n.p., 1955).

RUSSIAN	JAPANESE
Aniva (bay)	Aniwa
Aniva (cape)	Naka Shiretoko
Aniva (town)	Rūtaka
Boshniakovo	Nishi Shakutan
Chekhov	Noda
Chkalovo	Kitose
Dolinsk	Ochiai
Gastello	Nairo
Gornozavodsk	Naihoro
Iablochnyi	Rantomari
Iasnomorskii	Oko
Ilinskii	Kushunnai
Iuzhno-Sakhalinsk (formerly Vladimirovka)	Toyohara
Kholmsk	Maoka
Korsakov	Ōtomari
Krasnogorsk	Chinnai
Krilon (cape)	Nishi Notoro
La Pérouse (strait)	Sōya

RUSSIAN	JAPANESE
Leonidovo	Kami Shikuka
Lesogorsk	Nayoshi
Makarov	Shirutoru
Moneron (island)	Kaibatō
Nevelsk	Honto
Nevelskoi (strait)	Mamiya
Novikovo	Shiretoko
Novo Aleksandrovsk	Konuma
Orlovo	Ushiro
Ozerskii	Nagahama
Pobedino	Koton
Poronaisk	Shikuka (Shisuka)
Pravda	Ohadomari
Pugachevo	Maguntanhama
Sakhalin	Karafuto (used both to designate the entire island or just the southern half ruled by Japan, 1905–45).
Shakhtersk	Tōrō
Sinegorsk	Kawakami
Sokol	Ōtani
Starodubskoe	Sakaehama
Terpenie (bay)	Taraika
Terpenie (cape)	Kita Shiretoko
Tiulenii (island)	Kaihyōtō
Tomari	Tomarioru
Udarnyi	Taihei
Uglegorsk	Esutoru
Ugolnyi	Okuzawa
Ulianovskoe	Dorokawa
Vakhrushev	Tomarikishi
Vostochnyi	Mototomari
Vzmore	Shiraura

JAPANESE	RUSSIAN
Aniwa (bay)	Aniva
Chinnai	Krasnogorsk
Dorokawa	Ulianovskoe
Esutoru	Uglegorsk
Honto	Nevelsk
Kaibatō (island)	Moneron
Kaihyōtō (island)	Tiulenii

JAPANESE	RUSSIAN
Kami Shikuka	Leonidovo
Karafuto	Sakhalin or southern Sakhalin
Kawakami	Sinegorsk
Kita Shiretoko (cape)	Terpenie
Kitose	Chkalovo
Konuma	Novo Aleksandrovsk
Koton	Pobedino
Kushunnai	Ilinskii
Maguntanhama	Pugachevo
Mamiya kaikyō (strait)	Nevelskoi
Maoka	Kholmsk
Mototomari	Vostochnyi
Nagahama	Ozerskii
Naihoro	Gornozavodsk
Nairo	Gastello
Naka Shiretoko (cape)	Aniva
Nayoshi	Lesogorsk
Nishi Notoro (cape)	Krilon
Nishi Shakutan	Boshniakovo
Noda	Chekhov
Ochiai	Dolinsk
Ohadomari	Pravda
Okuzawa	Ugolnyi
Oko	Iasnomorskii
Ōtani	Sokol
Ōtomari	Korsakov
Rantomari	Iablochnyi
Rūtaka	Aniva
Sakaehama	Starodubskoe
Shikuka (Shisuka)	Poronaisk
Shiraura	Vzmore
Shiretoko	Novikovo
Shirutoru	Makarov
Sōya kaikyō (strait)	La Pérouse
Taihei	Udarnyi
Taraika (bay)	Terpenie
Tomarikishi	Vakhrushev
Tomarioru	Tomari
Tōrō	Shakhtersk
Toyohara	Iuzhno-Sakhalinsk (formerly Vladimirovka)
Ushiro	Orlovo

SELECT BIBLIOGRAPHY

I. GOVERNMENT DOCUMENTS AND PUBLICATIONS

DEGRAS, JANE, ed. *Soviet Documents on Foreign Policy*. 3 vols. London, 1951–3.

DENNET, RAYMOND, and KATHERINE D. DURANT, ed. *Documents on American Foreign Relations*, XIII (1951). Princeton, 1953.

GREAT BRITAIN, ADMIRALTY. *In-Letters* [Admirals' Despatches]. I–5629, I–5630, I–5656, I–5657 (1854–6).

—— FOREIGN OFFICE. *General Correspondence, China* F.O. 17. (1854–6).

—— FOREIGN OFFICE, HISTORICAL SECTION. *Sakhalin*. No. 56, British and Foreign State Papers. London, 1920.

—— NAVAL STAFF INTELLIGENCE DEPARTMENT. *A Handbook of Siberia and Arctic Russia*. London, 1918.

JAPAN. BŌEI CHŌ, BŌEI KENSHŪJO, SENSHI SHITSU [Defence Ministry, Defence Research Institute, War History Room], ed. *Hokutō hōmen rikugun sakusen* [North-east Region Army Operations], Vol. XXI of *Tōa senshi sōsho* [East Asia War History Series]. Tokyo, 1968.

—— FOREIGN OFFICE. *Saghalien (Karafuto) Island*. Tokyo, 1949.

—— FOREIGN OFFICE. *Treaties and Conventions between the Empire of Japan and other Powers together with Universal Conventions, Regulations, and Communications since March, 1854*. Rev. ed. Tokyo, 1884.

—— GAIMUSHŌ [Ministry of Foreign Affairs], ed. *Dai Nihon gaikō bunsho* [Documents of Japan's Foreign Relations], I–IX. Tokyo, 1936–40. Continued as *Nihon gaikō bunsho*, X– . Tokyo, 1949– .

—— GAIMUSHŌ, JŌHŌ BUNKA KYOKU [Public Information Bureau]. *Hoppō ryōdo* [The Northern Territories]. Tokyo, 1961.

—— GAIMUSHŌ, JŌHŌ BUNKA KYOKU. *Warera no hoppō ryōdo* [Our Northern Territories]. Tokyo, 1969.

—— GAIMUSHŌ, JŌYAKU KYOKU, CHŌSA SHITSU [Treaty Bureau, Research Room], ed. *Nihon tōjika no Karafuto* [Southern Sakhalin under Japanese Rule]. Tokyo, 1969.

—— GAIMUSHŌ, ŌA KYOKU [Europe and Asia Bureau]. *Nisso kōshō shi* [History of Japanese-Soviet Negotiations]. Tokyo, 1942. Reprinted in 1969.

—— HOKKAIDO CHŌ [Hokkaido Prefectural Office], ed. *Shinsen Hokkaido shi* [New History of Hokkaido]. 7 vols. Sapporo, 1936–7.

—— Hokkaido Sōmubu, Ryōdo Fukki Hoppō Gyogyō Taisaku Honbu [Hokkaido Prefectural Office, General Affairs Division, Central Planning Department for the Reversion of Territories and Northern Fisheries], ed. *Karafuto kankei shiryō mokuroku* [Catalogue of Sources relating to Southern Sakhalin]. 5 vols. Sapporo, 1963–9.

—— Hokkaido Sōmubu, Ryōdo Fukki Hoppō Gyogyō Taisaku Honbu, ed. *Karafuto shūsenshi nenpyō* [A Chronology of the End of the War in Southern Sakhalin]. Sapporo, 1968.

—— Karafuto chō [Karafuto Office], ed. *Karafuto enkaku shi* [A History of Karafuto's Development]. Toyohara, 1925.

—— Karafuto chō, ed. *Karafuto shisei enkaku* [The Development of Karafuto's Administration]. 2 vols. Toyohara, 1912.

—— Karafuto chō, ed. *Karafuto shisei sanjūnen shi* [A History of Thirty Years of Karafuto's Administration]. Toyohara, 1936.

—— Karafuto chō, ed. *Karafuto shokumin no enkaku* [The Development of Karafuto's Colonization]. Toyohara, 1929.

—— Karafuto chō, ed. *Karafuto sōsho* [Karafuto Series]. 7 vols. Toyohara, 1939–41.

—— Karafuto chō, ed. *Karafuto yōran*, 1936–42 [Karafuto Handbook]. Toyohara, 1937–43.

—— Ministry of Foreign Affairs, Public Information Bureau. *The Northern Islands: Background of Territorial Problems in the Japanese-Soviet Negotiations.* Tokyo, 1955.

—— Ministry of Foreign Affairs, Public Information Bureau. *The Northern Territorial Issue: Japan's Position on Unsettled Question between Japan and the Soviet Union.* Tokyo, 1968.

—— Takumushō [Ministry of Colonization], ed. *Takumu yōran, 1936* [Colonization Handbook]. Tokyo, 1937.

Kolesnikov, N. I., ed. *Sotsialisticheskoe stroitelstvo na Sakhaline 1925–1945 gg.* [Socialist Construction on Sakhalin, 1925–1945]. Iuzhno-Sakhalinsk, 1967.

A collection of government and party documents, press releases, and workers' resolutions.

Russia. Ministry of the Interior, Central Statistic Committee, Report No. 52. *Glavnishiia danniia po statistik naseleniia krainovo vostoka Sibiri: Primorskaia i Amurskaia oblast i ostrov Sakhalin* [Main Data on the Statistics of Peoples of the Maritime and Amur Districts and the Island of Sakhalin]. Ed., S. Patkanov. St. Petersburg, 1903.

Soviet Documents on Foreign Policy. Ed., Jane Degras. 3 vols. London, 1951–3.

UNITED STATES AIR FORCE, 6004th AIR INTELLIGENCE SERVICE SQUADRON, EVASION AND ESCAPE SECTION. *Gazetteer of Sakhalin.* n.p., 1956.

—— U.S. ARMY, HEADQUARTERS, FAR EAST, 8TH U.S. ARMY, OFFICE OF THE ASSISTANT CHIEF OF STAFF, G–2, INTELLIGENCE APO 343. *Gazetteer of Russian Place Names in Sakhalin and the Kurile Islands* (*Sakhalinskaia oblast*). 3rd ed. n.p., 1955.

—— U.S. ARMY, MILITARY HISTORY SECTION, HEADQUARTERS, ARMED FORCES, FAR EAST. *Japanese Monograph No. 155.* n.p., 1952.

—— DEPARTMENT OF STATE. *Bulletin*, IX. Washington, 1943.

—— DEPARTMENT OF STATE. *Foreign Relations of the United States.* For years 1905–45. Washington, 1906–60.

—— NAVAL RESERVE MIDSHIPMAN'S SCHOOL. *Project Report: Karafuto* (*Japanese Sakhalin*). New York, 1943.

—— SENATE. *Miscellaneous Documents.* No. 80, 30th Congress, 1st Session, 8 Mar. 1848.

U.S.S.R. MINISTERSTVO INOSTRANNYKH DEL SSSR [Ministry of Foreign Affairs of the U.S.S.R.], ed. *Dokumenty vneshnei politiki SSSR* [Documents of Exterior Politics of the U.S.S.R.]. Moscow, 1957–.

—— MINISTRY OF FOREIGN AFFAIRS, ed. *Correspondence between the Chairmen of the Council of Ministers of the U.S.S.R. and the Presidents of the U.S.A. and the Prime Ministers of Great Britain during the Great Patriotic War of 1941–45.* 2 vols. Moscow, 1957.

—— SAKHALINSKAIA OBLAST [Sakhalin District Office], ed. *Sakhalinskaia oblast v tsifrakh za 1946–1966 gody: statisticheskii sbornik* [Sakhalin Oblast in Figures from 1946 to 1966: Statistical Collection]. Iuzhno-Sakhalinsk, 1967.

—— SAKHALINSKAIA OBLAST, STATISTICHESKOE UPRAVLENIE [Statistical Administration], ed. *Narodnoe khoziaistvo Sakhalinskoi oblasti* [People's Economy of Sakhalin Oblast]. Iuzhno-Sakhalinsk, 1960.

—— TSENTRALNYI GOSUDARSTVENNYI ARKHIV, DALNEVO VOSTOKA, TOMSK [Central State Archive of the Far East at Tomsk], ed. *Pobeda Sovetskoi vlasti na Severnom Sakhaline, 1917–1925 gg.: sbornik dokumentov i materialov* [The Victory of Soviet Power in Northern Sakhalin, 1917–1925: A Collection of Documents and Materials]. Iuzhno-Sakhalinsk, 1959.

II. NEWSPAPERS, PERIODICALS, AND YEARBOOKS

Arctic Anthropology (Madison, Wisconsin).

Asahi nenkan [Asahi Annual] (Tokyo).

Asahi shimbun [Asahi Newspaper] (Tokyo).
Asia (New York).
The Asiatic Review (London).
Bibliotekar [Librarian] (Moscow).
Bōei nenkan [Defense Annual] (Tokyo).
Bolshevik (Moscow).
Bumazhnaia promyshlennost [Paper Industry] (Moscow).
Business Weekly (New York).
Chamber's Journal (London).
China Journal (Shanghai).
China Weekly Review (Shanghai).
Chiri shigaku [Historical Geography] (Tokyo).
Chūō kōron [Central Review] (Tokyo).
Contemporary Japan (Tokyo).
Current History (New York).
Dalnii Vostok [The Far East] (Khabarovsk).
Denki [Biography] (Tokyo).
Economic Geography (New York).
Far Eastern Review (Shanghai).
Far Eastern Survey (New York).
Fortnightly Review (London).
Gaikō jihō [Foreign Affairs Bulletin] (Tokyo).
Geografiia v shkole [Geography in School] (Moscow).
Great Britain and the East (London).
Hokkaido nenkan [Hokkaido Annual] (Sapporo).
The Imperial and Asiatic Quarterly Review (London).
Independent (New York).
Istoriia SSSR [History U.S.S.R.] (Moscow).
Iunyi naturalist [Young Naturalist] (Moscow).
Izvestiia (Moscow).
Izvestiia, Geograficheskoe obshchestvo SSSR [Bulletin, Geographical Society of the U.S.S.R.] (Leningrad).
Izvestiia, Seriia geograficheskaia, Akademiia nauk, SSSR [Bulletin, Geographical Series, U.S.S.R. Academy of Sciences] (Moscow).
Japan Times (Tokyo).
Journal of the Royal Artillery (Woolwich, England).
Journal of the Royal Central Asian Society (London).
Journal of the Royal Geographical Society (London).
Khudozhnik [Artist] (Moscow).
Kommunist (Moscow).
Literary Digest (New York).
Modern Asian Studies (London).
Morskoi sbornik [Maritime Collection] (St. Petersburg).

Moskva (Moscow).
Narodne obrazovanie [People's Education] (Moscow).
The Nation (New York).
Neftianik [Petroleum Worker] (Moscow).
New York Herald Tribune.
New York Times.
Nihon gaikō shi kenkyū [Research on the History of Japanese Foreign Affairs] (Tokyo).
Nihon rekishi [Japanese History] (Tokyo).
Ogoniok [Little Fire] (Moscow).
Oktiabr [October] (Moscow).
Outlook (New York).
Partiinaia zhizn [Party Life] (Moscow).
Pchelovodstvo [Beekeeping] (Moscow).
Pravda (Moscow).
Priroda [Nature] (Moscow).
Questions diplomatiques et coloniales (Paris).
Seikai ōrai [Political Affairs] (Tokyo).
Shin seimei [New Life] (Toyohara, later Iuzhno-Sakhalinsk).
Smena [Change] (Moscow).
Sobieto nenkan [Soviet Annual] (Tokyo).
Soobshcheniia, Sakhalinskii kompleksnyi nauchno-issledovatelskii institut, Akademiia nauk SSSR [Reports, Sakhalin Joint Scientific Research Institute, U.S.S.R. Academy of Sciences] (Novosibirsk).
Sovetskaia etnografiia [Soviet Ethnography] (Moscow).
Sovetskaia knizhnaia torgovlia [Soviet Book Trade] (Moscow).
Sovetskii Soiuz [Soviet Union] (Moscow).
Time (New York).
The Times (London).
Transactions of the Asiatic Society of Japan (Tokyo).
Trans Pacific (Tokyo).
Travel (New York).
Trudy, Sakhalinskii kompleksnyi nauchno-issledovatelskii institut, Akademiia nauk SSSR [Transactions, Sakhalin Joint Scientific Research Institute, U.S.S.R. Academy of Sciences]. (Novosibirsk).
Uchenye zapiski [Academic Notes] (Iuzhno-Sakhalinsk).
Vestnik, Akademiia nauk SSSR [Journal, U.S.S.R. Academy of Sciences] (Moscow).
Vestnik Azii [Journal of Asia, or Journal of the Russian Oriental Society] (Harbin, Manchuria).
Vitchyzna [Our Country] (Kiev).
Voenno-istoricheskii zhurnal [Military History Magazine] (Moscow).
Voprosy istorii [Problems of History] (Moscow).

World Today (London).
Yenching Journal of Social Studies (Peking).
Yomiuri shimbun [Yomiuri Newspaper] (Tokyo).

III. MEMOIRS AND TRAVELOGUES

ABE ETSURŌ. *Karafuto no tabi* [Karafuto Journey]. Toyohara, 1936.

ABOLTIN, V. Ia. *Ostrov sokrovishch: severnyi Sakhalin* [Island Treasure: Northern Sakhalin]. Vladivostok, 1928.

—— 'Vosstanovlenie Sovetskoi vlasti na severnom Sakhalin' [Restoration of Soviet Power in Northern Sakhalin], *Voprosy istorii* [Problems of History], XLI (Oct. 1966), 91–110.

ALEKSEEV, ALEKSANDR I. *Po taezhnim tropam Sakhalina* [Along the Taiga Paths of Sakhalin]. Iuzhno-Sakhalinsk, 1959.

ATKINSON, THOMAS WITLAM. *Travels in the Regions of the Upper and Lower Amoor and the Russian Acquisitions on the Confines of India and China*. New York, 1860.

BAIUKANSKII, A. 'U vostochnykh granits' [On the Eastern Frontier], *Ogoniok* [Little Fire], XXXI (June 1953), 2.

BELOUSOV, I. *Yuzhno-Sakhalinsk*. Moscow, 1968.

BENKOVSKII, L. M. 'Na Sakhalinskom poberezhe' [On the Shore of Sakhalin], *Priroda* [Nature], L (Nov. 1961), 127.

BERNARD, JEAN FREDERIC, ed. *Recueil de Voyages au Nord*. 8 vols. Amsterdam, 1715–27.

BIGELOW, POULTNEY. *Japan and Her Colonies: Extracts from a Diary made whilst visiting Formosa, Manchuria, Shantung, Korea, and Saghalin in the Year 1921*. London, 1923.

BORDEAUX, ALBERT. *Siberie et Californie: Notes de Voyage et de Séjour: Janvier 1889–Decembre 1902*. Paris, 1903.

BOSHNIAK, N. K. 'Ekspeditsiia v Priamurskom krae' [Expedition in the Priamur Region], *Morskoi sbornik* [Maritime Collection], XXXVIII (Dec. 1858), 179–94; XXXIX (Jan. 1859), 111–31.
Account of a Russian officer's exploration of central Sakhalin during the winter and spring of 1852.

BROUGHTON, W. R. *Voyage of Discovery in the North Pacific Ocean*. London, 1804.
Broughton describes his attempt and failure to discover a strait between Sakhalin and the mainland in 1796.

BUSSE, N. V. *Ostrov Sakhalin: Ekspeditsiia 1853–54 gg* [Sakhalin Island: Expedition of 1853–4]. St. Petersburg, 1872.
Major Busse commanded the pioneer Russian settlement (Muravevskii Post) established in 1853 in Aniwa Bay.

BUTKOVSKII, Ia. *O Sakhaline i evo znachenii* [Of Sakhalin and its Significance]. St. Petersburg, 1873.

A sanguine analysis of Sakhalin's rich economic potential together with a prediction that it would rival Sydney and Melbourne in growth.

CHAMBERLAIN, WILLIAM HENRY. 'Japan's Northern Outpost', *Christian Science Monitor Weekly Magazine*, 11 Nov. 1936, pp. 10, 20.
The author visited Japanese Karafuto in 1935.

CHEKHOV, ANTON P. 'Ostrov Sakhalin' [Sakhalin Island], in *A. P. Chekhov: sobranie sochinenii* [A. P. Chekhov: Collected Works], X. Moscow, 1963.
A classic description of Sakhalin as a penal colony, based on the author's visit during the summer of 1890. First published in 1895, it has been translated into several languages (see below).

—— *The Island: A Journey to Sakhalin.* Translated by Luba and Michael Terpak. New York, 1967.

CHEKHOV, S[ERGEI SERGEIVICH]. 'Poiezdka na ostrov Sakhalin: iz dnevnika khudozhnika' [Trip to Sakhalin: from an Artist's Diary], *Moskva*, IV (1960), 188–94.
A. P. Chekhov's grandnephew revisited the spots on Sakhalin described by his granduncle.

CHERNYSHEV, M. 'Na zemle Sakhalinskoi' [On the Soil of Sakhalin], *Iunyi naturalist* [Young Naturalist], II (Feb. 1961), 32–3.

CHISHOLM, W. S. 'Saghalien, the Isle of the Russian Banished', *Chamber's Journal*, VIII (April 1905), 301–4.

COLLINS, PERRY MCDONOUGH. *A Voyage Down the Amoor with a Land Journey through Siberia and Incidental Notices of Manchooria, Kamschatka, and Japan.* New York, 1860.
This account contains a description and drawings of Mongol-Chinese remains at Tyr on the lower Amur River.

DALTON, L. V. 'Sakhalin or Karafto [sic.]', *The Imperial and Asiatic Quarterly Review*, XX (Oct. 1905), 279–85.

DEMIN, L. M. *Za Tatarskim prolivom; Sakhalinskie ocherki* [Across the Tatar Strait; Sketches of Sakhalin]. Moscow, 1965.
The author spent 1943–5 on Sakhalin and revisited the island after an absence of twenty years.

DEWINDT, HARRY. 'The Island of Sakhalin', *Fortnightly Review*, New Series, LXI (Jan.–June 1897), 711–15.
A favourable report on prison conditions based on a short visit in 1893.

—— *The New Siberia.* London, 1896.

DIAKONOV, A. 'V boiakh na iuzhnom Sakhalin' [In the Battles in southern Sakhalin], *Voenno-istoricheskii zhurnal* [Military History Magazine], VIII (Aug. 1965), 58–63.
A firsthand account of the Soviet attack across the 50th parallel

upon the Japanese positions at Handenzawa, Koton, and Horomi Pass.

DOROSHEVICH, VASILII MIKHAILOVICH. *Sakhalin.* Moscow, 1903.
The author, a journalist, visited the penal colony in 1898. He maintained an intense interest in criminal types. The book is filled with remarkable portraits and photographs of individual convicts.

DU HAILLY, E. 'Une Campagne dans l'Océan Pacifique', *Revue des Deux Mondes*, 1 Sept. 1858, pp. 169–98.
A description of the unsuccessful attempt of the Anglo-French naval forces to capture a Russian convoy in the 'Bay of Tartary' during the Crimean War.

ELLINSKII, B. *Pod zvon tsepei: roman Sakhalinskikh politicheskikh silnikh* [In Clanging Chains: a Novel of the Lives of Sakhalin's Political Exiles]. Leningrad, 1927.
Based upon the author's experience as an exile in Sakhalin.

FURET, L. *Lettres á M. Léon de Roany sur l'archipel japonais et la Tartarie orientale.* Paris, 1857.
The author accompanied the French squadron which operated off the coasts of Sakhalin during the Crimean War. He explored the west central coast in July 1856 and studied the Gilyak language. A Gilyak glossary is the principal value of this book.

GAUNT, MARY. *A Broken Journey.* London, 1919.
Travelogue of an Australian lady who journeyed down the Amur River to Sakhalin in July 1914. While enjoying the hospitality of the governor, she called the island 'the end of the earth'.

GERASIMOV, I. P. 'Sakhalin', *Priroda* [Nature], LV (Aug. 1966), 84–92.
An optimistic appraisal of the island's agricultural potential. Based upon a visit in 1965.

GIZENKO, A. I. 'Na Sakhaline i Kurilskikh ostrovakh' [On Sakhalin and the Kurile Islands], *Priroda* [Nature], L (Mar. 1961), 125.

GOLOVNIN, VASILII MIKHAILOVICH. *Memoirs of a Captivity in Japan During the Years 1811, 1812, and 1813: with Observations on the Country and the People.* 3 vols. 2nd ed. London, 1824.

GREEY, EDWARD. *The Bear Worshippers of Yezo and the Island of Karafuto (Saghalin).* Boston, 1884.

—— *Young Americans in Yezo and the Island of Karafuto (Saghalin).* Boston, n.d. [*c. 1892*].

HABERSHAM, A. W. *The North Pacific Surveying and Exploring Expedition, or My Last Cruise.* Philadelphia, 1858.
The author visited Sakhalin in 1855.

HARRISON, MARGUERITE E. 'Red Bear, Yellow Dragon, and American Lady', *Literary Digest*, LXXXI (19 Apr. 1924), 38–44. Impressions of a lady journalist in Japanese-occupied northern Sakhalin. Sympathetic to Japanese.

HAWES, CHARLES H. *In the Uttermost East*. London, 1903.

HOWARD, B. D. *Life with Transsiberian Savages*. London, 1893. A Victorian gentleman relates the horrors of the penal colony and betrays his repugnance to Sakhalin's aborigines.

—— *Prisoners of Russia: A Personal Study of Convict Life in Sakhalin and Siberia*. New York, 1902.

ILATOVSKAIA, TAMARA. 'Kogda za plechami riukzak' [With a Knapsack on Your Shoulders], *Smena* [Change], XL (Feb. 1963), 16–17.
A young Russian tourist views Sakhalin's vacation resorts.

IZUMI TOMOSABURŌ. *Soren Minami Karafuto* [Soviet Southern Sakhalin]. Tokyo, 1952.
The author, formerly an official in the Karafuto Office, remained in southern Sakhalin until 1949, serving as an adviser in the Soviet military government. A rare and useful glimpse into the Russian occupation policies.

KALINICHENKO, IU. 'Na ostrove dalnem' [On an Island Far Away], *Neftianik* [Petroleum Worker], XI (June 1966), 18–20.
Describes the life of the oil workers at Okha.

KANTOROVICH, VLADIMIR I. *Sakhalinskie tetradi* [Sakhalin Notebooks]. Moscow, 1965.
Impressions of Sakhalin by a well-known critic who has had a forty-year association with the island.

—— *Soviet Sakhalin*. Moscow, 1933.
Eulogizes Soviet achievements in Sakhalin under the First Five-Year Plan.

KENNAN, GEORGE. *Siberia and the Exile System*. 2 vols. London, 1891.
While the author never visited Sakhalin, he knew its governor, General Kononovich, the commander of the Kara Prison.

KEPPEN, A. *Ostrov Sakhalin* [Sakhalin Island]. St. Petersburg, 1875.
A survey of the island's coal deposits and an optimistic appraisal of their potential exploitation.

KRUEGER, H. E. 'Present Day Conditions in Karafuto, Japanese-owned Saghalin', *China Journal*, XVII (Nov. 1937), 238–43.

KRUSENSTERN, A. J. von. *Voyage round the World in the Years 1803, 1804, 1805, 1806*. Translated from the German by R. B. Hoppner. 2 vols. London, 1813.

KUKUNIAN, S. *Poslednie dni na Sakhaline* [Last Days on Sakhalin]. Baku, 1910.
An account of Sakhalin on the eve of the Japanese attack of 1905.

LA PÉROUSE, JEAN FRANCOIS GALOUP DE. *A Voyage round the World in the Years 1785, 1786, 1787, 1788.* 3 vols. London, 1798.
Like Broughton and Krusenstern, La Pérouse failed to discover the strait between Sakhalin and the continent and concluded that Sakhalin was a peninsula.

LOBAS, N. S. *Katorga i poselenie na Ostrov Sakhalin* [Penal Servitude and Settlement on Sakhalin Island]. Pavlograd, 1903.

MAAK, RICHARD KARLOVICH. *Puteshestvie na Amur* [Journey on the Amur]. St. Petersburg, 1859.
A pioneer study of the lower Amur River region. Contains a sketch of Deren.

MAEDAKŌ HIROICHIRŌ. *Kokkyō Karafuto* [Frontier Karafuto]. Tokyo, 1939.

MALINOVSKII, L. Ia. *Kantōgun kaimetsu su* [The Destruction of the Kwantung Army]. Translated from the Russian by Ishiguro Hiroshi. Tokyo, 1968.
Originally appeared in the Soviet Union under the title *Finale* (Moscow, 1966). Marshall Malinovskii recalls the Far Eastern Campaign of August 1945 in Manchukuo, Korea, Karafuto, and the Kurile Islands.

MAMIYA RINZŌ. 'Kita Ezo zusetsu' [Illustrated Description of Sakhalin], in Ōtomo Kisaku, ed. *Hokumon sōsho* [Northern Gates Library], V. Tokyo, 1944, 279–380.
A useful description of Sakhalin and its natives.

—— 'Kita Yezo Zusetsu', *Proceedings of the American Philosophical Society*, IC. Part 2. 1955. 93–117. Translated by John A. Harrison.

MAMIYA RINZŌ. *Tōdatsu kikō* [Travels in Eastern Tartary]. Ed., Shimada Yoshi, Dairen, 1938.
Mamiya's account of his trip up the Amur River to the Manchu post at Deren in 1809.

MATSUDA DENJŪRŌ. 'Hokui dan' [Tales of Northern Savages], in Ōtomo Kisaku, ed. *Hokumon sōsho* [Northern Gates Library], V. Tokyo, 1944, 117–276.
Includes a description of Matsuda's exploration of Sakhalin with Mamiya Rinzō in 1808.

MATSUDA GENJI. 'Glimpses of Saghalien', *Trans Pacific*, XVIII (23 Oct. 1930), 5, 13.

MATSUKAWA KIKUNI. *Karafuto tankenki* [Karafuto Exploration Notes]. Tokyo, 1909.

'Matsumae shima kyōchō' [A Gazetteer of Matsumae], in Kokusho kankō kai, ed. *Zoku zoku gunsho ruiju*, IX. Tokyo, 1906, 323–5.
Dated 1700, the 'Matsumae Gazetteer' is one of the earliest extant Japanese sources concerning Sakhalin.

MATSUNAGA HIKOEMON. *Karafuto oyobi Kansatsuka* [Karafuto and Kamchatka]. Tokyo, 1905.

MIROLIUBOV, I. P. *Vosem let na Sakhalin* [Seven Years on Sakhalin]. St. Petersburg, 1901.
Memoirs of convict life on Sakhalin. Author's real name: Ivan Pavlovich Iuvachev.

MITSUL, M. S. *Ocherk ostrova Sakhalina v selskokhoziaistvennom otnoshenii* [Notes on Sakhalin Island with Respect to Agriculture]. St. Petersburg, 1873.
Mitsul shared with Butkovskii and Keppen the conviction that Sakhalin had a great economic potential.

MIYATAKE SHŌZŌ. *Shiberia* [Siberia]. Tokyo, 1965.
The author, a journalist from the Japan Broadcasting System, visited Sakhalin in 1964.

MOGAMI TOKUNAI. *Ezo sōshi* [Ezo Miscellaneous]. Ed., Yoshida Tsunekichi, Tokyo, 1965.
Dispatched by Japanese authorities, Mogami surveyed southern Sakhalin in 1792 and met there the Russian castaway Ivanov.

NOVOMBERGSKII, N. *Ostrov Sakhalin* [Sakhalin Island]. St. Petersburg, 1903.

OBZHIGALIN, K. P. *Sakhalin, chudesnyi krai: fotoalbom* (Sakhalin a Wonderful Country: an Album of Photographs]. Iuzhno-Sakhalinsk, 1965.

O'DRISCOLL, J. 'Report on Saghalin by J. O'Driscoll', in *Gaimushō* [Japan Foreign Ministry], ed. *Dai Nihon gaikō bunsho* [Documents of Japan's Foreign Relations], II. Part 3. Tokyo, 1938, 197–222.
Reveals the weak position of the Japanese in Sakhalin in 1869 while the Russians built up their forces on the island.

OGATA NAKABA. *Kurai rōka* [Dark Corridor]. Tokyo, 1957.
An account of arrest and eleven-year imprisonment by Karafuto's ex-chief of police.

OKUYAMA RYŌ. *Aa Karafuto*. Sapporo, 1966.
Memoirs of life in Karafuto before and during the Soviet occupation by a schoolteacher in Maoka.

OSIPOV, I. 'Na Sakhalin' [On Sakhalin], *Ogoniok* [Little Fire], XXXI (Dec. 1953), 4–5.

—— *Sakhalinskie zapisi: ocherki* [Sakhalin Notes: Sketches]. Moscow, 1955.

—— *Sakhalinskie zapisi: osen 1945 goda* [Sakhalin Notes: Fall, 1945]. Moscow, 1946.
A good first-hand account of the Soviet attack of 1945. Includes interviews with Japanese prisoners of war.

ŌTA CHŌBEI. 'Hakodate nikki' [Hakodate Diary]. Manuscript in the Hakodate Municipal Library. Dated 1807.
An eyewitness description of Khvostov's attack on the Japanese settlement of Kushunkotan in southern Sakhalin (1806).

ŌTOMO KISAKU, ed. *Hokumon sōsho* [Northern Gates Library]. 6 vols. Tokyo, 1943–4.
A valuable collection of Tokugawa period (1600–1868) sources concerning Hokkaido and Sakhalin. See Mamiya Rinzō, Matsuda Denjūrō.

PEROV, N. 'Na Sakhaline' [On Sakhalin], *Krylia rodiny* [Wings of the Motherland], II (June 1951), 16.

POLJAKOW [POLIAKOV], J. S. *Reise nach der Insel Sachalin in den Jahren 1881–1882*. Berlin, 1884.
A famous zoologist explores the island. Good descriptions of the Tym Valley and the Gilyak natives.

RAKOVSKII, S. N. 'Na iuzhnom Sakhaline' [On southern Sokhalin], *Geografiia v shkole* [Geography in School], III (May-June, 1947), 8–16.
An interesting Soviet view of Japanese in southern Sakhalin before their repatriation.

REIMERS, N. F. 'Zima na Sakhaline' [Winter in Sakhalin], *Priroda* [Nature], LIV (Feb. 1965), 126–7.

RIMSKII-KORSAKOV, V. 'Sluchai i zametki na vintovoi shkhune "Vostok"' [Events and notes on the screw schooner 'Vostok'], *Morskoi sbornik* [Maritime Collection], XXXV (May 1858), 1–45.
Describes the exploration of the Tatary Strait and Sakhalin's western shore during the summer and fall of 1853.

RYZHKOV, A. *Soviet Far East: A Tour of Sakhalin*. Moscow, 1966.

SALWEY, CHARLOTTE M. *The Island Dependencies of Japan*. London, 1913.

SCHRENK, LEOPOLD. *Ob inorodtsakh Amurskovo kraia* [Of the Natives of the Amur Region]. 3 vols. St. Petersburg, 1883–1903.
Contains stunning lithographs of the Gilyak and Goldi.

—— *Reisen und Forschungen im Amur-Lande in den Jahren 1854–56* [Travels and Researches in the Amur Territory in the Years 1854–56]. 2 vols. St. Petersburg, 1859–67.

SHERGOVA, GALINA. 'Na dalnem ostrove' [On a distant Island], *Ogoniok* [Little Fire], XXXIII (Sept. 1955), 7–9.

SHINJŌ NARIKICHI. *Fuyuzora no kiroku* [Record of Winter Skies]. Sapporo, 1949.
The author (real name: Izumi Tomosaburō) describes his experiences in southern Sakhalin under Soviet military rule (1945–9).

SHMIDT [SCHMIDT], P. Iu. *Ostrov izgnaniia, Sakhalin* [Sakhalin, Island of Banishment]. St. Petersburg, 1905.
A biologist's impression of the island on the eve of the Russo-Japanese War.

SLIOTOV, PETR V. *Na Sakhaline* [On Sakhalin]. Moscow, 1933.

STALIN, I. V. *O velikoi otechestvennoi voine Sovetskovo Soiuza* [On the Great Patriotic War of the Soviet Union]. Moscow, 1946.
Contains a justification for the Soviet attack on Japanese Karafuto in 1945 (pp. 205–6).

STARKOV, A. 'Na Tikhom Okeane' [On the Pacific Ocean], *Ogoniok* [Little Fire], XXXVI (Sept. 1958), 14–19.

SUDZUKI SHIGEHIRA. *A Journal Kept in Karafuto.* Ed., Matsuura Takeshirō. Excerpt from *Transactions of the Japan Society*, IV (1895).

SUGAWARA MICHITARŌ. *Akai rōgoku* [Red Prison]. Sapporo, 1949.
Memoir of life in Khabarovsk's Krasnaia Rechka Prison by the former chief of Karafuto's Imperial Rule Assistance Association (Taisei yokusankai).

SUGIMOTO ZENNOSUKE. *Karafuto no omoide o kataru* [Speaking of Memories of Karafuto]. Iwashiro (Fukushima Prefecture), 1959.

SUGIMURA AKIRA. *Shin Karafuto fudoki* [A Description of New Karafuto]. Toyohara, 1936.

TAKANO AKIRA. 'Fubuosutofu bunsho kō' [Documents of Khvostov], *Waseda daigaku toshokan kiyō* [Waseda University Library Bulletin], VI (Dec. 1964), 1–28.
Documents left by Lieutenant Khvostov at Kushunkotan in southern Sakhalin (1806) are presented and annotated.

TEELING, WILLIAM. 'Migration to Sakhalin', *Great Britain and the East*, XLVIII (14 Jan. 1937), 62–3.

TILLEY, HENRY ARTHUR. *Japan, the Amoor, and the Pacific.* London, 1861.

TORII RYŪZŌ. *Kokuryūkō to kita Karafuto* [The Amur River and northern Sakhalin]. Tokyo, 1943.
The author accompanied the Japanese Army into the Russian Far East and northern Sakhalin during 1919–20.

TRONSON, J. M. *Personal Narrative of a Voyage to Japan, Kamtschatka, Siberia, Tartary, and Various Parts of the Coast of China, in H.M.S. Barracouta.* London, 1859.

VENIUKOV, COLONEL. 'On the Island of Sakhalin', *Journal of the Royal Geographical Society*, XLII (1872), 373–88.

Veniukov stressed Sakhalin's strategic importance to Russia's military posture in the Far East.

VINOKUROV, I., and F. FLORICH. *Po iuzhnomu Sakhalinu* [In southern Sakhalin]. Moscow, 1950.

VRIES, MAERTEN GERRITSZOON. *Reize van Maarten Gerritzoon Vries in 1643.* Amsterdam, 1858.
Includes Vries' account of his sighting of Sakhalin in 1643.

WHITTINGHAM, BERNARD. *Notes on the Expedition against the Russian Settlements in Eastern Siberia, and of a Visit to Japan and to the Shores of Tartary and of the Sea of Okhotsk.* London, 1856.
Contains an eyewitness account of Commodore Elliot's failure to trap the Russian convoy in the 'Bay of Tartary' (1855).

WOODROFFE, CAPTAIN C. R. 'Four Weeks in Saghalien', *Journal of the Royal Artillery*, XXXV (1908–9), 349–72.
Camping in Japanese Karafuto in the summer of 1907.

YAKOVLEV, N. 'A Visit to the Ainu in Southern Sakhalin', *The Asiatic Review*, New Series, XLIII (July 1947), 276–9.
A Soviet ethnographer investigates the condition of the Sakhalin Ainu immediately after the 1945 invasion.

YANAGIDA KUNIO. 'Karafuto kikō' [Karafuto Journey], in *Yanagida Kunio shū* [Collection of the Works of Yanagida Kunio], II. Tokyo, 1962, 443–63.
The famous Japanese folklorist visited Karafuto in September 1906 and left a diary of his impressions.

ZASUKHA, A. 'Na Sakhalin' [On Sakhalin], *Sovetskaia knizhnaia torgovlia* [Soviet Book Trade], I (1955), 16–17.

—— 'Sredi vekovoi taigi' [Among the eternal Taiga], *Bibliotekar* [Librarian], II (Feb. 1958), 30–1.

IV. SECONDARY STUDIES

ABE KŌZŌ. 'Bakumatsu ki Nichiro kankei' [Russo-Japanese Relations in the End of the Tokugawa Period], *Nihon gaikō shi kenkyū* [Research on the History of Japanese Foreign Affairs] (Dec. 1960), pp. 44–58.

ABE MAKOTO. 'Edo makki ni okeru Karafuto tanken' [Exploration of Karafuto in the End of the Tokugawa Period], *Chiri shigaku* [Historical Geography], LXIII (Mar. 1934), 51–8.

ADACHI KINNOSUKE. 'Sakhalin: What it means to Japan', *Independent*, LIX (14 Sept. 1905), 618–22.

AKADEMIIA NAUK SSSR, SIBIRSKOE OTDELENIE, SAKHALINSKII KOMPLEKSNYI NAUCHNO-ISSLEDOVATELSKII INSTITUT [U.S.S.R. Academy of Sciences, Siberian Branch, Sakhalin Joint

Scientific Research Institute]. *Atlas Sakhalinskoi oblasti* [Atlas of Sakhalin Oblast]. Moscow, 1967.

AKIOKA TAKESHIRŌ. *Nihon chizu shi* [History of Japanese Maps]. Tokyo, 1955.

AMIDON, W. C. 'The Issue of Sakhalin in Russo-Japanese Relations', in University of Michigan, Centre of Japanese Studies, ed. *Occasional Papers*, VII. Ann Arbor, 1957, pp. 60–9.

ARMAND, D. L. *Ostrov Khokkaido* [Hokkaido Island]. Moscow, 1947.

ASTON, W. G. 'Russian Descents into Saghalien and Itorup', *Transactions of the Asiatic Society of Japan*, First Series, I (1882), 78–86.

BABA HIDEO. 'Japanese Oil Wells in North Sakhalin', *Far Eastern Review*, XXXII (Feb. 1936), 79–80, 83.

BAGROV, V. N. *Iuzhno-Sakhalinskaia i Kurilskaia operatsii, avgust* 1945 *goda* [Southern Sakhalin and Kurile Operations, Aug. 1945]. Moscow, 1959.

BALIAEVSKII, V. F., and IA. L. MARKOVICH. 'Bumazhnaia promyshlennost Sakhalina v poslevoennyi period' [Sakhalin Paper Industry in the Postwar Period], *Bumazhnaia promyshlennost* [Paper Industry], XXXII (Dec. 1957), 15–18.

BARSKAIA, V. 'Moia sovest ne pozvoliaet molchat' [My Conscience does not allow Me to be Silent], *Partiinaia zhizn* [Party Life], V (Mar. 1965), 59–61.

BARSUKOV, IVAN. *Graf Nikolai Nikolaevich Muravev Amurskii*. 2 vols. Moscow, 1891.

BERTON, PETER A. *Nichiro ryōdo mondai*, 1850–1875 [The Russo-Japanese Boundary Problem, 1850–1875]. Translated by Tamura Kōsaku. Tokyo, 1967.

Bibliografiia Iaponii [Bibliography of Japan]. Ed. Akademiia nauk SSSR [U.S.S.R. Academy of Sciences]. 2 vols. Moscow, 1960–5.

Bolshaia Sovetskaia entsiklopediia [Great Soviet Encyclopedia]. Second edition. Moscow, 1949–57.

'Bolshe vnimaniia pchelovodstvo na Sakhaline' [Greater Attention to Beekeeping in Sakhalin], *Pchelovodstvo* [Beekeeping], XXIX (May 1952), 58–9.

BUITOVOI, S. *Sadi i okeana* [Gardens and Oceans], Leningrad, 1957.

BURIATOV, B. N., and M. V. TEPLINSKII. *A. P. Chekhov na Sakhaline* [A. P. Chekhov in Sakhalin]. Iuzhno-Sakhalinsk, 1957.

BURNEY, JAMES. *A Chronological History of Northeastern Voyages of Discovery and of the Early Eastern Navigations of the Russians*. London, 1819.

CHARD, CHESTER S. 'A New Look at the Ainu Problem.' Mimeograph. University of Wisconsin, 1969.

—— 'Time Depth and Culture Process in Maritime Northeast Asia', *Asian Perspectives*, V (Winter 1961), 213–16.

CH'EN, AGNES FANG-CHIH. 'Chinese Frontier Diplomacy: the Eclipse of Manchuria', *Yenching Journal of Social Studies*, V (July 1950), 69–141.

CHŌ ZAI JUTSU. *Gokumontō* [Prison Island]. Tokyo, 1966.

CHUBAROVA, R. V. 'K istorii drevneishevo naseleniia Sakhalina' [Towards the History of the Ancient Population of Sakhalin], *Sovetskaia etnografiia*, IV (1957), 60–75.

CONOLLY, VIOLET. 'The Sino-Soviet Conflict and the Soviet Far Eastern Region', *Journal of the Royal Central Asian Society*, XIV (June 1967), 146–50.

COXE, WILLIAM. *Account of the Russian Discoveries between Asia and America, to which are added the Conquest of Siberia and the History of the Transactions and Commerce between Russia and China*. London, 1780.

DE SABIR, C. *Le Fleuve Amour*. Paris, 1861.

DU HALDE, J. B. *Description de l'Empire de la Chine*. 4 vols. Paris, 1735.

EIDUS, KH. T. *Ocherki novoi i noveishei istorii Iaponii* [Essays on the Recent History of Japan]. Moscow, 1955.

ENDŌ HARUHISA. *Hoppō ryōdo mondai no shinsō: Chishima rettō to Yaruta kaidan* [The Truth of the Northern Territories Problem: the Kurile Islands and the Yalta Talks]. Tokyo, 1968.

ETTER, CARL. *Ainu Folklore*. Chicago, 1949.

FAINBERG, E. IA. *Russko-Iaponskie otnosheniia v 1697–1875 gg.* [Russo-Japanese Relations from 1697 to 1875]. Moscow, 1960.

FEIS, HERBERT, *Churchill, Roosevelt, Stalin*. Princeton, 1957.

FEOKTISTOV, SERGEI. 'Sakhalinskoe utro' [Sakhalin Morning], *Oktiabr* [October], VI (June 1950), 122–3.

FISCHER, LOUIS. 'The Greased Wheels of Diplomacy', *The Nation*, CXIX (8 Oct. 1924), 357–8.

—— 'Sinclair vs. Standard Oil in Russia', *The Nation*, CXIX (6 Aug. 1924), 138–40.

FORSTER, JOHN REINHOLD. *History of the Voyages and Discoveries made in the North*. London, 1786.

FRIIS, HERMAN R. 'Pioneer Economy of Sakhalin Island', *Economic Geography*, XV (Jan. 1939), 55–79.

FUNKE, MAX. 'Die Insel Sachalin', *Angewandte Geographie*, Serie 2, Heft 12 (Nov. 1906).

GALTSEV-BEZIUK, S. D. 'O soedinionii Sakhalina c materikom i o. Khokkaido v chetvertichnoe vremia' [Junction of Sakhalin with the Mainland and Hokkaido Island in the Quaternary Period], Akademiia nauk SSSR, *Izvestiia, seriia geograficheskaia*

[U.S.S.R. Academy of Sciences, Bulletin, Geographical Series], No. 1 (Jan.–Feb. 1964), 56–62.

GIZENKO, A. I. *Ptitsi Sakhalinskoe oblasti* [Birds of Sakhalin Oblast]. Moscow, 1955.

GOLDER, F. A. *Russian Expansion on the Pacific*, 1641–1850. Cleveland, 1914.

GOR, G., and V. LESHKEVICH. *Sakhalin.* Moscow, 1949.

GRAJDANZEV, ANDREW J. 'Soviet Position in the Far East'. *Far Eastern Survey*, XIV (21 Nov. 1945), 334–7.

GULKOV, A. 'Nasledniki boevykh traditsii' [Heirs to Our Battle Traditions], *Professionalno-tekhnicheskoe obrazovanie* [Vocational Technical Education], XXIV (Feb. 1967), 21.

HANAMI TATSUJI. 'Hoppō zen ryōdo ga Nihon ryō da' [All the Northern Territories are Japanese Territory], *Seikai ōrai* [Political Affairs], XXXVI (Jan. 1970), 36–41.

HARRISON, JOHN A. *Japan's Northern Frontier.* Gainesville, 1953.

—— 'The Saghalien Trade: a Contribution to Ainu Studies', *Southwestern Journal of Anthropology*, X (Autumn 1954), 278–93.

HAYASHI SHIGERU, ed. *Nihon shūsen shi* [The History of the End of the War for Japan]. 3 vols. Tokyo, 1962.

HIRAOKA MASAHIDE. *Nichiro kōshō shiwa* [Historical Discourses on Russo-Japanese Relations]. Tokyo, 1944.

Hokkaido shi jimmei jiten [Biographical Dictionary of Hokkaido History]. Ed., Tachibana Bunshichi, 4 vols. Sapporo, 1953–7.

HOKKAIDO SHIMBUNSHA [Hokkaido Newspaper Co.], ed. *Hokkaido hyakunen* [Hokkaido's 100 Years]. 3 vols. Sapporo, 1967–8.

HORA TOMIO. *Karafuto shi kenkyū* [Studies of Sakhalin's History]. Tokyo, 1956.

—— *Mamiya Rinzō.* Tokyo, 1960.

IAKOVLEVA, P. T. 'Pervootkryvateli Sakhalina' [The First Discoverers of Sakhalin], *Istoriia SSSR* [History U.S.S.R.], VIII (Mar.–Apr. 1964), 181–2.

IANKELEVICH, IA. 'Ostrov Sakhalin' [Sakhalin Island], *Vestnik Azii* [Journal of Asia], XLIX (1922), 195–96.

IGURO YATARŌ. *Kuroda Kiyotaka.* Sapporo, 1965.

ILIN, A. K. 'K likvidatsii Iaponskikh kontsessii na severnom Sakhalin i prolongatsii na piatlet rybolovnoi konventsii' [Liquidation of the Japanese Concessions on northern Sakhalin and the 5-Year Prolongation of the Fishing Convention], *Bolshevik*, No. 9 (1944), 69–73.

IMAMURA TAKESHI, ed. *Karafuto.* Vol. V of *Dai Nihon takushoku shi*

[History of Japan's Colonization]. Ed., Nihon gyōsei gakkai [Japan Administrative Studies Society]. Tokyo, 1934.

IRVING, WALTER. 'Why Japan took Saghalien', *Current History*, XVI (July 1922), 628.

ISBERT, HEINRICH. *Geschichte, Natur und Bedeutung der Insel Sachalin*. Bonn, 1907.

ITŌ TASABURŌ. 'Nihonjin no tankenteki seishin' [Exploratory Spirit of the Japanese], *Nihon bunka kenkyū* [Studies in Japanese Culture], VII (1959).

JONES, F. C. *Hokkaido*. London, 1958.

KAMANIN, L. G. *Pervie issledovateli Dalnevo Vostoka* [First Explorers of the Far East]. Moscow, 1946.

'Kampaniia Sovetskikh vooruzhennykh sil na Dalnem Vostoke v 1945 g.: fakty i tsifry' [Campaign of Soviet Armed Forces in the Far East in 1945: Facts and Figures], *Voenno-istoricheskii zhurnal* [Military History Magazine], VIII (Aug. 1965), 64–73.

'Karafuto and Sakhalin', *Asia*, XXXVII (June 1937), 430–2.

KARAFUTO RINGYŌ SHI HENSAN KAI [Society for the Compilation of the History of Karafuto's Forestry], ed. *Karafuto ringyō shi* [History of Karafuto's Forestry]. Tokyo, 1960.

KATŌ KYŪZŌ. *Shiberia no rekishi* [History of Siberia]. Tokyo, 1963.

KAWAKAMI, K. K. 'Oil: the Key to Russo-Japanese Agreement', *Outlook*, CXXXIX (4 Feb. 1925), 180–1.

KENNEDY, M. D. 'Japan and the Problem of Oil in the Pacific', *World Today*, XLV (June 1925), 573–82.

KEPPEN, A. *Mining and Metallurgy*. Vol. IV in Chicago, World's Columbian Exposition, ed. *The Industries of Russia*. St. Petersburg, 1893.

KHODZHER, GRIGORII. 'Sem let spustia' [Seven Years Later], *Dalnii Vostok* [Far East], XXIV (Nov.–Dec. 1956), 142–8.

KIKUCHI KIEJI. *Kita Nihon no hanashi* [Talks of northern Japan]. Tokyo, 1944.

KINDAI'ICHI KYŌSUKE. *Ainu no kenkyū* [Research on the Ainu]. Tokyo, 1925.

KLAPROTH, H. J. *Observations sur la Carte de l'Asie publiée en 1822 par M. Arrowsmith*. Paris, 1826.

KNIAZEV, K. I., ed. *Sakhalinskaia oblast: sbornik statei* [Sakhalin Oblast: a Collection of Articles]. Iuzhno-Sakhalinsk, 1960.

KOBAYASHI YOSHIO. 'Nihon no tai So shōnin to keizai mondai' [Japan's Diplomatic Recognition of the U.S.S.R. and the Economic Problem], *Kokusai seiji* [International Politics], No. 2 (1965), 86–98.

KOKURYŪKAI [Black Dragon Society], ed. *Tōa sengaku shishi kiden* [Biographies of East Asian Patriot Pioneers]. 2 vols. Tokyo, 1934.

KOLARZ, WALTER. *The Peoples of the Soviet Far East.* New York, 1954.

KOMISSARENKO, B. T. *Mineralnye istochniki i lechebnye griazi Sakhalina i Kuril* [Mineral Springs and Medicinal Muds of Sakhalin and the Kuriles]. Iuzhno-Sakhalinsk, 1964.

KONDŌ JŪZŌ. *Kondō seisai zenshū* [Complete Works of Kondō Jūzō]. Ed., Kokusho Kankokai. 3 vols. Tokyo, 1905–6.

KOUDREY, V. 'Island of Ill Repute', *Asia*, XXXV (Mar. 1935), 143–8.

KOZYREVA, R. V. *Drevneishee proshloe Sakhalina* [Remote Past of Sakhalin]. Iuzhno-Sakhalinsk, 1960.

—— *Drevnii Sakhalin* [Ancient Sakhalin]. Leningrad, 1967.

KRIUKOVA, T. N., and T. A. ZIMINA. 'Opyt introduktsii zhenshenia na Sakhaline' [Experimental Introduction of Ginseng on Sakhalin], Sakhalinskii kompleksnyi nauchno-issledovatelskii institut, *Trudy* [Sakhalin Joint Scientific Research Institute, *Transactions*], XVII (1966), 180–7.

KUCHEROV, L. 'Dla tekh, kto v more' [For Those Who are at Sea], *Bibliotekar*, V (May 1968), 23–5.

KUTAKOV, L. N. *Nisso gaikō kankei shi* [History of Japanese-Soviet Diplomatic Relations]. 3 vols. Tokyo, 1965–9.

KUZNETSOV, VIACHESLAV. 'Sakhalin literaturnyi' [Literary Sakhalin], *Oktiabr* [October], XLI (Dec. 1964), 211–13.

LABBÉ, PAUL. 'Sakhaline', *Questions diplomatiques et coloniales*, XX (Oct. 1905), 422–35.

LANGER, PAUL F. 'Japan and Her Soviet Neighbors during the Interwar Years: Japanese Images and Reactions.' Mimeograph. Rand Corporation. Santa Monica, California. December 1961.

LARKIN, V. G. *Orochi*. Moscow, 1964.

LATTIMORE, OWEN. *Studies in Frontier History: Collected Papers, 1928–1958.* Paris, 1962.

LEBEDEV, P. A. 'Ekonomika i kultura severnovo Sakhalina v gody dovoennykh piatiletok' [Economy and Culture of northern Sakhalin during the prewar Five-Year Plans], in K. I. Kniazev, ed. *Sakhalinskaia oblast* [Sakhalin Oblast]. Iuzhno-Sakhalinsk, 1960, pp. 185–205.

LEE, ROBERT H. G. *The Manchurian Frontier in Ch'ing History.* Cambridge (Mass.), 1970.

LENSEN, GEORGE ALEXANDER. *Japanese Recognition of the U.S.S.R.: Soviet-Japanese Relations, 1921–1930.* Tokyo, 1970.

—— *The Russian Push toward Japan: Russo-Japanese Relations*, 1697–1875. Princeton, 1959.

LEONOV, P. 'Vospityvat ubezhdennykh stroitelei kommunizma' [Let Us Train the Convinced Builders of Communism], *Kommunist*, XXXXV (May 1968), 52–61.

LINDNER, LUDWIG. 'Entdeckungsgeschichte der Insel Jesso und der Halbinsel Sagalien', *Allgemeine Geographische Ephemeriden*, XXXVIII (July 1812), 249–85, 393–425.

Literaturnyi Sakhalin; literaturno-khudozhestvennyi sbornik [Literary Sakhalin; Literary-artistic Collection]. Ed., I. E. Belousov and A. S. Tkachenko. Iuzhno-Sakhalinsk, 1959.

LOGAN, R. F. 'Survey of Sakhalin', *Far Eastern Survey*, XIV (1 Aug. 1945), 209–13.

LOPACHEV, A. M. 'Severnyi Sakhalin v period Iaponskoi okkupatsui: aprel 1920–mai 1925 gg. '[Northern Sakhalin in the Period of the Japanese Occupation: April 1920–May 1925], in K. I. Kniazev, ed. *Sakhalinskaia oblast* [Sakhalin Oblast]. Iuzhno-Sakhalinsk, 1960. pp. 139–56.

LOPATIN, IVAN A. *The Cult of the Dead among the Natives of the Amur Basin*. The Hague, 1960.

LUTSKII, S. L. *Ostrov Sakhalin* [Sakhalin Island]. Moscow, 1946.

MCALEAVY, HENRY. 'China and the Amur Provinces', *History Today*, XIV (June 1964), 381–90.

MCCARTHY, J. W. 'Saghalin from a Japanese Source', *The Geographical Magazine*, V (Aug. 1878), 205–9.

MARUYAMA KUNIO. *Nihon hoppō hatten shi* [History of Japan's Northern Expansion]. Tokyo, 1942.

MATSUI MASATO and SHIMANAKA KATSUMI. *Research Resources on Hokkaido, Sakhalin, and the Kuriles at the East-West Center Library*. Honolulu, 1967.

MEERSON, E. G. 'Sakhalinskaia oblast' [Sakhalin Oblast], in Akademiia nauk, institut geografii [U.S.S.R. Academy of Sciences, Geographical Institute], ed. *Dalnii Vostok: ekonomiko-geograficheskaia karakteristika* [The Russian Far East: Economic and Geographical Characteristics]. Moscow, 1966, pp. 365–88.

MEKLER, G. K. *Khokkaido* [Hokkaido]. Moscow, 1967.

MINAGAWA SHINSAKU. 'Karafuto hantō setsu to Sagarin hantō setsu' [The Peninsular Theory of Karafuto and the Peninsular Theory of Sakhalin], *Denki* [Biography], X (Mar. 1943), 9–25.

MINAMI KARAFUTO HENKAN KISEI DŌMEI [Alliance for the Realization of the Return of Southern Sakhalin]. 'Zenshin no shuisho' [Manifesto of the Advance]. Tokyo, 1 Apr. 1969.

MIYAZAKI RAIHACHI. *Karafuto shi monogatari* [The Story of Karafuto's History]. Tokyo, 1944.

MOLL, HERMAN. *Atlas Geographus or a Compleat System of Geography.* 5 vols. London, 1711–12.

MOORE, HARRIET L. *Soviet Far Eastern Policy*, 1931–1945. Princeton, 1945.

MORIZAWA MASATERU. 'Chishima minami Karafuto mondai no shōten' [The Focus of the Kurile-Southern Sakhalin Problem], *Chūō kōron* [Central Review] (Aug. 1955), 158–68.

MORLEY, JAMES W. 'Soviet-Japanese Peace Declaration', *Political Science Quarterly*, LXXII (Sept. 1957), 370–9.

MOTOYAMA KEISEN. *Roshia shinkan sanbyakunen* [Three Hundred Years of Russian Aggression]. Tokyo, 1939.

MUSHKAREVA, E. V. 'Vosstanovlenie i uprochenie Sovetskoi vlasti na severnom Sakhaline: 1925–1928 gg.' [The Restoration and Consolidation of Soviet Authority on Northern Sakhalin, 1925–1928], in K. I. Kniazev, ed. *Sakhalinskaia oblast* [Sakhalin Oblast]. Iuzhno-Sakhalinsk, 1960, pp. 159–82.

NANPŌ DŌHO ENGO KAI [Society for the Assistance of Compatriots in Southern Regions], ed. *Hoppō ryōdo no chi'i* [The Position of the Northern Territories]. Tokyo, 1962.

NISHIZURU SADAYOSHI. 'Shijitsu ni motozuku hoppō ryōdo mondai ni tsuite' [Concerning the Northern Territorial Problem as Based on Historical Fact]. Unpublished MS. n.d.

—— *Karafuto tanken no hitobito* [Explorers of Karafuto]. Tokyo, 1939.

NUMATA ICHIRŌ. *Nichiro gaikō shi* [History of Russo-Japanese Relations]. Tokyo, 1943.

OBUKHOV, V. 'Nepravnie metodi' [Incorrect Methods], *Partiinaia zhizn* [Party Life], XXI (Nov. 1956), 57–9.

OHMAE TOSHIKAZU. 'The Kuriles and Sakhalin', in M. G. Saunders, ed. *The Soviet Navy*. New York, 1958, pp. 274–84.

OKA SAKAE. *Kita Karafuto* [Northern Sakhalin]. Tokyo, 1942.

ŌKUMA RYŌ'ICHI. *Hoppō ryōdo mondai no rekishiteki haikei* [Historical Background of the Northern Territories Problem]. Tokyo, 1964.

ŌSAKA MAINICHI SHIMBUNSHA [Ōsaka Mainichi Newspaper Company], ed. *Kita Karafuto* [Northern Sakhalin]. Ōsaka, 1925.

OSHIMA SEIJI. *Karafuto shima zenzu* [A Complete Map of Karafuto]. Hakodate, 1940.

OSKORBIN, L. S., A. A. POPLAVSKII, AND V. N. ZANIUKOV. *Noglikskoe zemletriasenie 2 oktiabria 1964 goda* [Nogliki Earthquake of 2 Oct. 1964]. Iuzhno-Sakhalinsk, 1967.

ŌTA SABURŌ. *Nichiro Karafuto gaikō sen* [Russo-Japanese Diplomatic Struggle Regarding Karafuto]. Tokyo, 1941.

PADERIN, G. *Rediscovered Country*. Moscow, n.d. [*c*. 1966].

PANOV, A. A. *Shokuminchi to shite no Sagaren* [Sakhalin as a Colony]. Translated from the Russian by the Takumushō [Japanese Ministry of Colonization]. Tokyo, 1942.

PHILLIPS, CLAUDE S., JR. 'Some Forces Behind the Opening of Japan', *Contemporary Japan*, XXIV (1956), 431–59.

PILSUDSKI, BRONISLAW. *Materials for the Study of the Ainu Language and Folklore*. Cracow, 1912.

POLEVOI, B. P. 'Istoriia Russkikh issledovaniia' [History of Russian Exploration], in Akademiia nauk SSSR, Sibirskovo otdeleniia, Sakhalinskii kompleksnyi nauchno-issledovatelskii institut [U.S.S.R. Academy of Sciences, Siberian Branch, Sakhalin Joint Scientific Research Institute]. *Atlas Sakhalinskoi oblasti* [Atlas of Sakhalin Oblast]. Moscow, 1967, p. 5.

—— *Pervootkryvateli Sakhalina* [The First Discoverers of Sakhalin]. Iuzhno-Sakhalinsk, 1959.

—— 'Zabytye svedeniia sputnikov V. D. Poiarkova o Sakhaline (1644–1645 gg.)' [Forgotten Information from Traveling Companions of V. D. Poiarkov about Sakhalin (1644–1645)], *Geograficheskoe obshchestvo SSSR, Izvestiia* [Geographical Society of the U.S.S.R., Bulletin], XC (Nov.–Dec. 1958), 547–51.

POLEVOI, P. I., AND D. V. SOKOLOV. 'Materiali po issledovaniiu Russkovo Sakhalina' [Material on the Exploration of Russian Sakhalin], *Trudi geologicheskovo komiteta* [Transactions of the Geological Committee], New Series, No. 97. St. Petersburg, 1914.

POZDNEEV, DIMITRII M. *Materialy po istorii severnoi Iaponii i eia otnoshenii k materiku Azii i Rossii* [Material on the History of Northern Japan and Her Relations with the Asian Continent and Russia]. 2 vols. Tokyo, 1909.

QUESTED, R. K. I. *The Expansion of Russia in East Asia*, 1857–1860. Kuala Lumpur, 1968.

RACHKOV, D. A. *Pisateli Sakhalina* [Writers of Sakhalin]. Iuzhno-Sakhalinsk, 1962.

RAVENSTEIN, E. G. *The Russians on the Amur; Its Discovery, Conquest, and Colonization, with a Description of the Country, Its Inhabitants, Productions, and Commercial Capabilities; and Personal Accounts of Russian Travelers*. London, 1861.

RENDEL, K. 'Uvolit po sobstvennomu zhelaniiu' [Dismiss at One's Own Request], *Sovetskie profsoiuzy* [Soviet Trade Unions], XXII (May 1966), 36.

Russkii Sakhalin kak novaia Iaponiia [Russian Sakhalin as New Japan].

Ed., General Kojima. Vladivostok, 1921.

RYZHKOV, A. N. 'Iz istorii otkrytiia, issledovaniia i osvoeniia Sakhalina i Kurilskikh ostrovov' [History of the Discovery, Exploration, and Struggle for Sakhalin and the Kurile Islands], in K. I. Kniazev, ed. *Sakhalinskaia oblast* [Sakhalin Oblast]. Iuzhno-Sakhalinsk, 1960, pp. 43–90.

—— 'Sakhalinskaia oblast v gody Velikoi Otechestvennoi Voiny Sovetskovo Soiuza: 1941–1945 gg.' [Sakhalin Oblast during the Great Patriotic War of the Soviet Union, 1941–1945], in K. I. Kniazev, ed. *Sakhalinskaia oblast* [Sakhalin Oblast]. Iuzhno-Sakhalinsk, 1960, pp. 207–44.

SATA HAKUBŌ. 'Karafuto hyōron' [Karafuto Reviewed], in Yoshino Sakuzō, ed. *Meiji bunka zenshū* [Collection of Meiji Period Works], XXII. Tokyo, 1929, 13–22.

SCHWIND, MARTIN. *Die Gestaltung Karafutos zum japanischen Raum.* Gotha, 1942.

SEMYONOV, YURI. *Siberia: Its Conquest and Development.* Translated from the German by J. R. Foster. Baltimore, 1963.

SENCHENKO, I. A., ed. *Issledovateli Sakhalina i Kuril* [Explorers of Sakhalin and the Kuriles]. Iuzhno-Sakhalinsk, 1961.

SENCHENKO, I. A. *Ocherki istorii Sakhalina; vtoraia polovina XIX v., nachalo XX v.* [Outline History of Sakhalin; Second Half of the 19th Century, Beginning of the 20th Century]. Iuzhno-Sakhalinsk, 1957.

—— *Revoliutsionery Rossii na Sakhalinskoi katorge* [Russian Revolutionists in Penal Servitude in Sakhalin]. Iuzhno-Sakhalinsk, 1963.

—— 'Severnyi Sakhalin v 1905–1916 gg.' [Northern Sakhalin in 1905–1916], in K. I. Kniazev, ed. *Sakhalinskaia oblast* [Sakhalin Oblast]. Iuzhno-Sakhalinsk, 1960, pp. 93–111.

SENCHENKO, I, A., AND P. A. LEBEDEV. 'Borba za ustanovlenie Sovetskoi vlasti na severnom Sakhaline: mart 1917–aprel 1920 gg.' [Struggle for the Restoration of Soviet Authority on Northern Sakhalin, March 1917–April 1920], in K. I. Kniazev, ed. *Sakhalinskaia oblast* [Sakhalin Oblast]. Iuzhno-Sakhalinsk, 1960, pp. 115–36.

SHAKHNAZAROV, B. 'Khudozhniki Sakhalina' [Artists of Sakhalin], *Khudozhnik* [Artist], V (1959), 16–19.

SHEPELENKO, M. 'Prolivom druzhbi' [Via the Strait of Friendship], *Sovetskie profsoiuzy* [Soviet Trade Unions], XXII (May 1966), 41–3.

SHEREMET, MYKOLA. 'Na Sakhalini' [On Sakhalin], *Vitchyzna* [Our Country], XXVI (Dec. 1958), 115–24.

SHIMOIDE SHIGEO. *Kinsei Karafuto shiyō* [An Outline of Karafuto History]. Tokyo, 1962.

SHINKAWA KŌZŌ. *Hokkaido e no shōtai* [An Invitation to Hokkaido]. Tokyo, 1965.

SHIRANI UKICHI. *Karafuto kaihatsusaku* [A Policy for Developing Karafuto]. Ōtomari, 1909.

SHIRATORI KURAKICHI. 'Tō jidai no Karafuto shima ni tsuite' [Concerning Sakhalin Island during the T'ang Period], *Rekishi chiri* [Historical Geography], IX (1907), 329–42, 423–34.

SHTERNBERG, L. IA. *Giliaki, orochi, goldy, negidaltsy, ainy* [Gilyak, Oroki, Golki, Negidal, Ainu]. Khabarovsk, 1933.

SIEBOLD, PHILIPP FRANZ VON. *Geographical and Ethnographical Elucidations to the Discoveries of Maerten Gerrits Vries, A.D. 1643, in the East and North of Japan.* Translated from the Dutch by F. M. Cowan. Amsterdam, 1859.

—— *Nippon. Archiv zur Beschreibung von Japan.* 20 vols. Leyden, 1832–52.

SIRYK, I. M. *Neftegazonosnost vostochnykh sklonov Zapadno-Sakhalinskikh gor* [Oil and Gas Potentials of the Eastern Slopes of the Zapadno-Sakhalinski Mountains]. Moscow, 1968.

SMOLIAK, A. V. 'O sovremennom etnicheskom razvitii narodov nizhnevo Amura i Sakhalina' [Present-day Development of the Peoples of the Lower Amur Valley and Sakhalin], *Sovetskaia etnografiia* [Soviet Ethnography], III (May–June 1967), 95–102.

STEPHAN, JOHN J. 'The Crimean War in the Far East', *Modern Asian Studies*, III (July 1969), 257–77.

—— 'Ezo under the Tokugawa Bakufu, 1799–1821: an Aspect of Japan's Frontier History.' Unpublished Ph.D. dissertation. University of London, 1969.

—— 'Sakhalin Island: Soviet Outpost in Northeast Asia', *Asian Survey* (Dec. 1970).

STONE, E. 'North Pacific Outposts of Japan', *Travel*, LXXXIII (May 1944), 10–13, 32.

SUEMATSU YASUKAZU. *Kinsei ni okeru hoppō mondai no shinten* [The Evolution of the Northern Problem in Recent Times]. Tokyo, 1928.

SUGIMOTO ZENNOSUKE. *Karafuto gyosei kaikaku enkaku shi* [The Reform and Development of Karafuto's Fishing Industry]. Maoka, 1936.

SUSLOV, S. P. *Physical Geography of Asiatic Russia.* Translated from the Russian by Noah D. Gershevsky and edited by Joseph E. Williams. Second revised edition. New York, 1956.

TAKADA GINJIRŌ. *Karafuto kyōiku hattatsu shi* [The Development of Education in Karafuto]. Toyohara, 1936.

TAKAKURA SHIN'ICHIRŌ. *Chishima gaishi* [A General History of the Kurile Islands]. Tokyo, 1962.

TAKAKURA SHIN'ICHIRŌ. *Ezo chi* [Hokkaido before 1869]. Tokyo, 1959.

—— *Hokkaido takushoku shi* [History of Hokkaido's Colonization]. Sapporo, 1947.

TAKAKURA SHIN'ICHIRŌ AND SHIBATA SADAKICHI. 'Waga kuni ni okeru Karafuto chizu sakusei shi' [History of Karafuto Maps in Our Country], *Hoppō bunka kenkyū hōkoku* [Reports on Research of Northern Cultures], II (Oct. 1939), 273–320.

TAKSAMI, CHUNER, M. *Nivkhi* [The Gilyak People]. Leningrad, 1967.

TELEKI, PAUL GRAF. *Atlas zur Geschichte der Kartographie der japanischen Inseln*. Budapest, 1909.

TEPLINSKII, M. V. *Sakhalinskie puteshestviia* [Sakhalin Journeys]. Iuzhno-Sakhalinsk, 1962.

THIEL, ERICH. *The Soviet Far East*. Translated from the German by Annelie and Ralph M. Rockwood. New York, 1957.

TIERNEY, EMIKO OHNUKI. 'A Northwest Coast Sakhalin Ainu World View.' Unpublished Ph. D. dissertation. University of Wisconsin, 1968.

TIKHOMIROV, N. E. 'Greipfrut na severe Sakhalina' [Grapefruit in the north of Sakhalin], *Priroda* [Nature], XLII (Mar. 1953), 119.

TIKHONINA, L. 'Ordenonosnii ostrov' [An Order-bearing Island], *Bibliotekar* [Librarian] (Sept. 1968), 32.

TIURIN, V. S., ed. *Sakhalin, Kurily, rodnye ostrova, sbornik ocherkov* [Sakhalin and the Kuriles, Our Native Islands, a Collection of Sketches]. Iuzhno-Sakhalinsk, 1967.

TRUBACHEV, D. N., *et. al.* 'Ekonomika i kultura oblasti v poslevoennye period' [Economy and Culture of the Oblast in the Postwar Period], in K. I. Kniazev, ed. *Sakhalinskaia oblast* [Sakhalin Oblast]. Iuzhno-Sakhalinsk, 1960. pp. 247–365.

URSYN-PRUSZYNSKI, S. VON. *Die Kämpfe auf der Insel Sachalin während des russisch-japanischen Krieges*. Vienna, 1910.

URYVSKII, F. 'Kraevedenie v shkolakh Sakhalina' [Local History Classes in Sakhalin's Schools], *Narodne obrazovanie* [People's Education] (Aug. 1966), pp. 54–8.

VEND, VERA. *L'Amiral Nevelskoi et la Conquete definitive du fleuve Amour*. Paris, 1894.

VINOKUROV, I., AND F. FLORICH. *Podvig Admirala Nevelskovo* [The Exploit of Admiral Nevelskoi]. Moscow, 1951.

VLADIMIROVA, G. 'Sluzhba tsunami' [Tidal Wave Service], *Ogoniok* [Little Fire], XXXV (Feb. 1957), 24.

WADA KIYOSHI. 'Shina no kisai ni arawaretaru Kokuryūkō karyū iki no genjumin' [The Natives of the Lower Amur River as Described in Chinese Sources], *Tōa shi ronsō* [Discussions on East Asian History]. Tokyo, 1942.

WATSON, FRANCIS. *The Frontiers of China*. London, 1966.

WHITE, JOHN A. *The Diplomacy of the Russo-Japanese War*. Princeton, 1964.

WITSEN, NICOLAES. *Noord en Oost Tartaren*. Amsterdam, 1705.

YAMASHITA RYŪMON. *Karafuto ron* [Views on Karafuto]. Tokyo, 1929.

YAMASHITA SHŪNOSUKE, ed. *Hokkaido, Karafuto, Chishima rettō* [Hokkaido, Karafuto, and Kurile Islands]. Tokyo, 1943.

YANAI WATARU. *Tōyō dokushi chizu* [Historical Atlas of the Orient]. Tokyo, 1925.

YOSHIDA SHIEN. *Hoppō ryōdo* [The Northern Territories]. Revised edition. Tokyo, 1968.

YOSHIDA TAKEZŌ. *Matsuura Takeshirō*. Tokyo, 1967.

YOSHIZAKI MASAKAZU. 'Prehistoric Culture in Southern Sakhalin in the Light of Japanese Research', *Arctic Anthropology*, I, 2 (1963), 131–58.

ZADORNOV, NIKOLAI. P. *Daliokii krai* [Distant Country]. Leningrad, 1950.

ZAKHAROV, S. E., M. N. ZAKHAROV, V. N. BAGROV, AND M. P. KOTUKHOV. *Tikhookeansky flot* [The Soviet Pacific Fleet]. Moscow, 1966.

ZEMTSOVA, A. I. *Klimat Sakhalina* [The Climate of Sakhalin]. Leningrad, 1968.

ZENKOKU KARAFUTO RENMEI [National Karafuto League], ed. *Minami Karafuto o wasureru na* [Do Not Forget Southern Sakhalin]. Tokyo, 1969.

ZHUKOV, IURII. *Russkie i Iaponiia* [Russians and Japan]. Moscow, 1945.

INDEX